Television in American Society

Biographies

Television in American Society

Biographies

Laurie Collier Hillstrom
Allison McNeill Gudenau, Project Editor

U·X·L
An imprint of Thomson Gale,
a part of The Thomson Corporation

THOMSON
GALE

Detroit • New York • San Francisco • New Haven, Conn. • Waterville, Maine • London

THOMSON
★
GALE™

Television in American Society: Biographies

Laurie Collier Hillstrom

Project Editor
Allison McNeill Gudenau

Rights and Acquisitions
Shalice Shah-Caldwell,
Emma Hull

Imaging and Multimedia
Leitha Etheridge-Sims, Lezlie Light,
Dan Newell

Product Design
Kate Scheible, Deborah van Rooyen

Composition
Evi Seoud

Manufacturing
Rita Wimberley

LIBRARY OF CONGRESS CATALOGING-IN-PUBLICATION DATA

Hillstrom, Laurie Collier, 1965–
   Television in American society. Biographies / Laurie Collier Hillstrom; Allison McNeill,
project editor.
      p. cm. -- (Television in American society reference library)
   Includes bibliographical references and index.
   ISBN-13: 978-1-4144-0223-9 (hardcover : alk. paper) -- ISBN-13: 978-1-4144-0221-5
(set : alk. paper)
      ISBN-10: 1-4144-0223-6 (hardcover : alk. paper) -- ISBN-10: 1-4144-0221-X (set : alk. paper)
   1. Television broadcasting -- United States -- Biography -- Dictionaries -- Juvenile literature.
I. Title. -- II. Series.
   PN1992.4.A2H55 2006
   302.23' 450973 -- dc22
                                                                          2006011889

This title is also available as an e-book.
ISBN-13: 978-1-4144-1075-3, ISBN-10: 1-4144-1075-1
Contact your Thomson Gale sales representative for ordering information.

Printed in the United States of America
10 9 8 7 6 5 4 3 2

Contents

Reader's Guide **vii**

Timeline **ix**

Words to Know **xix**

Roger Ailes **1**

Roone Arledge **7**

      Howard Cosell (sidebar) **12**

Lucille Ball **17**

Milton Berle **25**

      Ed Sullivan (sidebar) **29**

Mark Burnett **33**

Joan Ganz Cooney **41**

Bill Cosby **47**

Walter Cronkite **55**

Philo T. Farnsworth **63**

Larry Gelbart **73**

Merv Griffin **81**

Don Hewitt **87**

Robert L. Johnson **93**

      Judy McGrath (sidebar) **96**

Norman Lear **101**

      Sherwood Schwartz (sidebar) **102**

Lorne Michaels **111**

Mary Tyler Moore **119**

Agnes Nixon **125**

William S. Paley **131**

     Edward R. Murrow (sidebar) **134**

David Sarnoff **141**

     Peter Goldmark (sidebar) **148**

Fred Silverman **151**

Aaron Spelling **157**

Brandon Tartikoff **165**

Ted Turner **171**

     Gerald Levin (sidebar) **174**

Barbara Walters **181**

Oprah Winfrey **187**

Vladimir Zworykin **195**

Where to Learn More **xxxi**

Index **xxxiii**

Reader's Guide

Television in American Society: Biographies presents profiles of twenty-six men and women who influenced the development of television in a significant way. The volume includes a diverse mix of personalities who played a key role in television history, including inventors, broadcast industry leaders, network executives, cable TV pioneers, program producers, TV news journalists, and entertainers.

Television in American Society: Biographies covers such key figures as inventor Philo T. Farnsworth, who came up with a design for the world's first all-electronic television system at the age of fourteen; Radio Corporation of America (RCA) chairman David Sarnoff, a Russian immigrant whose ambition and vision propelled him to the most powerful position in the American broadcasting industry; network executive Roone Arledge, whose ideas revolutionized sports on television; cable TV pioneer Robert L. Johnson, who introduced Black Entertainment Television (BET); children's program producer Joan Ganz Cooney, the creator of *Sesame Street*; TV writer Agnes Nixon, known as the queen of the modern soap opera; influential TV news journalist Walter Cronkite, who reported on some of the most important events of the television era; and television personality Lucille Ball, the star of the beloved 1950s comedy series *I Love Lucy* and the first woman to run a major TV production studio.

Features

Television in American Society: Biographies includes informative sidebars containing brief biographies of influential people in the world of television. Approximately sixty black-and-white photographs enliven the work. *Television in American Society: Biographies* also includes a timeline of important events and a section defining important words to know.

The volume concludes with a bibliography of sources for further reading, and a subject index.

Television in American Society Reference Library

Television in American Society: Biographies is only one component of a three-volume Television in American Society Reference Library. The other two titles in this multivolume set are:

- *Television in American Society: Almanac* presents a comprehensive overview of the development of television technology, the growth of the broadcast and cable industries, the evolution of television programming, and the impact of television on American society and culture. The volume's eleven chapters cover all aspects of television in the United States, from the invention of the technology in the 1920s to programming trends in the 2000s. The main emphasis of the volume concerns the many ways in which television has both reflected and influenced American life throughout its history.

- *Television in American Society: Primary Sources* presents fifteen full or excerpted documents relating to the development and impact of television. These documents range from notable speeches that mark important points in TV history to critical analyses of television's influence on American culture. The documents are arranged chronologically, beginning with longtime RCA chairman David Sarnoff's 1936 remarks to the press at his company's first demonstration of television technology, and ending with former vice president Al Gore's 2005 speech about the effects of television on democracy.

- A cumulative index of all three titles in Television in American Society Reference Library is also available.

Acknowledgments

The author extends thanks to the following writers who prepared biographies for this volume: Brian Escamilla, Tina Gianoulis, Margaret Haerens, Carolyn Hembree, and Rhoda Wilburn.

Comments and Suggestions

We welcome your comments on *Television in American Society: Biographies* and suggestions for other topics in history to consider. Please write: Editors, *Television in American Society: Biographies,* U*X*L, 27500 Drake Road, Farmington Hills, MI 48331-3535; call toll-free 800-877-4253; fax to 248-699-8097; or send e-mail via http://www.gale.com.

Timeline

1835 Samuel Morse invents the telegraph.

1876 Alexander Graham Bell invents the telephone.

1880 *Scientific American* magazine runs an article about the possibility of distance vision (television).

1884 German scientist Paul Nipkow invents the optical scanning disk used in mechanical television systems.

1887 Heinrich Rudolph Hertz discovers radio waves.

1895 Guglielmo Marconi develops a wireless or radio telegraph.

1897 German scientist Karl Ferdinand Braun develops the first cathode ray tube.

1900 Russian scientist Constantin Perskyi coins the term "television" at the Paris World's Fair.

1900 David Sarnoff immigrates to the United States from Russia.

1901 Guglielmo Marconi sends and receives radio signals across the Atlantic Ocean.

1907 Russian physicist Boris Rosing designs an electronic television receiver with a cathode ray tube.

1911 Boris Rosing and his assistant, Vladimir Zworykin, achieve the first successful transmission of crude television images, using a mechanical transmitter and an electronic receiver.

1912 The Radio Act of 1912 allows the U.S. government to issue licenses to people who wish to broadcast signals over radio waves.

1912 David Sarnoff, working as a telegraph operator, claims to have received distress signals from the sinking luxury oceanliner *Titanic*.

1919 The Radio Corporation of America (RCA) is formed.

1921 American inventor Philo T. Farnsworth, age 14, has a vision of an all-electronic television system.

1921 Commercial radio broadcasting begins in the United States.

1922 Philo T. Farnsworth explains his television system to his high school science teacher.

1923 Vladimir Zworykin applies for a patent on an all-electronic television system.

1925 Vladimir Zworykin demonstrates a TV system for his bosses at Westinghouse, but they decide against funding further TV research.

1926 Philo T. Farnsworth gathers investors and opens a television research laboratory in San Francisco, California.

1926 The National Broadcasting Company (NBC) is formed as a radio network.

1926 American Charles Francis Jenkins and Scotsman John Logie Baird independently invent working mechanical television systems.

1927 Philo T. Farnsworth builds his all-electronic TV system and successfully transmits an image.

1927 The Columbia Broadcasting System (CBS) is founded as a radio network.

1927 Secretary of Commerce Herbert Hoover appears in the first long-distance transmission of television signals, between Washington, D.C., and New York City.

1927 William S. Paley becomes president of CBS.

1927 The Radio Act of 1927 first mentions broadcasters' duty to serve the public interest.

1928 The U.S. government issues the first permits for experimental TV stations.

1928 Philo T. Farnsworth demonstrates his TV system for the press.

1929 Vladimir Zworykin goes to work for RCA and begins developing his Kinescope electronic television receiver.

1929 The Great Depression begins in the United States.

1930 David Sarnoff becomes president of RCA.

1930 Philo T. Farnsworth receives a patent for his Image Dissector television camera.

1931 CBS begins experimental TV broadcasting.

1932 NBC begins experimental TV broadcasting.

1934 The Communications Act of 1934 established the Federal Communications Commission (FCC).

1935 Philo T. Farnsworth wins the patent battle against Vladimir Zworykin, preventing RCA from gaining total control over electronic television technology.

1935 David Sarnoff announces RCA's million-dollar television research and testing program.

1936 RCA demonstrates an all-electronic television system.

1936 Philo T. Farnsworth begins experimental TV broadcasts from his Philco laboratory in Philadelphia, Pennsylvania.

1936 The Olympic Games in Berlin, Germany, are televised using both RCA and Farnsworth equipment.

1936 About 200 television sets are in use worldwide.

1938 Vladimir Zworykin and RCA introduce an improved Iconoscope television camera that is ten times more sensitive to light than the original version.

April 20, 1939 David Sarnoff introduces television to the public at the New York World's Fair.

April 30, 1939 Franklin D. Roosevelt becomes the first U.S. president to be televised.

May 1, 1939 RCA begins selling television sets to the public, followed by DuMont, General Electric, and Philco.

October 2, 1939 RCA pays a licensing fee to Philo T. Farnsworth for use of his television patents.

1940 Peter Goldmark of CBS develops the first working color television system, which uses both mechanical and electronic elements.

March 1941 The FCC's National Television Standards Committee (NTSC) announces a technical standard for monochrome (black-and-white) television sets.

July 1, 1941 NBC makes the first commercial television broadcast in the United States.

December 7, 1941 Japanese fighter planes attack the U.S. naval base in Pearl Harbor, Hawaii, drawing the United States into World War II.

1942–45 Most television broadcasting and manufacturing stops for the duration of the war.

1942–45 About 10,000 television sets had been sold, and 23 TV stations exist in the United States.

1943 The American Broadcasting Company (ABC) is formed when NBC is forced to sell its Blue radio network.

1946 Postwar production of television sets begins.

1946 CBS demonstrates its color television system for the FCC.

1948 Don Hewitt joins the CBS news division.

1948 The first cable TV systems (known as Community Antenna Television or CATV) are installed to improve reception in rural areas of the United States.

1948 The FCC places a temporary freeze on new broadcast licenses in order to study interference between stations and develop an orderly system for assigning licenses.

1948 There are 107 television stations operating in 63 markets.

1949 Philo T. Farnsworth sells his company, Farnsworth Radio and Television, to ITT and leaves the television industry.

1949 The Academy of Television Arts and Sciences creates the Emmy Awards to honor excellence in TV performance and production.

1950 The FCC approves the CBS mechanical-electronic color television system.

June 1951 CBS begins broadcasting TV programs in color; only a few hundred TV sets can receive the broadcasts.

June 1951 RCA demonstrates its all-electronic color television system.

October 1951 Color TV production stops during the Korean War (1950–53).

December 1951 The National Association of Broadcasters (NAB) adopts its Code of Practices for Television Broadcasters.

1952 The FCC ends its freeze on new broadcast licenses and approves broadcasting on UHF channels.

1952 The first political campaign advertisements appear on television.

1953 The FCC reverses its 1950 decision and approves the RCA color television system.

1953 NBC begins broadcasting in color.

1954 Broadcast journalist Edward R. Murrow exposes Joseph McCarthy (1908–1957), a U.S. Senator from Wisconsin who had ruined the careers of many American politicians and entertainers by falsely accusing them of being Communists, on his news program *See It Now*.

1954 Engineer Vladimir Zworykin retires after twenty-five years of television development at RCA.

1956 Ampex Corporation demonstrates videotape recorder (VTR) technology, which makes it possible to record television programs for immediate viewing.

1959 The U.S. Congress uncovers the quiz show scandal, in which producers and sponsors provided answers to some game show contestants in advance.

1959 Congress adds the Fairness Doctrine, written by the FCC in 1949, as an amendment to the Communications Act of 1934.

1960 John F. Kennedy and Richard M. Nixon take part in the first televised presidential debates.

1960 Approximately 87 percent of American homes contain at least one television set.

1961 Roone Arledge increases the entertainment value of sports with *ABC's Wide World of Sports*.

1961 Newton N. Minow becomes chairman of the FCC under President John F. Kennedy.

1962 The Telstar communications satellite is launched into orbit, allowing for the first international transmission of television images.

1962 The All-Channel Receiver Act requires all new television sets to be equipped to receive both UHF and VHF broadcasts.

1962 The FCC decides that it has the authority to regulate cable television.

1962 Merv Griffin becomes host of a talk show called *The Merv Griffin Show*.

1962 Broadcast journalist Walter Cronkite becomes anchor of the *CBS Evening News*.

1963 President John F. Kennedy is assassinated; television news provides around-the-clock coverage of the story for four days.

1964 Merv Griffin creates the hugely successful game show *Jeopardy!*

1965 Bill Cosby becomes the first African American star of a prime-time drama series by appearing in *I Spy*.

1967 ABC Sports introduces slow-motion and stop-action features to sports telecasts.

1967 Most television broadcasts are now in color.

1967 The Public Broadcasting Act of 1967 creates the framework for public radio and television in the United States.

1968 Don Hewitt introduces the news magazine format to television by creating *60 Minutes*.

1968 Agnes Nixon creates the long-running soap opera *One Life to Live*.

1968 Walter Cronkite criticizes U.S. involvement in the Vietnam War in a powerful on-air editorial.

1969 A worldwide television audience estimated at 600 million watches American astronaut Neil Armstrong become the first human being to set foot on the Moon.

1969 PBS programmer Joan Ganz Cooney creates the popular children's show *Sesame Street.*

1970 Roone Arledge brings sports to prime-time television with *Monday Night Football.*

1970 Mary Tyler Moore stars as an independent career woman in *The Mary Tyler Moore Show.*

1970 Agnes Nixon introduces current events and issues to the soap opera format with *All My Children.*

1970 The Public Broadcasting Service (PBS) is established.

1970 The invention of fiberoptic cable increases the amount of information that can be transmitted through wires.

1971 Norman Lear creates the working-class family comedy *All in the Family.*

1972 Larry Gelbart creates *M*A*S*H,* one of the first programs to combine drama and comedy.

1972 The FCC issues its open-skies decision, allowing commercial use of satellites.

1972 The U.S. government releases the results of a large-scale study which shows that viewing violent programs on television tends to increase children's aggressive behavior.

1975 The pay-cable channel Home Box Office (HBO) broadcasts a heavyweight championship fight between Muhammad Ali and Joe Frazier live via satellite from Manila, in the Philippines.

1975 Merv Griffin creates the popular game show *Wheel of Fortune.*

1975 Lorne Michaels launches the late-night comedy/variety series *Saturday Night Live.*

1975 As the head of programming at ABC, Fred Silverman introduces a number of popular shows featuring beautiful women in skimpy clothing.

1976 The first videocassette recorders (VCRs) are introduced for home use.

1976 Ted Turner turns his Atlanta-based independent TV station into the national cable network Superstation TBS by arranging to deliver his signal to cable systems across the country via satellite.

1976 Broadcast journalist Barbara Walters becomes the first female anchor of a major network newscast at ABC, and also launches her popular series of interview specials.

1978 PBS becomes the first network to deliver all of its programming via satellite.

1979 The Entertainment and Sports Programming Network (ESPN) becomes the first sports network on cable TV.

1980 Ted Turner launches the Cable News Network (CNN), television's first twenty-four hour news channel.

1980 Brandon Tartikoff becomes head of programming at NBC and increases the quality of the network's lineup of shows.

1980 Robert L. Johnson starts the cable TV network Black Entertainment Television (BET).

1981 Electronic News Gathering (ENG) technology gives a boost to local television newscasts.

1981 Mark S. Fowler becomes chairman of the FCC under President Ronald Reagan.

August 1, 1981 Cable channel MTV (Music Television) makes its debut.

1982 The FCC authorizes Direct Broadcast Satellite (DBS) services.

1983 The series finale of *M*A*S*H* becomes the most-watched television episode of all time.

1984 Bill Cosby stars in the popular family comedy *The Cosby Show*.

1984 The FCC deregulates broadcasting under President Ronald Reagan, eliminating rules about the number of commercials allowed per hour of programming and increasing the limits on ownership of TV stations.

1984 The FCC authorizes stereo TV broadcasting, and sales of stereo TV sets begin.

1984 The U.S. Supreme Court rules in favor of Sony in the *Betamax* case, making VCR technology legal for home use.

1986 *The Oprah Winfrey Show* reaches a nationwide audience.

1987 Fox becomes the fourth broadcast TV network operating in the United States.

1989 The FCC eliminates the Fairness Doctrine.

1990 General Instrument (GI) develops the world's first all-digital TV broadcasting system.

1990 The U.S. Congress passes the Children's Television Act (CTA), which requires all television networks to broadcast at least three hours of educational/informational (E/I) programming per week and limits the amount of advertising allowed during children's programs.

1990 Producer Aaron Spelling introduces *Beverly Hills, 90210,* one of the first prime-time dramas aimed at teenagers.

1992 The broadcast networks adopt a ratings system, modeled after that used for theatrical films, to inform parents about program content that might be inappropriate for younger viewers.

1994 The FCC establishes technical standards for high-definition television (HDTV) in the United States.

1995 The first television program is delivered over the Internet.

1995 Broadcast networks WB (the Warner Brothers Network) and UPN (the United Paramount Network) are formed.

1996 The Telecommunications Act of 1996 reduces limits on TV station ownership and removes barriers between different areas of the communication industry, leading to increased media consolidation.

1996 Approximately one billion television sets are in use worldwide.

1997 The FCC establishes a schedule for the transition to digital television broadcasting.

1997 Barbara Walters creates the daytime talk show *The View.*

2000 Producer Mark Burnett launches the reality-TV craze with *Survivor.*

2000 All new television sets sold in the United States are required to contain a V-chip to allow parents to block programs electronically based on their content ratings.

2000 Television news comes under criticism for its coverage of the 2000 presidential election, after several broadcast and cable networks report results before they have enough information to do so accurately.

2004 During the presidential campaign, Democratic Senator John Kerry and Republican President George W. Bush, combined, spend more than $600 million on television and radio advertising.

2006 The ABC network charges advertisers $2.5 million for each 30-second commercial that airs during Super Bowl XL; these ads reach more than 100 million people in the United States and hundreds of millions more around the world.

2006 The WB and UPN networks merge, forming a new network, The CW.

Words to Know

affiliate: A local television station that is connected or grouped together with a major network. Local affiliate stations are required to carry the network's programs according to a regular schedule.

airwaves: Naturally occurring waves of electromagnetic energy that travel through the air and can be used to carry information, such as television signals. In the United States, the airwaves belong to the American people, and the FCC grants individuals and companies the right to use the public airwaves by issuing broadcast licenses.

American Broadcasting Company (ABC): One of the major U.S. broadcast television networks, formed in 1943.

analog: A naturally occurring form of electromagnetic energy that is composed of waves and can be used to carry information, such as television signals.

anchor: The main host or presenter on a television news program.

animated: A type of television program that features cartoon characters rather than live actors.

bandwidth: A measurement of the amount of space on the airwaves needed to carry a television signal, based on the frequency and wavelength characteristics of that signal.

Big Three: The major networks (ABC, CBS, and NBC) that controlled television broadcasting in the United States from the 1940s until the 1980s.

broadcast: The act of sending communication signals, such as radio or television programs, over a large area to be received by many people. The term is also used to distinguish television networks that deliver their signals over the airwaves from those that deliver their signals by cable or satellite.

broadcast license: A permit granted by the FCC that gives an individual or company the right to operate a radio or television station that sends communications signals over the public airwaves.

C

cable television: A type of service that delivers television signals to customers through cables, or long wires buried underground or strung along electrical poles, rather than through the airwaves.

cathode ray tube: The part of a television set that makes it possible to see an image on the screen. Invented in 1897, it works by shooting a beam of electrons (tiny, negatively charged particles) toward the inside of the TV screen, which is coated with a substance that glows when struck by the beam of radiation. Also known as a picture tube.

coaxial cable: A type of line or wire used to transmit electronic communication signals, consisting of a copper wire surrounded by insulation, with an aluminum coating.

Columbia Broadcasting System (CBS): One of the major U.S. broadcast television networks, formed in 1927 as a radio network.

commercial television broadcasting: A type of service, approved by the FCC in 1941, in which television networks sell commercial time to advertisers. The networks use advertising money to create and distribute programs according to a regular schedule. Before 1941, television broadcasting was experimental, and it was paid for by the television networks and TV set manufacturers.

Communications Act of 1934: The first major U.S. law that covered television. It created the Federal Communications Commission to oversee and regulate all forms of electronic communication, including radio, television, telephone, and telegraph.

consolidation: The combination or merger of several different companies that each operate in one part of the media industry to form a large communications firm that controls many types of media outlets.

content: The topics or subject matter included in a television program.

content ratings: A labeling system for television programs that provides viewers with information about the types of subject matter they contain. The system in effect in 2006 included warnings about violence (V), strong language (L), and sexuality (S).

D

deregulation: The process of reducing or eliminating government rules and regulations affecting a business or industry.

digital: A method of storing and transmitting electronic information as a binary code consisting of long strings of the digits zero and one. The main advantage of digital television signals is that they can be understood, changed, and enhanced by computers.

digital video recorder (DVR): A device that saves television programs onto a computer hard drive, making it easy for users to record shows for later viewing.

Direct Broadcast Satellite (DBS): A technology that allows television signals to be sent from satellites orbiting Earth directly to small, individual dish antennas on the roofs of houses and buildings.

E

electronic television: The type of television system used in the United States, which has no moving parts and works using the properties of electricity.

Emmy Awards: Annual honors presented by the Academy of Television Arts and Sciences for excellence in television programming. There are separate Emmy Awards for prime time and daytime programs.

experimental television broadcasting: A type of service provided by early television networks and manufacturers in order to test their facilities and equipment and try out different kinds of programming. It was used in the United States until 1941, when the

FCC approved commercial (advertiser-supported) television broadcasting.

F

Fairness Doctrine: An FCC rule, in effect from 1949 to 1989, that required broadcasters to present opposing viewpoints on controversial issues of public importance.

Federal Communications Commission (FCC): The U.S. government agency, created in 1934, charged with regulating all forms of electronic communication, including television, radio, telephone, and walkie-talkie.

fiberoptic cable: A type of line or wire consisting of clear rods of glass or plastic, which transmits electronic communication signals as rapid pulses of light.

Fox: The fourth major U.S. broadcast television network, formed in 1987 by Australian businessman Rupert Murdoch.

frequency: A characteristic of radio waves that refers to how often the wave pattern repeats itself. The entire range of frequencies is called the radio spectrum. The FCC assigns every television station a specific operating frequency within the radio spectrum to broadcast its signal.

G

game show: A type of television program in which contestants answer questions, solve puzzles, or complete physical challenges in an effort to win money or prizes.

genre: A general type or format of television program, such as a drama, situation comedy, talk show, or soap opera.

H

high-definition (HD): A technology that scans and transmits a visual image at a higher resolution, or number of horizontal lines per screen, than the original U.S. technical standard of 525 lines. The U.S. standard for high-definition television established in 1994 divides a TV screen into 1,080 lines, creating a picture twice as sharp as the old system.

interactive: A technology that allows two-way communication between the sender and receiver of TV signals. It gives viewers more control over programming by enabling them to select, respond to, and change the content of shows.

Internet Protocol Television (IPTV): The process of delivering television signals over the vast computer network known as the Internet.

![M]

market: A geographic area that is served by a distinct group of television stations.

mechanical television: An early type of television system that used a spinning disk with holes punched in it to measure the light reflected off a moving image and turn it into an electrical impulse. It required extremely bright lights to create a decent image, and it was replaced by electronic television in the 1940s.

media: Plural of medium; often used to refer to all sources of news and information, or all types of mass communication.

media outlets: Specific modes or systems of mass communication, such as radio and TV stations, cable TV systems, newspapers, and magazines.

medium: A mode or system of communication, information, or entertainment.

miniseries: A type of television program in which the story continues over several episodes, but then ends rather than extending for a full season.

![N]

National Association of Broadcasters (NAB): An industry organization made up of representatives of U.S. radio and television networks and local stations.

National Broadcasting Company (NBC): One of the major U.S. broadcast television networks, formed by the Radio Corporation of America (RCA) in 1926 as a radio network.

network: A business organization that creates programs and distributes them to a group of affiliated or linked local stations.

news magazine: A type of television program that features several different segments, like the articles in a print magazine, ranging from investigative news reports to celebrity interviews.

on the air: Short for "on the airwaves," referring to the airwaves that carry television and radio signals. Slang term for the broadcast of a program.

patent: A form of legal protection that gives an inventor the exclusive right to use or make money from an invention for a period of seventeen years.

pilot: An initial test episode of a television program, which is used to determine whether the program will attract enough viewers to become a continuing series.

prime time: The evening hours, roughly between 8 P.M. and 11 P.M., when television programs generally reach the largest number of viewers.

Public Broadcasting Service (PBS): A national nonprofit organization, consisting of more than 350 member stations, designed to air TV programs that serve the public interest. Instead of selling commercial time to make money, PBS stations receive funding from individual viewers, businesses, charities, and the federal government.

public interest: A phrase that was included in the Communications Act of 1934, which said that people who received licenses to use the public airwaves had a duty to serve the public interest. Although never fully defined by the U.S. government, the phrase was generally taken to mean that the broadcast industry had a responsibility to benefit American society by providing informative and educational programming.

Radio Corporation of America (RCA): A company that was formed in 1919 and became the nation's leading producer of televisions, operator of TV stations, and broadcaster of TV programs (through its ownership of the NBC network) in the 1940s and 1950s.

radio spectrum: The entire range of frequencies, or repeating patterns, in which radio waves exist. Television signals are broadcast over a small part of the radio spectrum.

radio wave: A form of electromagnetic energy that travels through the air and can be used to carry communication signals.

ratings: Measurements of the percentage of all television viewers who watched a particular program. A program's ratings determine how much money the network can charge advertisers to place commercials on that program. Ratings also influence whether programs are renewed for another season or canceled.

reality TV: A type of program that features regular people, rather than actors, who compete against one another or experience unusual situations together, while television cameras film their interactions. Reality shows are also known as unscripted programs, because the participants use their own words instead of reading lines from a script.

regulate: To establish rules or guidelines to control the operation of a business or industry.

rerun: A repeat showing of a television program that has already been broadcast.

S

satellite: A man-made object that orbits around Earth and can be used to relay television signals.

signal: A set of instructions that tells a television set how to display an image. A TV set can receive video signals from a broadcast network, a cable box, a satellite dish, or a VCR/DVD player. A complete video signal consists of three parts: picture, color, and synchronization (which forces the TV set to lock onto the signal in order to reproduce the image correctly).

situation comedy (sitcom): A type of television program that draws humor from continuing characters and their environment.

soap opera: A type of television program, also known as serial drama or daytime drama, that involves continuing characters and a complex story line.

spin-off: A television series that centers around a character who first appeared on another TV series.

sponsor: An individual or business that provides the money to create or broadcast a television program. Sponsors want their products and services to be associated with a television program for advertising purposes.

standard: A basic rule or guideline established by the U.S. government that applies to an entire industry.

syndication: The process of selling the legal rights to a television program to customers other than the major broadcast networks, such as independent TV stations and cable channels. First-run syndication describes programs that are created especially for independent distribution, or are syndicated when they appear on television for the first time. Off-network syndication occurs when programs that originally ran as network series are sold for a second time in syndication.

T

talk show: A type of television program that features a host, whose name often appears in the title, and includes some discussion of current events in the fields of news and entertainment.

transmit: To send or broadcast.

U

Ultra-High Frequency (UHF): A portion of the radio spectrum used to broadcast television signals. When most TV signals were sent over the airwaves, rather than by cable or satellite, UHF channels were generally considered technically inferior to VHF channels because they sent a weaker signal over a smaller area.

V

variety show: A type of television program that features a wide range of entertainment, such as music, comedy, and skits.

Very-High Frequency (VHF): A portion of the radio spectrum used to broadcast television signals. When most TV signals were sent over the airwaves, rather than by cable or satellite, VHF channels were generally considered technically superior to UHF channels because they sent a stronger signal over a wider area.

videocassette recorder (VCR): A device that saves television programs on videotape enclosed in a plastic cassette, allowing users to record shows at home for later viewing. By the 2000s it was being replaced by digital video recorder (DVR) technology.

wavelength: A characteristic of radio waves that refers to the time or distance between waves.

Television in American Society

Biographies

Roger Ailes

BORN: May 15, 1940 • Warren, Ohio

*American chief executive officer,
president of Fox News*

Roger Ailes.
© GENE BLEVINS/CORBIS.

"I worked hard, and I was always taught that you work hard, and you use your brain, and you provide a value to whoever you're working for."

In a career that has spanned more than four decades, Roger Ailes has succeeded in U.S. politics and journalism. From the late 1960s through the late 1980s, he ranked as one of the Republican Party's most effective campaign advisors. Some critics claimed that his work on behalf of various political candidates distorted the records of Republican opponents and appealed to voters' prejudices (opinions or ideas formed without knowing all the facts). But Ailes flatly rejected these claims, and his campaign efforts often ended in victory for his candidates.

Ailes moved into the world of television as a producer in the early 1990s. He first worked as an executive for the cable news channels CNBC and America's Talking (which later became MSNBC). But Ailes became well-known for his work as the head of Fox News. Hired by Fox owner Rupert Murdoch (1931–) to build up the new network, which began broadcasting in 1996, Ailes turned Fox into the most popular cable news network in the United States. Critics say that he did this by developing a news operation that routinely agreed with conservative and Republican points of view (also known as right-wing political views). But Fox and its defenders insisted that the network is the only one that does not present the news with a liberal or Democratic bias (also known as left-wing political views). Ailes insisted that Fox News's slogan, "fair and balanced," accurately represents its news-gathering philosophy.

Youth marked by illness and ambition

Roger Eugene Ailes was born in Warren, Ohio, on May 15, 1940. He was the son of a factory foreman at the local Packard Electric plant and a stay-at-home mother. As a youngster, Ailes suffered from hemophilia, a disease in which the blood does not clot properly, leaving sufferers prone to excessive bleeding from even minor scratches. He was an average student, but his grades were good enough for him to enroll at Ohio University in Athens, Ohio, in 1958.

Over the next four years, Ailes divided his time between campus life and summer and vacation work on area road crews. He joined the campus Air Force ROTC (a training program for military officers), but his hemophilia disqualified him from service. He also worked at the university radio station as a disk jockey (a person who selects music to be played on the radio). This job gave him a taste for broadcasting, and when he graduated from Ohio University in 1962 with a bachelor's degree, he sought work in the field.

Within a few months of graduating, Ailes had secured a job as property assistant on *The Mike Douglas Show*, a television talk show that was filmed in Cleveland, Ohio. Over the next few years, the program expanded to a national audience, and Ailes rose to the position of executive producer. "I worked hard, and I was always taught that you work hard, and you use your brain, and you provide a value to whoever you're working for," he later told *U.S. News and World Report*.

Moves into political consulting

Ailes eventually received two Emmy Awards for his production work on *The Mike Douglas Show*, in 1967 and 1968. During this same time, he met Republican presidential candidate Richard Nixon (1913–1994). Nixon was reportedly so impressed with Ailes that he invited the young man to join his campaign as a media consultant (a person who helps candidates present a positive image in the media).

Ailes accepted the invitation, and during the last few months of the campaign, he became Nixon's most visible media advisor. Among other Nixon advisors and journalists, Ailes became known as a confident and brash individual who understood the growing importance of television to political campaigns. When Nixon narrowly won the November 1968 presidential election over Democratic candidate Hubert Humphrey (1911–1978), Ailes received a fair amount of the credit. "Ailes became a national political player virtually overnight, and he had not yet turned thirty," wrote television historian Scott Collins in *Crazy Like a Fox.*

During the 1970s, Ailes divided his time between serving as a consultant for Republican politicians and working as a theater and television producer. His most successful experience in theater was the hit play *Hot-L Baltimore,* which enjoyed a highly successful multi-year run. Ailes received four Obie Awards (annual honors presented to Off-Broadway theatrical productions) from 1973 to 1976 for his work as a producer on the show.

In addition, Ailes produced a handful of television specials from the late 1960s through the early 1980s. In 1984, Ailes won an Emmy Award (annual honors recognizing excellence in television programming) as executive producer and director of a television special, *Television and the Presidency.* He also served as executive producer of three television programs: *Allen Ludden's Gallery* (1969), *Steve Allen's Laugh-Back* (1976), and *Tomorrow: Coast to Coast* (1981).

Returns to presidential political consulting

Ailes provided consulting services to several Republican political candidates during the 1970s and early 1980s. In 1984, he signed up for his first presidential campaign since the 1968 Nixon campaign. As media advisor to President Ronald Reagan (1911–2004; served 1981–89), Ailes helped lift the Republican president to an easy November 1984 re-election victory over Democratic candidate Walter Mondale (1928–). According to campaign insiders, Ailes played a particularly valuable role as a debating coach for Reagan. When Mondale scored a victory in the first presidential debate between the two candidates, Ailes stepped in. He helped Reagan regain his focus and sharpen his debating skills, and the president gave a much stronger performance in the second presidential debate. Reagan's showing reassured voters and stalled Mondale's effort to pull off a come-from-behind victory.

The Republican Party called on Ailes again four years later, when Reagan's vice president, George H. W. Bush (1924–), gained the party's presidential nomination. Bush's Democratic opponent in the general election was Massachusetts governor Michael Dukakis (1933–). As the presidential campaign heated up in early 1988, Dukakis held the lead in most polls. By mid-summer, however, Dukakis's lead had vanished in the face of a series of harshly negative political ads sponsored by the Bush campaign.

Ailes was one of the leading creators of this campaign, which described Dukakis as unpatriotic and out of step with ordinary American values. Many of the campaign ads put together by Ailes and his fellow Republican media consultants reduced public support for Dukakis. Perhaps the most effective—and controversial—negative campaign commercial was the so-called Willie Horton ad. This ad blamed Dukakis for a Massachusetts program that allowed certain criminals to be released from prison when authorities determined that they were not likely to pose a threat to other citizens. This program had led to the release of a convicted murderer named Willie Horton, who proved to be a threat to others when he committed rape and armed robbery following his release. Supporters of the much-debated commercial claimed that it raised a valid point about the Democratic nominee's positions on crime. But critics charged that the Republican ad appealed to prejudices among white voters who were then inclined to vote for Bush.

Bush ultimately won the November 1988 presidential election over Dukakis, and in January 1989 he was sworn in as the forty-first president of the United States. Midway through his first term in office, it appeared that Bush (served 1989–93) would easily win re-election. But concerns about the U.S. economy enabled Democratic nominee Bill Clinton (1946– served 1993–2001)to defeat Bush in the 1992 election. Unlike Bush's presidential campaign of 1988, Ailes was not heavily involved in the 1992 election battle.

Producing television news

After Bush's victory in 1988, Ailes decided to focus his energies on television news programming. He later acknowledged that he had no doubts that he would become a powerful figure in the business once he set his mind to it. After all, he had already worked in most areas of the television industry, from director and producer to salesman and technical assistant. These jobs helped him develop the gut instincts needed to create news programs that would appeal to viewers.

In 1992, Ailes combined his interests in media and Republican politics for the first time, serving as executive producer of a television show featuring right-wing radio commentator Rush Limbaugh (1951–). One year later, Ailes was named president of CNBC, a cable financial news channel owned by the NBC TV network. Around this same time, NBC executives asked Ailes to help begin another cable channel, called America's Talking. The new network debuted on July 4, 1994. Within a matter of months, Ailes actually had his own talk show on the channel, called *Straight Forward with Roger Ailes*.

Ailes received credit for boosting the ratings and profits of CNBC, but in 1996, he and NBC parted ways. NBC canceled America's Talking and announced plans to partner with Microsoft to create a new cable news network, called MSNBC, in its place. Meanwhile, Australian media tycoon Rupert Murdoch (1931–) convinced Ailes to head a proposed new 24-hour cable news operation called the Fox News Channel.

Ailes spent the next several months overseeing all aspects of Fox News's development, including the construction of studios, the arrangement of licensing deals, and the hiring of reporters, news anchors, and other staff. "It's probably the toughest thing I've ever done in my career," he admitted to *Multichannel News*. "But pressure doesn't effect me the way it does some people. I started out digging ditches for the county highway department—this beats that."

Architect of Fox News

When Fox News made its debut on October 7, 1996, Ailes promoted the channel as the only major television news outlet that was impartial in its reporting on political events. He made heavy use of such marketing slogans as "fair and balanced" and "we report, you decide" to suggest that Fox was the only reliable source of news that was not tainted by a liberal slant. Within months of the channel's launch, this strategy helped Ailes establish Fox as the favored network of Americans who described themselves as conservatives or Republicans.

But Fox News was also criticized for this approach. Critics claimed that Fox exaggerated the issue of liberal bias in other media as a way of excusing its own bias in favor of conservative political beliefs and the Republican Party. From the first day of the Fox News Channel's existence, Ailes has denied this charge. "[Fox] is not a conservative network!" he declared in the October 1999 issue of *Brill's Content*.

Still, some media critics continued to claim that Ailes and other Fox executives provided slanted news coverage. "Since its 1996 launch, Fox has become a central hub of the conservative movement's well-oiled media machine," declared the liberal advocacy group Fairness and Accuracy in Reporting (FAIR). Liberal media critic Eric Alterman, meanwhile, believes that Ailes and his Fox News Channel have influenced all news reporting in America. "The conservative orientation of Fox is invaluable to the right, not merely because Fox offers the spin [interpretation] on reality conservatives prefer to have people see and hear, but also because it helps pull the rest of the not-terribly-liberal media in its direction," he claimed in *What Liberal Media?*

As the controversy continued over whether Fox News inappropriately favored conservative causes and politicians, there was no debating the success of Ailes's time at the network. Since January 2002, Fox has regularly beaten CNN and all other cable news networks in the ratings, often by large margins. As chairman of the board, chief executive officer, and president of the network, Ailes usually receives most of the credit for Fox's stunning rise to the top.

For More Information

BOOKS

Alterman, Eric. *What Liberal Media? The Truth about Bias and the Media.* New York: Basic Books, 2003.

Collins, Scott. *Crazy Like a Fox: The Inside Story of How Fox News Beat CNN.* New York: Portfolio, 2004.

PERIODICALS

Ailes, Roger. "Campaign Strategy." *Time,* May 11, 1992.

Hass, Nancy. "Rogers Ailes: Embracing the Enemy." *New York Times Magazine,* January 8, 1995.

Hayden, Thomas. "Natural-Born Networker." *U.S. News & World Report,* October 31, 2005.

Karz, Richard. "Ailes Talks Tough on Fox Launch." *Multichannel News,* September 23, 1996.

WEB SITES

Ackerman, Seth. "The Most Biased Name in News: Fox News Channel's Extraordinary Right-Wing Tilt." *Fairness and Accuracy in Reporting (FAIR).* http://www.fair.org/index.php?page=1067 (accessed on May 22, 2006).

"Ailes, Roger." *Museum of Broadcast Communications.* http://www.museum.tv/archives/etv/A/htmlA/ailesroger/ailesroger.htm (accessed on May 22, 2006).

Roone Arledge

BORN: July 8, 1931 • Forest Hills, New York

DIED: December 5, 2002 • New York, New York

American television producer

"We are going to add show business to sports!"

As the president of ABC Sports and later ABC News, Roone Arledge helped turn the smallest of the three major television networks (NBC and CBS are the other two) into a respected leader. He came up with so many original ideas and created so many new shows during his forty-year career that a *Newsweek* obituary described him as "the most innovative TV producer ever." As the head of ABC Sports, Arledge created many production techniques that became routine in televised sporting events, such as instant replay, slow motion, and "up close and personal" portraits of athletes. After taking over ABC's news division in 1977, he launched the careers of numerous top television journalists and created such highly rated programs as *Nightline, Prime Time Live,* and *20/20.*

Changing the look of televised sports

Roone Pinckney Arledge Jr. was born on July 8, 1931, in Forest Hills, New York. He was the son of Roone Arledge Sr., a successful lawyer, and his wife Gertrude (Stritmater) Arledge. Arledge earned a bachelor's

Roone Arledge.
© NAJLAH FEANNY/CORBIS.

degree in business from Columbia College in 1952. He briefly attended Columbia University's School of International Affairs, but then he was drafted into the U.S. Army. During his two years of military service, he produced several radio commercials. In 1955, Arledge took a job with the NBC television network as a producer of children's and public affairs programming. In 1958, he won an Emmy Award (an annual honor recognizing excellence in television programming) as the producer of a puppet show called *Hi, Mom*.

In 1960, Arledge moved to the ABC television network. At that time, ABC was the smallest and least influential of the three national broadcast networks. It trailed CBS and NBC in both entertainment and news programming. In fact, it was jokingly referred to as the Almost Broadcasting Company. But young Arledge saw an advantage in ABC's weak position in the broadcast industry. In its efforts to catch up to the competition, the network was more open to bold new ideas.

Arledge started out working in the sports division. ABC Sports faced a challenge in reaching viewers because its competitors already controlled the legal rights to broadcast America's most popular sporting events. But ABC did manage to win the contract to broadcast college football games. In preparing for the start of the season, Arledge began thinking of ways that ABC Sports could make its football telecasts stand out from the competition.

Arledge came up with a plan to make the game more interesting and exciting for viewers. He described his vision in a famous memo to his colleagues, which was quoted by Charles Hirshberg in *ESPN 25*. Arledge proposed using portable cameras "to get the impact shots that we cannot get from a fixed camera—a coach's face as a man drops a pass in the clear—a pretty cheerleader after her hero has scored a touchdown—a coed who brings her infant baby to the game—the referee as he calls a particularly difficult play—two romantic students sharing a blanket late in the game on a cold day—the beaming face of a substitute halfback as he comes off the field after running seventy yards for a touchdown. . . . In short—WE ARE GOING TO ADD SHOW BUSINESS TO SPORTS!"

Creating *ABC's Wide World of Sports*

In 1961, Arledge used these ideas as the basis for an innovative new sports program, *ABC's Wide World of Sports*. Since ABC's competitors held the rights to televise all the major U.S. sporting events, Arledge decided that ABC Sports should take a different approach and focus on the wide variety of sports available in the rest of the world. He believed that these lesser-known sports might attract a solid audience, as long as the events were presented in an entertaining way. The show's well-known introduction, read by host Jim McKay (1921–), explained its mission: "Spanning the globe to bring you the constant variety of sport. The thrill of victory, and the agony of defeat. The human drama of athletic competition. This is *ABC's Wide World of Sports*."

ABC Sports sent camera crews all over the world to provide coverage of such little-known events as table tennis, badminton, curling, cliff diving, and drag racing. It also showed international gymnastics and ice-skating competitions at a time when these sports received minimal coverage. The most notable aspect of *Wide World of Sports* was that it presented sporting events as entertainment. It was the first show to provide "up close and personal" profiles of athletes, for example, and to use technical innovations like instant replay and slow motion.

Wide World of Sports earned forty-seven Emmy Awards during its forty-year run on ABC. Its influence can be seen in many aspects of later sports broadcasting, especially in the coverage of multi-event athletic contests such as the Olympic Games. Rather than simply providing viewers with film footage of the event itself, all of the networks started offering special features that turned sports into high-quality television entertainment.

Launching *Monday Night Football*

In 1963, Arledge was promoted to vice president of ABC Sports. The following year, he served as executive producer for the network's telecast of the Olympic Games. As it turned out, it was the first of ten Olympic broadcasts that he would produce for ABC. Arledge introduced a number of innovations that gave the Games a broad appeal to television viewers. For instance, he produced special features that gave viewers an in-depth look at the personal background of individual athletes. He also convinced the network to move its Olympic telecasts from the afternoon, when sporting events were usually broadcast, into the evening, when more people could watch. His coverage of the 1976 Olympics attracted such a large audience that it helped lift ABC to its first number one finish in the annual TV ratings in network history.

In 1968, Arledge was promoted to president of ABC Sports. Two years later, he negotiated a deal for ABC to broadcast National Football League (NFL) games. Until this time, NFL games had always been

Monday Night Football announcers, from left, Don Meredith, Howard Cosell, and Frank Gifford, during the 1972 season. AP IMAGES.

broadcast on Sunday afternoons. Among television industry experts, conventional wisdom said that women controlled the TV set during the evening hours and that female audiences did not watch sports. But Arledge did not agree with these assumptions and believed that professional football could do well in the weekly prime-time schedule.

In 1970, Arledge launched a new sports program called *Monday Night Football.* Building on the success of *Wide World of Sports,* he continued to offer viewers a combination of sports and entertainment. For instance, Arledge put together an unusual team in the broadcast booth in order to increase viewer interest in the games. He combined Howard Cosell (1918–1995)—a hard-driving, opinionated journalist who tended to stir up strong feelings (both positive and negative) in TV audiences—with Don Meredith (1938–)—a funny, relaxed former quarterback for the Dallas Cowboys. The team also included an experienced play-by-play announcer, first Keith Jackson and later Frank Gifford (1930–). The

Monday Night Football announcers became the talk of the nation on Tuesday mornings, as viewers discussed the interactions among the three very different personalities.

Before long, *Monday Night Football* became so popular that restaurants and sports bars across the country started hosting parties around it. For many years, the program included special appearances by prominent athletes, entertainers, and politicians, who promoted their projects as they chatted with the show's hosts. *Monday Night Football* remained a winner in the ratings into the 2000s, despite numerous changes in the hosts who occupied the broadcast booth.

Taking charge of ABC News

Arledge's record in turning ABC Sports into a ratings success convinced network management to make him the president of ABC News in 1977 (he also remained president of ABC Sports). Up to this point, ABC had lagged behind the other broadcast networks in news coverage, and management hoped that Arledge could improve this situation. But his appointment upset many people in the news division. Arledge did not have a background in journalism, and he had gained a reputation over the years for creating flashy, dramatic sports telecasts. Many people worried that he did not understand the seriousness of the news and would tend to emphasize entertainment over journalism.

Despite such doubts, however, Arledge quickly began putting his successful ideas to work on the news division. He reshaped ABC's news coverage by adding attractive graphics, introducing the new practice of split-screen interviews (which divided the screen so that viewers could see the interviewer and interviewee at the same time), expanding news coverage to new time periods, and raiding other networks to hire top journalistic talent. Some of the television anchors (news presenters) whose careers he helped launch include Peter Jennings (1938–2005), Ted Koppel (1940–), David Brinkley (1920–2003), **Barbara Walters** (1931–; see entry), Sam Donaldson (1934–), and Diane Sawyer (1945–). Arledge also created several new programs that combined news and entertainment, such as *20/20* and *Prime Time Live*.

In 1979, ABC launched a late-night news program to provide viewers with updates on the Iran hostage crisis. Earlier that year, revolutionaries in the Middle Eastern nation of Iran had overthrown the U.S.-supported government. The new leader, Ayatollah Khomeini (1902–2003), had encouraged his followers to demonstrate against American

Sportscaster Howard Cosell

Howard Cosell. AP IMAGES.

Howard Cosell is one of the most famous sports broadcasters in the history of television. He earned both fans and critics with his intellectual approach to sports and his willingness to express his opinion. In fact, a survey of television viewers conducted by *TV Guide* in the 1970s named Cosell both the most popular and least popular sportscaster in the United States.

Cosell was born as Howard William Cohen on March 25, 1918, in Winston-Salem, North Carolina. His family name was originally Kozel, but it had been changed to Cohen when his father immigrated to the United States from Poland. Cosell changed it back, with a slightly different English spelling, around 1940.

Cosell's family moved to Brooklyn, New York, when he was a child. He was an excellent student, and he served as a sportswriter for his high school newspaper. Cosell earned a law degree from New York University in 1941 and opened a law office in New York City. Specializing in labor issues, he represented several actors and athletes, including the famous New York Giants baseball player Willie Mays. Another client of Cosell's law practice was Little League Baseball of New York. In 1953 the ABC radio network asked Cosell to host a program in which Little League players would interview Major League Baseball stars. The show attracted a great deal of attention, partly because Cosell provided the children with interesting questions to ask.

and Israeli interests. In November a group of Iranian students captured the U.S. Embassy in the capital city of Tehran and took fifty-two American diplomats and citizens hostage. Most of these people were held for over a year before they were finally released in early 1981.

During the hostage crisis, Arledge reserved a nightly time slot for news bulletins. Anchor Ted Koppel discussed current events and interviewed prominent people from around the world. Once the hostage situation was resolved, Arledge decided to turn it into a regular news program called *Nightline*. From 1981 into the 2000s, *Nightline* received critical praise for covering complex issues, particularly regarding foreign

In 1956 Cosell gave up his law practice to work for ABC full time. By the 1960s he had become one of the network's main announcers for television coverage of boxing matches and the Olympic Games. Cosell was very different in appearance and manner from most TV sportscasters of that time. He spoke with a strong Brooklyn accent, for instance, and often showed off his intelligence by using big words. Unlike the good-looking former athletes who often served as TV commentators, Cosell was not considered physically attractive and had never played competitive sports. Cosell also provided viewers with unusually in-depth coverage of various issues in sports. When people objected to his hard-hitting approach, he always insisted, "I'm just telling it like it is."

Cosell first came to fame by covering the sport of boxing. In the minds of many TV viewers, his career became linked with that of Muhammad Ali, a great fighter who reached the height of his talent and popularity in the 1960s and 1970s. Cosell interviewed Ali on television countless times during these years. The two men often teased and insulted each other on camera, but they developed a deep mutual respect and friendship behind the scenes. Cosell stopped covering boxing in 1982, following an especially brutal and one-sided match between heavyweight champion Larry Holmes and challenger Randall "Tex" Cobb. Afterward, Cosell openly criticized the sport and called for it to be outlawed.

Cosell is probably best known as the longtime co-host of *Monday Night Football*. This innovative program, which started in 1970, marked the first time that a television network tried to air regular-season sporting events during the weekday evening hours known as prime time. In order to compete against the entertainment programs airing on other channels, ABC selected a team of hosts whose widely differing personalities often made their interactions more interesting than the game itself. Cosell especially clashed with co-host Don Meredith, a funny, laid-back former quarterback for the Dallas Cowboys. Cosell finally quit *Monday Night Football* in 1984.

The following year Cosell started hosting a newsmagazine program called *Sportsbeat* on ABC. Although the show received praise from critics, it went off the air after only three months. Television insiders claimed that ABC executives canceled the show out of anger at Cosell, who had criticized many co-workers in his 1985 book *I Never Played the Game*. Cosell never worked in TV again. He wrote several other books, including *Cosell on Cosell, Like It Is,* and *What's Wrong with Sports*. After suffering from poor health for the last decade of his life, Cosell died on April 23, 1995, in New York City.

affairs. Even though it faced tough competition from entertaining late-night talk shows hosted by Johnny Carson, Jay Leno, and David Letterman, *Nightline* became the highest-rated program in its time slot in 1995. "I'm prouder of that show than of almost anything I've ever done," Arledge told *Newsweek*. "It gives us a dimension no other network has ever had."

Over the course of his long career as a television executive, Arledge won thirty-six Emmy Awards. In 1990, he was inducted into both the Academy of Television Arts and Sciences Hall of Fame and the U.S. Olympic Hall of Fame. In addition, a *Life* magazine poll released that year listed him among the one hundred most important Americans of the twentieth century. In 1994, *Sports Illustrated* ranked Arledge third (behind boxer Muhammad Ali and basketball player Michael Jordan) among individuals who had the greatest impact on the world of sports since 1950. Arledge was promoted to chairman of ABC News in 1997, but his influence began to decline when he was diagnosed with cancer. He died on December 5, 2002, at the age of 71.

For More Information

BOOKS

Arledge, Roone. *Roone: A Memoir.* New York: HarperCollins, 2003.

Cosell, Howard, with Peter Bonventre. *I Never Played the Game.* New York: William Morrow, 1986.

Gunther, Marc. *The House That Roone Built: The Inside Story of ABC News.* Boston: Little, Brown, 1994.

Gunther, Marc, and B. Carter. *Monday Night Mayhem: The Inside Story of ABC's Monday Night Football.* New York: William Morrow, 1988.

Hirshberg, Charles. *ESPN 25: 25 Mind-Bending, Eye-Popping, Culture-Morphing Years of Highlights.* New York: Hyperion, 2004.

Kindred, Dave. *Sound and Fury: Two Powerful Lives, One Fateful Friendship.* New York: Free Press, 2006.

Powers, Ron. *Supertube: The Rise of Television Sports.* New York: Coward-McCann, 1984.

Rader, Benjamin G. *In Its Own Image: How Television Has Transformed Sports.* New York: Free Press, 1984.

Spence, Jim, and Dave Giles. *Up Close and Personal: The Inside Story of Network Television Sports.* New York: Atheneum, 1988.

PERIODICALS

Alter, Jonathan. "Roone Arledge: July 8, 1931–December 5, 2002." *Newsweek,* December 16, 2002.

Arledge, Roone. "It's Sport . . . It's Money . . . It's TV." *Sports Illustrated,* April 25, 1966.

Jicha, Tom. "The Sporting Life: Monday Night Football Revitalized the Game and the Network." *Television Week,* May 19, 2003.

Roberts, Randy. "Roone Arledge and the Rise of Televised Sports." *USA Today,* January 1992.

"Roone Arledge on ABC's Wide World of News." *Broadcasting and Cable,* October 10, 1994.

Rubinstein, Julian. "The Emperor of the Air." *New York Times Magazine.* December 29, 2002.

Shapiro, Leonard. "Howard Cosell Dies at 77." *Washington Post,* April 24, 1995.

WEB SITES

Baran, Stanley J. "Sports and Television." *Museum of Broadcast Communications.* http://www.museum.tv/archives/etv/S/htmlS/sportsandte/sportsandte.htm (accessed on May 23, 2006).

Tedesco, John. "Roone Arledge." *Museum of Broadcast Communications.* http://www.museum.tv/archives/etv/A/htmlA/arledgeroon/arledgeroon.htm (accessed on May 23, 2005).

Lucille Ball

BORN: August 6, 1911 • Jamestown, New York
DIED: April 26, 1989 • Los Angeles, California

American comedian, actress

"I never thought I was funny. I don't think funny."

Widely considered one of the greatest comedians of all time, Lucille Ball created an early television character that still enjoys great popularity around the world after more than fifty years. In October 1951, when she made her debut as the zany housewife Lucy Ricardo in the situation comedy (a type of program that draws humor from continuing characters and their environment) *I Love Lucy,* she was a forty-year-old actress with more than sixty movies to her credit. But Ball made her greatest impact on the small screen. As the first female superstar of the television era, she changed the course of TV history and had a lasting influence on American culture. "Quite simply, the show was better written, performed, and photographed than anything else the audience had ever seen," Vince Waldron wrote in *Classic Sitcoms.* "Even today—more than four decades after the series ended its run—few situation comedies can match the look, pacing, and precision of the best episodes of *I Love Lucy,* television's first classic sitcom."

Lucille Ball.
© BETTMANN/CORBIS.

A young actress and model

Lucille Desiree Ball was born in Jamestown, New York, on August 6, 1911. She was the eldest of two children born to Henry Durell Ball and Desiree (DeDe) Hunt. Ball's father was a telephone lineman for the Bell Company, and the family moved to Montana and then Michigan before Ball was four years old. In 1915, Henry Ball died, and the family moved back to Jamestown to live with Ball's grandparents.

Ball showed an early interest in acting, and her mother and grandfather encouraged her to develop her talents. Throughout her teen years, she participated in as many school and community plays as she could. When she was seventeen, Ball attended the John Murray Anderson–Robert Milton School of Theater in New York City. After only one term, however, the instructors told Ball that she did not have the special qualities needed to become an actress and asked her to leave the school. But Ball refused to simply accept the rejection and go back home. "Although lonely, homesick, and lost, I couldn't face the sneers and snickers I felt would be waiting for me back in Jamestown," she wrote in her autobiography, *Love, Lucy*. "This was the day of the Ziegfeld Follies and Shubert spectacles [popular stage shows featuring costumed dancing girls]; hundreds of girls were hired to decorate the stage in fur and feathers. So I decided to become a showgirl."

Ball struggled as a showgirl, too, and was repeatedly fired from various chorus lines. She eventually found her first show-business success as a model. After a bout of rheumatoid arthritis sent her back to Jamestown for almost a year, Ball returned to New York in 1931 to continue modeling. Her big break came when the Chesterfield cigarette company selected her portrait for a major advertising campaign. Ball became the new Chesterfield Girl, and her face appeared on billboards all over New York City. A talent agent recognized her from the ads and recommended her for a role in a movie starring Eddie Cantor called *Roman Scandals*. She got the part and moved to Hollywood, California, in 1933.

For the next fifteen years, Ball appeared in a number of small movies. She also occasionally received minor parts in major films, such as *Stage Door* with Katharine Hepburn (1907–2001) and Ginger Rogers (1911–1995). While working on the set of *Too Many Girls* in 1940, Ball met a young Cuban bandleader named Desi Arnaz (1917–1986). Arnaz had arrived in the United States just five years earlier. At that time, he was penniless, but he soon found work as a musician and bandleader. He got a part in the Broadway version of *Too Many Girls,* which led to a role in the movie with Ball. The two fell in love immediately. "Everyone at the studio knew I was starry-eyed over Desi, and most of them warned me against him," Ball remembered in her autobiography. "But I had flipped." The couple was married a few months later, on November 30, 1940.

For the next ten years, Ball worked on movies in Hollywood and on various film locations, while Arnaz toured the country with his band. Being away from each other so much took a toll on their marriage. At one point, Ball decided that the only way to save her marriage was to find a way that she and her husband could work together. Approached by CBS Radio to appear on a radio show about a married couple, Ball proposed that Arnaz play her husband. CBS executives worried that the audience would not believe they were married, but Ball managed to convince them to give it a try. The radio show, *My Favorite Husband,* made its debut in 1948. Although the show was successful, it soon began losing listeners to the new medium of television, which was rapidly increasing in popularity in the late 1940s.

I Love Lucy

In 1950, CBS approached Ball with a plan to move *My Favorite Husband* to television. Once again, Ball suggested that Arnaz play her husband, but network executives claimed that TV audiences would not find them believable as a couple. In an effort to prove that viewers would accept them, Ball and Arnaz created a stage act of comedy and music that they performed around the country. The tour was a big success. When they returned to California, CBS agreed to produce a TV show starring Ball and Arnaz.

From the debut of the series in 1951, Ball and her husband played important roles in shaping their TV characters. "We called my radio writers on *My Favorite Husband* and together dreamed up a set of television characters," Ball remembered in *Love, Lucy.* "Originally, we were Lucy and Larry Lopez. . . . Desi would be a Cuban bandleader who worked in New York City. I would play a housewife with burning stage ambition." This initial idea proved to be a good one, but getting a sponsor to agree to their plan was a bit difficult.

The pilot, or initial test episode, of the show was filmed quickly, adapting parts from the successful stage act. Ball, who was carrying their first child, wore baggy clothing to conceal her pregnancy. The pilot attracted the attention of cigarette manufacturer Philip Morris,

A scene from I Love Lucy, *starring, from left, Lucille Ball, Vivian Vance, William Frawley, and Desi Arnaz.* © BETTMANN/ CORBIS.

which agreed to sponsor the program on the condition that it be broadcast live from CBS network studios in New York City. Most television programs were produced in New York at that time. The East Coast was the most heavily populated area of the country, and early television pictures declined in quality the further the signals were sent from the original source. Naturally, advertisers wanted to base shows where the most viewers could receive their messages. But this rather ordinary location request by the sponsor created problems for Ball and Arnaz, who refused to move to New York.

The couple wanted to produce the show in Hollywood, using technically superior film rather than less-expensive videotape. They also suggested building a soundstage large enough to hold a live audience and using a multiple-camera technique that would give the actors more freedom to play to the audience. Both CBS and Philip Morris felt that filming the show in California and using the innovative camera style would be too difficult and expensive. In order to make the arrangement work, Ball and Arnaz agreed to take a cut in pay. But they also demanded that their new production company, Desilu, be granted ownership of the show.

Following the successful pilot episode, the creative team decided to add more regular characters in order to balance the personalities of Ball and Arnaz, who played Lucy and Ricky Ricardo. They came up with an older couple, Fred and Ethel Mertz, who became landlords and best friends of the Ricardos. Veteran actor William Frawley (1887–1966) was cast as Fred Mertz, and Vivian Vance (1909–1979) was cast as his wife Ethel.

A smash hit

The first episode of *I Love Lucy* was broadcast on October 15, 1951. It was an immediate hit, and over time it came to be regarded as the standard for all future situation comedies. By April 1952, nearly 10.6 million television sets were tuned to *I Love Lucy* each week, marking the first time a TV show had reached so many people. In fact, stores and restaurants across the country would close for the half-hour broadcast, placing a sign on the door that said, "We love Lucy, too. See you after the show." Over the course of its six-year run, the show was nominated for twenty-three Emmy Awards and won five. Emmy Awards are annual honors recognizing excellence in television programming.

When Ball was pregnant with her second child, she and the producers decided to write her pregnancy into the show. A pregnant woman had rarely appeared on television before, and certainly never as the lead in a comedy series. Although CBS was nervous about offending viewers with what was considered a private experience at that time, the plans moved forward. On January 19, 1953, both Lucille Ball and Lucy Ricardo had a baby. Ball's real-life delivery took place on the same day the groundbreaking episode "Lucy Goes to the Hospital" aired. By some estimates more than 44 million people watched that episode, setting a record for a television audience that lasted for decades.

Original weekly episodes of *I Love Lucy* ran until May 1957. Once the series ended, Desilu Productions sold the rights to air reruns of the show to CBS for the record price of $4 million. This business deal allowed Ball and Arnaz to buy RKO Pictures, a movie-production studio. In November 1957, the characters of Lucy, Ricky, Fred, and Ethel returned to television in *The Lucille Ball–Desi Arnaz Show* (also known as *The Lucy-Desi Comedy Hour*). The hour-long program, which aired until April 1960, kept the same format as *I Love Lucy* but was set in Westport, Connecticut, where the Ricardos and Mertzes had moved in the last season of the original show. Shortly after this program concluded its run, Ball and Arnaz were divorced. They remained good friends, though, and each retained 25 percent ownership of Desilu Productions.

The first female head of a TV production company

In 1962, following a successful run on Broadway in the musical *Wildcat,* Ball decided to return to television. She bought out Arnaz's share of Desilu Productions for $3 million and thus became the first female president of a major television production company. Ball then produced a new series, called *The Lucy Show,* in which she and Vivian Vance played two widowed best friends who shared a house with their children. The show was not as successful as *I Love Lucy,* though it did earn high ratings. Vance left the show in 1965, but it continued running until 1968. Then Ball starred in another show, *Here's Lucy,* which also featured her real-life children, Lucie Arnaz and Desi Arnaz Jr. This program aired until September 1974. When it finally ended its run, it marked the conclusion of nearly twenty-three years of original weekly television programming starring Lucille Ball.

In 1967, Ball sold Desilu Productions to the Gulf and Western Industries for $17 million. While she experienced some success as president of Desilu, overseeing the production of such popular shows as *Mission: Impossible* and *Star Trek,* she ultimately found the work of a studio head to be too demanding. With the $10 million she earned from the sale as Desilu's major stockholder, she formed a smaller company called Lucille Ball Productions.

During the 1970s and 1980s, Ball continued to appear on television specials and in occasional films. In 1986, she tried to launch a new TV series called *Life with Lucy.* It turned out to be an unfortunate way to end her career in television, as the show was canceled after only eight episodes. Later that year, her ex-husband Desi Arnaz died. A deeply saddened Ball traveled to Washington, D.C., a few days later to receive the Kennedy Center Award from President Ronald Reagan. In 1988, Ball suffered a stroke, becoming partially paralyzed. She died on April 26, 1989, after undergoing heart surgery.

Throughout her long career, Lucille Ball became known as the "first lady of television." The landmark 1950s comedy she helped develop and starred in, *I Love Lucy,* is often mentioned among the best TV programs of all time. In an era when women were expected to play traditional roles as housewives and mothers, Ball created a female character who constantly tried to become more independent and add some excitement to her life. Although Lucy Ricardo's struggles always had humorous results, Lucille Ball's career as an actress, producer, and president of a major television studio stood as a real-life example for American women.

For More Information

BOOKS

Ball, Lucille, with Betty Hannah Hoffman. *Love, Lucy.* New York: G. P. Putnam's Sons, 1996.

Fidelman, Geoffrey Mark. *The Lucy Book.* Los Angeles: Renaissance Books, 1999.

Halberstam, David. *The Fifties.* New York: Villard, 1993.

Higham, Charles. *Lucy: The Life of Lucille Ball.* New York: St. Martin's Press, 1986.

Morella, Joe, and Edward Z. Epstein. *Forever Lucy: The Life of Lucille Ball.* Secaucus, NJ: Lyle Stuart, 1986.

Sanders, Coyne Steven, and Tom Gilbert. *Desilu.* New York: William Morrow, 1993.

Waldron, Vince. *Classic Sitcoms: A Celebration of the Best Prime-Time Comedies,* 2nd ed. Los Angeles: Silman-James Press, 1997.

WEB SITES

"Lucille Ball." Museum of Broadcast Communications. http://www.museum.tv/archives/etv/B/htmlB/balllucille/balllucille.htm (accessed on May 22, 2006).

PBS American Masters. http://www.pbs.org/wnet/americanmasters/database/ball_l.html (accessed on May 22, 2006).

Milton Berle

BORN: July 12, 1908 • New York, New York
DIED: March 27, 2002 • Beverly Hills, California

American comedian

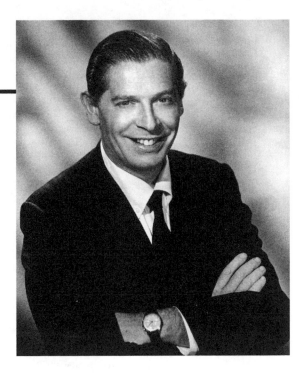

Milton Berle.
© BETTMANN/CORBIS.

"I learned quickly that I couldn't do anything small, because the studio audience couldn't see it, and if the studio audience didn't laugh, chances were the home audience wouldn't either."

Milton Berle was the first superstar of the television age. His variety show (a program that features many different types of entertainment), *Texaco Star Theater,* was a huge hit in the late 1940s and early 1950s, attracting up to 75 percent of American TV audiences each week. Berle's brand of outrageous physical humor took full advantage of the visual element that television made possible. In the earliest years of TV, friends and neighbors gathered around their sets to watch him wear ridiculous costumes, tell bad jokes, and appear on stage with trained animals and jugglers. Although the popularity of *Texaco Star Theater* helped promote the tremendous growth of television, Berle's appeal faded as the new technology developed beyond its novelty stage.

A boyhood in show business

Born Milton Berlinger on July 12, 1908, in New York City, Berle spent virtually his entire life in show business. When he was only five years

25

old, his mother began entering him in amateur talent contests. Soon after, Berle began appearing in silent movies, such as *The Perils of Pauline* and Charlie Chaplin's *Tillie's Punctured Romance.* Berle's mother, though not in show business herself, was determined to see her son succeed and get noticed. "My name got shortened," Berle explained to the *Chicago Tribune,* "because Mother figured that way it could be displayed in bigger letters on a marquee [the lighted overhead display sign on the front of a theater]."

Berle started to make a name for himself as a performer in vaudeville. Vaudeville was a circuit of theaters around the country that featured a variety of live entertainment, such as comedians, musical acts, skits, jugglers, and just about anything else that could be performed on a stage. In 1920, the twelve-year-old Berle teamed with Elizabeth Kennedy to create a youthful comedy act called *Kennedy and Berle.* By the following year, the act was appearing in vaudeville's most prestigious theaters.

Traveling around the country and performing in vaudeville shows was not an easy life for the young performers, as Berle recalled in his autobiography: "On the Orpheum Circuit, one of the best, you did two shows a day, seven days a week. You finished one theater on Sunday and you packed and traveled to get to the next theater in time for the Monday opening. A typical Orpheum route would be Minneapolis to Winnipeg to Calgary to Vancouver. From there you went to Seattle and Portland and then to San Francisco, where you played two dates. First you played the Orpheum, which was the big-time house, and then you moved to the Golden Gate, which was murder because you did continuous performances."

When he grew too tall to continue performing in the child act with Kennedy, Berle struck out on his own. A gifted joke teller, he abandoned any formal education and began honing his stage act. By 1924, at the age of sixteen, he was earning $600 per week, which was a lot of money in the 1920s. Through the remainder of the decade, Berle's success in vaudeville only increased.

In the early 1930s, the growing popularity of movies began to take its toll on vaudeville, and audiences for live entertainment started to decline. Hoping to repeat his stage success in the movies, Berle went to Hollywood. Though he appeared in a handful of movies over the next ten years—including *Gags to Riches, RKO's New Faces of 1937, Rise and Shine,* and *Whispering Ghosts*—his film career did not flourish. Berle's emphasis on physical humor and visual comedy also failed to translate to radio, where vaudeville stars such as Jack Benny (1894–1974) and Bob Hope (1903–2003) found success. Instead, Berle took his act to nightclubs, where he earned as much as $10,000 per week after World War II (1939–45).

Taking his act to television

In 1948, Berle was hired to host a radio show sponsored by the Texaco Oil Company called *Texaco Star Theater*. Within a few months, the sponsor decided to transfer the show to the brand new medium of television. Berle auditioned before the TV cameras along with two other comedians, and he was eventually selected to continue in his role as host. *Texaco Star Theater* made its television debut on the NBC network on September 21, 1948. The show was an immediate hit. In fact, it was so popular among viewers that NBC actually delayed broadcasting the results of the November 1948 presidential election until after the end of the program.

Despite his instant success, Berle soon realized that he had a lot to learn about television. "Since there were no monitors on which the audience could watch the show," he wrote in his autobiography, "they had to do as well as they could by looking around the cameras, which blocked their view of the stage. I learned quickly that I couldn't do anything small, because the studio audience couldn't see it, and if the studio audience didn't laugh, chances were the home audience wouldn't either."

During the five years that Berle's show appeared on the air, the number of American homes that contained television sets grew from 500,000 to nearly 20 million. Some historians attribute the rapid growth of television to the popularity of *Texaco Star Theater*. "The early history of television and the story of Berle's show are close to being one and the same thing," David Halberstam wrote in *The Fifties*. "Those who didn't have television sets visited those who did. The very success of Berle's show accelerated the sale of television sets; those Americans who did not yet own sets would return home after watching him at their neighbors' houses and decide that, yes, it was finally time to buy a television." Berle's impact on the early sales of TV sets helped him earn the nickname Mr. Television.

Fearing Berle would leave for a rival network, in 1951 NBC signed the popular comic to a thirty-year contract that paid him $200,000 a year, whether he appeared on TV or not. As more people bought televisions, however, more programs came on the air, which meant that Berle faced increased competition. When the ratings for his show began to decline, NBC imposed a more rigid format, which did not allow Berle to be as outrageous or freewheeling as he had been in earlier years. Texaco dropped its sponsorship in 1953, and Buick took over. *The Buick-Berle Show* only lasted until June 1955, though, before Berle was fired.

Milton Berle often dressed in outrageous costumes and makeup to entertain audiences watching his program, Texaco Star Theater. © BETTMANN/ CORBIS.

Television's first superstar thus became the first casualty of the changing tastes of television audiences.

Berle accepted responsibility for the failure of his show. "I had violated one of my basic rules of work," he explained in his autobiography. "For years I had told new young comics that they decide on their own personal image before they work, and that they must never violate that image in the public's mind. . . . But when I cooperated . . . and turned the aggressive, pushy 'Milton Berle' into a passive straight man for the 'Buick' format, I had broken my image and hurt myself."

Variety Show Host Ed Sullivan

Ed Sullivan served as the host of one of the most popular and longest-running entertainment programs in television history, *The Ed Sullivan Show*. Airing more than one thousand episodes on the CBS network between 1948 and 1971, it showcased a wide variety of entertainment—from opera singers, ballet dancers, and classical violinists to rock 'n roll bands, comedians, and trained animals.

Edward Vincent Sullivan was born on September 28, 1901, in the Harlem section of New York City. When he was a boy, his family moved to the distant suburb of Port Chester, New York. At Port Chester High School, Sullivan was a good student, especially in English, and an excellent athlete.

After graduating from high school in 1917, Sullivan got a job writing about high-school sporting events for a local newspaper, the *Port Chester Daily Item*. This job turned out to be the first of many that Sullivan would hold in the field of journalism. He went on to cover sports, entertainment, and gossip for a number of New York City newspapers, including the *New York Daily News*.

Sullivan enjoyed going to nightclubs around the city, where he often came in contact with well-known athletes and actors. During the 1930s, the young newspaper writer began organizing and hosting events to raise money for charity. He convinced many big-name entertainers to appear at these events. In 1937 Sullivan moved to Hollywood, California, hoping to expand his career to include writing and acting in films. His efforts received very poor reviews, however, and he returned to New York three years later.

Back in New York, Sullivan continued writing for newspapers and hosting charity benefits. In 1947 he served as the host of an event called the Harvest Moon Ball at Madison Square Garden. This event was broadcast on television, which was just starting out at that time. An executive at the CBS television network saw the show and asked Sullivan to host a new TV program called *Toast of the Town*. The network wanted the show to compete against *Texaco Star Theater,* a popular variety show on the NBC network that was hosted by the comedian Milton Berle.

Toast of the Town premiered on June 20, 1948, and soon became a huge hit with viewers. Although Sullivan appeared somewhat stiff and awkward on stage—and mostly stood around with his hands in his pockets—the show benefited from his remarkable ability to recognize and promote talent. He featured many young artists who went on to rank among the biggest names in American music, including Elvis Presley and the Beatles. He also featured a number of African American entertainers, such as jazz musician Louis Armstrong and comedian Richard Pryor, at a time when few blacks appeared on TV.

Sullivan served as the executive editor of the program from the beginning. In this role, he decided what acts to feature and how many minutes of air time each one would receive. CBS recognized his importance in 1955, when it changed the name of the program to *The Ed Sullivan Show*.

The appeal of the program began to fade in the mid-1960s, when many viewers felt that it failed to keep up with changing times and musical tastes. CBS finally canceled *The Ed Sullivan Show* in 1971. By this time, Sullivan had introduced more than 10,000 performers to American television audiences. Sullivan appeared in a couple of TV specials after his show ended. He died of cancer on October 13, 1974, in New York City.

Settling for guest appearances

After his show went off the air, Berle and his wife moved to California. Since he was contractually tied to NBC, he was unable to work for other TV networks. Berle appeared in three more short-lived series for NBC over the next few years: *The Milton Berle Show* in 1956; *Kraft Music Hall* in 1958; and a game show called *Jackpot Bowling* in 1961. In 1965, Berle and NBC changed his contract to allow Berle to work for other networks, and his yearly salary was cut to $120,000. In 1966, he appeared in another *Milton Berle Show* for the ABC network, but the series lasted less than one year. For the next thirty-five years, Mr. Television would make only occasional guest appearances on the medium that made him a star.

When his television career stalled, Berle returned to the nightclub circuit and played some of the biggest stages in Las Vegas. He also appeared in a number of movies, such as *It's a Mad, Mad, Mad, Mad World; The Oscar; Where Angels Go, Trouble Follows;* and Woody Allen's *Broadway Danny Rose*. Capitalizing on the fact that he was known for stealing other people's jokes, Berle published a number of joke books over the years. In 1974 he published *Milton Berle: An Autobiography,* which provided an intimate account of his life in show business.

In the 1980s and 1990s, Berle returned to television to make a series of guest appearances on shows geared toward much younger viewers. In 1985, for instance, Berle appeared in an episode of *Amazing Stories,* a science-fiction series produced by Steven Spielberg. The episode centered on aliens from outer space who intercept American television signals and travel to Earth in order to meet 1950s TV stars, such as Lucille Ball, Jackie Gleason, and Milton Berle. Berle, speaking gibberish, turns out to be the only person who can communicate with the aliens. Berle also appeared in episodes of the popular teen-oriented programs *The Fresh Prince of Bel-Air,* starring Will Smith, and *Beverly Hills, 90210.*

Berle received many awards and honors toward the end of his long show-business career. In 1984, for instance, he was the first person inducted into the Television Hall of Fame, and in 1992, he was the first person inducted into the Comedy Hall of Fame. Berle died in his sleep on March 27, 2002, at the age of 93. He was married four times and had two adopted children and two stepchildren.

For More Information

BOOKS

Berle, Milton, with Haskel Frankel. *Milton Berle: An Autobiography.* New York: Delacourte, 1974.

Bowles, Jerry. *A Thousand Sundays: The Story of the Ed Sullivan Show.* New York: Putnam, 1980.

Halberstam, David. *The Fifties.* New York: Villard, 1993.

PERIODICALS

Brownfield, Paul. "Milton Berle 1908–2002: Legendary Comedic Trouper Dies." *Los Angeles Times,* March 28, 2002.

Grossman, Ron. "Gags to Riches." *Chicago Tribune,* January 4, 1991.

Reed, J. D. "Favorite Uncle: Schticking Together Old Radio and Vaudeville Bits—and Purloining Gags from Everyone—Milton Berle Became Television's First Superstar." *People,* April 15, 2002.

Smith, J. Y. "Milton Berle, 'Mr. Television,' Dies at 93: Comic Sparked American Love Affair with Small Screen." *Washington Post,* March 28, 2002.

Van Gelder, Lawrence. "Milton Berle, TV's First Star as 'Uncle Miltie,' Dies at 93." *New York Times,* March 28, 2002.

WEB SITES

"Berle, Milton." *Museum of Broadcast Communications.* http://www.museum.tv/archives/etv/B/htmlB/berlemilton/berlemilton.htm (accessed on May 22, 2006).

Schaeffer, Eric. "Ed Sullivan." *Museum of Broadcast Communications.* http://www.museum.tv/archives/etv/S/htmlS/sullivaned/sullivaned.htm (accessed on June 19, 2006).

Mark Burnett

BORN: July 17, 1960 • London, England

British television producer

"I don't really consider myself doing reality TV.... I'm making dramatic television. It's all about the storytelling, it's all about the visual art, and I approach it in that way."

Mark Burnett is the television producer most responsible for launching the popular type of programming known as reality TV in the early 2000s. The innovative programmer created several popular reality shows, including *Survivor* and *The Apprentice,* that inspired many imitators and helped make reality programming a major part of the television schedule in the United States and around the world.

A soldier and businessman

Mark Burnett was born on July 17, 1960, in London, England. He grew up as the only child of working-class parents and credited much of his later success to the supportive atmosphere in which he was raised. The athletic Burnett enjoyed swimming, basketball, and soccer. When he was eighteen years old, he entered the British Army, and his desire for adventure led him to become an elite paratrooper (a highly trained

Mark Burnett.
WIREIMAGE.

33

soldier who parachutes into hostile situations). During his four years in the military, he served in Northern Ireland and participated in the British invasion of the Falkland Islands in the South Atlantic, eventually rising to the rank of section commander.

In 1982, Burnett left both the army and his native land and headed for Central America, where he planned to seek work as a military advisor. After his mother expressed concerns about his safety, though, he reconsidered his decision. When the plane taking him to Central America stopped over in Los Angeles, California, Burnett chose to remain in the capital of the U.S. entertainment industry. Over the next ten years, he did whatever work he could find. For example, he worked as a nanny/bodyguard for a wealthy family, as an insurance salesman, and as a used-clothing vendor in the resort town of Venice Beach. A natural as a businessman, Burnett soon found himself running five profitable T-shirt stands. He invested the money from that venture in real estate, and he also started his own credit card company.

Entering the world of television

Burnett became a U.S. citizen in 1990. Around the same time, he read a newspaper article about an extreme adventure race called the *Raid Gauloises*. Created in 1989 by French journalist Gerald Fusil, the *Raid* is a long-distance endurance race in which five-person teams combine their strength and intelligence to reach a series of destinations on foot, boat, camelback, and horseback. Burnett had been something of a thrill-seeker since his army days, and the idea of testing his skills and stamina in such a race appealed to him. In 1992, he assembled the first American team to compete in the *Raid Gauloises,* which was being held in the Middle Eastern nation of Oman.

In addition to competing in the *Raid,* Burnett also filmed the event. He then sold edited footage to the cable television sports network ESPN in exchange for half the commercial rights. With the money he made selling commercials for the televised *Raid Gauloises,* he began to work on producing and filming his own race, which he called the *Eco Challenge.* Although Gerald Fusil did not approve of the commercialization of endurance racing, he sold Burnett the right to create a similar competition.

The first *Eco Challenge* was held in Utah in 1995. Four-person coed teams raced over a grueling three-hundred-mile course, alternately backpacking, swimming, paddling kayaks, or riding horses or bicycles. Burnett produced the *Eco Challenge* until 2002, and the race was televised on various cable networks, including the Discovery Channel, MTV, and USA. The race became a popular athletic event for participants and spectators and an enormous moneymaker for its creator.

One lesson Burnett learned from his work on the *Eco Challenge* was that the most interesting aspect of the race was not the athletic skill of the contestants or the challenge of the course but the personal dynamics within the teams. He heard that another TV producer and writer named Charlie Parsons had an idea for a television program that would place a group of people on a deserted island in order to observe their reactions. Burnett worked with Parsons to turn the idea into a new television show.

Inventing reality TV with *Survivor*

The show that resulted from their efforts was *Survivor*, a sort of extreme game show. Although there had been a few earlier reality-based television series—such as MTV's *The Real World*, which made its debut in 1992—no major network had aired one in prime time. In the summer of 2000, Burnett convinced a reluctant CBS to broadcast *Survivor*, and audiences were immediately captivated.

On the first season of *Survivor*, sixteen contestants from diverse backgrounds were taken by boat to the remote tropical island of Pulau Tiga, near Borneo in the South China Sea. They were given two minutes to pack as many supplies as they could carry on two small rafts, then they were forced to paddle to shore and set up makeshift camps.

TV cameras followed the contestants for the next thirty-nine days, as they struggled to find food and shelter, competed in physical and mental challenges, and formed and dissolved alliances (cooperative groups or partnerships). Every three days they held a tribal council ceremony in which they voted to eliminate one contestant from the island. The drama of the program came from the contestants' interactions with each other, as they struggled to endure the difficult living conditions and plotted their strategies for winning the game. On the show's Web site, Burnett described *Survivor* as "two parts adventure contest, eight parts surviving the peer group."

An amazing 51 million people watched the final episode of the season, in which scheming advertising executive Richard Hatch became the last "survivor" and won a million dollars. The season finale thus became the second-highest rated show of the year after the Super Bowl. The

Mark Burnett's creation, Survivor, *pits contestants against their harsh living conditions and against one another.* THE KOBAL COLLECTION.

popularity of *Survivor* continued the following season, when the second edition of the series became the highest-rated show of 2001. Other successful seasons were set in a variety of exotic locations, from the Australian Outback to Guatemala.

Reality takes over prime time

The success of *Survivor* encouraged the other networks to launch their own reality series. Several of these shows enjoyed great popularity as well. In fact, by 2002, five of the top ten programs on television were reality shows. Burnett took advantage of this situation to start his own TV production company, Mark Burnett Productions (MBP).

In addition to producing new seasons of *Eco Challenge* and *Survivor,* Burnett came up with ideas for other successful unscripted dramas (shows in which participants use their own words instead of reading lines of dialogue from a script). He believed that audiences were drawn to this type of programming because it offered lively and unpredictable action. Each of Burnett's programs was based on what he described to Cynthia Littleton of the *Hollywood Reporter* as "contrived [artificial] situations creating genuine emotions."

One of Burnett's most-watched productions was *The Apprentice,* which premiered in 2004. In each episode of *The Apprentice,* contestants undertook various business-related challenges under the supervision of multi-billionaire businessman Donald Trump (1946–). The winner received a one-year contract for a high-paying job within Trump's corporation. Just as audiences had tuned in to *Survivor* week after week to see who would be voted off the island, millions of viewers watched each episode of *The Apprentice* to see the famous executive tell another contestant, "You're fired!"

MBP created a number of other unscripted programs. Along with competition shows like *Rock Star,* in which the well-known band INXS sought a new lead singer from among sixteen contestants, Burnett introduced behind-the-scenes shows such as *The Restaurant* and *The Casino,* which gave viewers a glimpse of the inner workings of businesses. Some Burnett shows were less successful than others. For instance, he failed to attract viewers with a version of *The Apprentice* starring home and garden expert Martha Stewart, as well as with *The Contender,* a behind-the-scenes look at the world of boxing. Even with the failures, though, Burnett's programs inspired dozens of imitators.

The reality show format has attracted a number of critics. Some point out that reality programming is not real or spontaneous at all. Instead, producers carefully manipulate the shows and contestants to achieve the highest dramatic impact. In 2001, a group of *Survivor* contestants filed a lawsuit against MBP, accusing the producers of urging competitors to act and vote in certain ways in order to create a desired outcome.

Other critics complain that reality programming humiliates contestants and appeals to base emotions in the viewing audience. For example, they claim that reality shows value competition over cooperation and often reward lying, cheating, and other negative behavior. TV audiences, however, seem to care little about behind-the-scenes maneuvering or possible negative messages. The majority of viewers tune in for entertainment, and many find reality television programs to be highly entertaining. In 2003, the Academy of Television Arts and Sciences recognized the impact of the Burnett-style reality show by adding the category Outstanding Reality/Competition Program to the Emmy Awards (annual honors recognizing excellence in television programming).

Blurring the boundaries between shows and commercials

Another of Burnett's major innovations in television programming has been his skillful management of commercial time. His earnings from advertising sales for the *Raid Gauloises* allowed him to start his television empire, and advertising dollars became a major source of his future income. When major networks were unenthusiastic about airing his new reality show, Burnett convinced CBS to take a chance on *Survivor* by agreeing to take half of the commercial time for the show as his payment. What appeared to be a good deal for CBS turned out to be a very profitable decision for Burnett, who sold the advertising time at increasingly high rates as the show gained popularity.

In addition to making sharp business decisions about selling commercial time, Burnett also anticipated a problem that new technology would create for advertisers. With the introduction of TiVo and other digital video recording systems, more television viewers began recording programs to watch later and fast-forwarding through commercials. Advertisers, who paid high prices for their commercial time, became concerned that their messages were being lost. Burnett solved this problem by developing the use of product placement in his shows.

Product placement is the use of a brand-name product within the content of a television show or film. Manufacturers of various consumer products make arrangements with TV producers so that characters will use their products on screen during a show. For instance, the characters might talk about or drink a certain beverage. Even a truck driving by on the street with a brand name on the side can be a result of a product placement agreement. Product placement seemed to fit naturally into Burnett's reality shows, and he became famous for incorporating brand-name goods into his programs. For example, the contestants on *Survivor* eagerly awaited a well-labeled delivery of supplies from Target, a national discount retail chain. *The Apprentice* provided an even better showcase for product placement, as teams of contestants were directed to design a new toy for Mattel or an ad campaign for Crest toothpaste.

Burnett has not only continued to create new seasons of his popular shows, but he continually comes up with ideas for new television programming. In 2006 he worked with film director Steven Spielberg (1946–) to develop a show for the Fox network, called *On the Lot,* which was expected to give contestants a chance to direct their own movies. Another of his ideas for a new program involved a competition for would-be astronauts, in which contestants would try to win a spot on a space shuttle mission.

Despite his success in reality television, Burnett does not rule out working in more traditional plot-based formats. In 2004, he combined reality and fiction by creating a situation comedy pilot (initial test episode) based on his own life. *Commando Nanny* follows the adventures of a discharged British soldier who takes a job as a nanny for a wealthy Beverly Hills family. No network decided to turn the pilot into a series, but Burnett took the loss in stride and continued to look forward to the next profitable new idea.

Burnett's phenomenal rise in the entertainment industry has provided inspiration for many people who seek business success. He is in high demand as a motivational speaker in a variety of corporate settings, and he has written about his life and his business philosophy in two books: *Dare to Succeed: How to Survive and Thrive in the Game of Life* (2001) and *Jump In! (Even if You Don't Know How to Swim)* (2005). As of 2006, Burnett lived in Los Angeles with his second wife, actress Roma Downey. He has two sons, James and Camcron, with his first wife, Diane Burnett.

For More Information

BOOKS

Burnett, Mark. *Dare to Succeed: How to Survive and Thrive in the Game of Life.* New York: Hyperion, 2001.

Burnett, Mark. *Jump In! (Even If You Don't Know How to Swim).* New York: Ballantine Books, 2005.

PERIODICALS

"Burnett Likes Mad Ave." *Advertising Age,* May 19, 2003.

Boyles, Denis, and Alicia Ault. "Ultimate Survivor." *Reader's Digest,* February 2001.

Downey, Kevin. "A Dreamer of Real Dreams: Burnett Launched a Television Genre and Has Seen It Gain Respect." *Multichannel News,* January 19, 2004.

Grainger, David. "Hollywood Hitman." *Fortune,* August 23, 2004.

Orens, Geoff. "Mark Burnett." *Current Biography,* May 2001.

Wassermann, Todd. "Mark Burnett: An Adventure with No Ending." *Brandweek,* October 11, 2004.

WEB SITES

Littleton, Cynthia. "Dialogue with Producer Mark Burnett." *Hollywood Reporter.* http://www.hollywoodreporter.com/thr/article_display.jsp?vnu_content_id=1000518943 (accessed on May 24, 2006).

"Survivor." *CBS.com.* http://www.cbs.com/primetime/survivor/show/about.shtml (accessed on June 6, 2006).

Joan Ganz Cooney

BORN: November 30, 1929 • Phoenix, Arizona

American television producer

"As an education device, television has important strengths: it is accessible, it is cost effective, and it works."

Joan Ganz Cooney is the founder of the Children's Television Workshop, an organization that has created educational programming for children's television for more than three decades. Her best-known work is *Sesame Street,* an original children's TV program that features such beloved characters as Big Bird, Elmo, Oscar, and Bert and Ernie. The show enjoyed such great popularity in the United States that a number of other countries developed their own versions. By the mid-2000s, *Sesame Street* reached more than 235 million people in 120 countries around the world.

Using the media to help others

Joan Ganz Cooney was born on November 30, 1929, in Phoenix, Arizona. Her father, Sylvan Ganz, worked as a banker, and was born Jewish. Her mother, Pauline Ganz, was Roman Catholic. Joan was raised as a Catholic, and she went to parochial elementary schools as a child. She then attended North Phoenix High School, participating in tennis and drama productions. It was in high school that her life was changed by a teacher. Classroom discussions about such important social issues as poverty, race, and class inspired her to become involved in social activism.

Another early influence in Cooney's life was Father James Keller, a Roman Catholic priest who founded the Christopher movement in 1945. Father Keller used his position as a religious leader, writer, and radio and television personality to encourage Catholics to become involved in mass communication (media like television, radio, magazines, and newspapers) as a means to help people. In several interviews, Cooney noted that Father Keller's message motivated her to become involved with children's television in order to help deprived kids and make a difference in the world.

After graduating from high school, Cooney attended the Dominican College of San Rafael in California. She later transferred to the University of Arizona, where she earned a bachelor's degree in education in 1951. With little interest in becoming a teacher, she decided to pursue a career in journalism.

Cooney worked as a writer for the *Arizona Republic* newspaper for a year, then decided to move to New York City. Her first job in television came when she was hired as a publicist (someone who promotes a business or product in the news media) for a soap opera at the NBC television network. She then took a job at the CBS television network, where she served as a publicist for a variety show called the *U.S. Steel Hour* from 1955 to 1962.

During Cooney's first year at CBS, her father committed suicide. His death profoundly affected Cooney, who then suffered from a long and dangerous bout of anorexia (a type of eating disorder). She later told a reporter that she considered her struggle with anorexia to be a passive form of suicide. Fortunately, she was eventually able to get her eating disorder under control. In 1964, she married Timothy Cooney.

Becoming involved in children's programming

During the 1960s, animated cartoons started to dominate children's programming on the major television networks, particularly on Saturday mornings. This emphasis on cartoons led to increased concerns about the quality of children's TV programming. Critics complained that cartoons had no educational value and pointed out that they often included violence, stereotyped characters (generalized, usually negative portrayals of a group of people), and commercial tie-ins (products for sale which are linked to characters in the cartoons). Many people felt that the networks did not offer enough educational programming for children.

In 1967, the U.S. Congress responded to growing concerns about the quality of television programming by passing the Public Broadcasting Act, which provided government funding to create a national broadcasting service. The Public Broadcasting Service (PBS) focused on creating programs that would educate, inform, and enrich the television viewers. Cooney's strong interest in education and social issues helped her get a job as a producer of documentaries (fact-based films) for a public television station in New York City. Even though Cooney had no experience working on films, she soon received an Emmy Award (an annual honor presented for excellence in TV programming) for producing a highly praised documentary on poverty in America.

A short time later, Cooney received a grant from the Carnegie Corporation to study the impact of educational programming on disadvantaged children. Her study, titled *The Potential Uses of Television in Preschool Education,* found significant differences in what middle-class and lower-class children knew by the time they started preschool. Most middle-class children were already familiar with letters and numbers by the time they started school, for instance, while the majority of poorer children were not. The study concluded that television could be used as a tool to teach disadvantaged children basic skills, such as counting and the alphabet, through programs that were both educational and entertaining.

In an editorial for *Electronic Learning,* Cooney expressed her belief that television can serve as a valuable tool for teachers in the classroom:

> *As an education device, television has important strengths: it is accessible, it is cost effective, and it works. Fifty years ago, a teacher could only point to a map and say, "Here's Africa." Today, with broadcast channels devoted to schools, television can bring Africa itself into the classroom. And VCRs can make rich video libraries available to teachers when they want it, for as long as they need it. . . . Research has found that carefully designed educational programming can help children learn—motivate them to read and write, improve their mathematical problem-solving skills, or encourage them to get involved in science-related activities—even after the set is turned off.*

Along with Lloyd Morrisett from the Carnegie Corporation, Cooney founded the Children's Television Workshop to create this kind of children's programming. She recruited educators, psychologists, child development experts, and creative personnel to develop a fast-paced and enjoyable TV show that would add to existing educational programs in schools. The result of this work was *Sesame Street*.

Sunny days on *Sesame Street*

Sesame Street made its debut in November 1969. It aired on about 190 public television stations nationwide and was watched by an estimated 11 million weekly viewers in the United States. Filmed in Queens, New York, the show featured a racially and ethnically diverse cast of characters living in an urban setting. It also included the imaginative puppets of Jim Henson (1936–1990), as well as songs, skits, guest stars, cartoons, and instruction in such topics as the alphabet, counting, colors, and geography. Based on Cooney's research into the way children learn, the show was divided into short segments, and the key concepts were repeated in various segments.

As *Sesame Street* evolved, it also began to address current social issues, such as changing gender roles, child abuse, illness, aging, sibling rivalry, race relations, and death. When Will Lee (1908–1982), the actor who played the beloved character Mr. Hooper, died, the show not only paid tribute to the character but discussed how his death affected the other characters. Many television critics praised the show for its sensitive handling of the issue, pointing out that the character's death gave parents a valuable opportunity to discuss a difficult topic with their children.

Studies on the impact of *Sesame Street* have demonstrated that children who watch the program show improvement in their skills and level of school readiness. As Cooney predicted in her study, the show benefits poor children by teaching them the alphabet, counting, and reasoning skills at a crucial time in their lives. This knowledge allows them to start school without a distinct disadvantage compared to middle-class children.

Sesame Street has remained popular for more than three decades. As of 2006, approximately 8 million people tuned in to watch the show each week in the United States, and versions appeared in over 120 countries around the world. In fact, *Sesame Street* was the most widely viewed children's television program in the world. The show received 97 Emmy Awards (annual honors recognizing excellence in television)—more than any other show in television history—as well as numerous other honors.

Growing the Children's Television Workshop

Spurred by the overwhelming success of *Sesame Street,* the Children's Television Workshop went on to produce several other popular educational

Joan Ganz Cooney (fifth from the left) was among the women honored at the Museum of Television and Radio's premiere of "She Made It: Women Creating Television and Radio" exhibit in 2005. PHOTO BY EVAN AGOSTINI/GETTY IMAGES.

programs for children, including *The Electric Company,* a show for grade-school children; *3-2-1 Contact,* a science show targeted at young girls; *Ghostwriter,* a detective show featuring a multicultural cast; and *Square One TV,* a program about math.

In 1975, Cooney and her husband divorced. That same year, she was diagnosed with breast cancer. She underwent a radical mastectomy (the surgical removal of both breasts) and emerged from a series of treatments cancer-free. In 1980, she married Peter G. Peterson, the former U.S. secretary of commerce and chairman of the New York investment firm Lehman Brothers. The couple established a foundation to support children's television programming.

With the rise of cable television in the 1990s, the Children's Television Workshop teamed up with the Nickelodeon cable network to launch an educational channel for children called NOGGIN. Cooney's organization also published books and magazines; produced computer software, toys, and films; and sponsored community outreach programs.

Cooney has served as a member of several notable boards and commissions, including the Council on Foreign Relations, the President's Commission on an Agenda for the 1980s, and the Governors' Commission on the Year of the Child. She has also received a number of respected awards for her work in children's television programming. In 1990, she was named to the Hall of Fame of the Academy of Television Arts and Sciences, and she also received an Emmy Lifetime Achievement Award from the Academy. In 1995, she was awarded the Presidential Medal of Freedom, the nation's highest civilian (non-military) honor. In 2003 she received the National Humanities Award.

For More Information

PERIODICALS

Cooney, Joan Ganz. "Not a Moment to Waste: The Power of Television in Education." *Electronic Learning,* March 1993.

WEB SITES

"Joan Ganz Cooney." *Museum of Broadcast Communications.* http://www.museum.tv/archives/etv/C/htmlC/cooneyjoan/cooneyjoan.htm (accessed on May 22, 2006).

"Sesame Street Facts." *Sesame Street Workshop.* http://www.sesameworkshop.org/press_kit/facts.php (accessed on May 22, 2006).

Bill Cosby

BORN: July 12, 1937 • Philadelphia, Pennsylvania

American actor, comedian

Bill Cosby.
© KIM KULISH/CORBIS.

"I don't think you can bring races together by joking about the differences between them. I'd rather talk about the similarities, about what's universal in their experiences."

Bill Cosby is one of the best known and most respected African American comedians and actors. In the 1960s, when very few racial minorities were featured on television, he won three Emmy Awards for his pioneering role as a secret agent in the action-adventure series *I Spy*. In the 1970s, he created a popular animated cartoon series called *Fat Albert and the Cosby Kids,* which followed the experiences of a group of black children living in an urban neighborhood. Cosby also created and starred in a successful situation comedy, *The Cosby Show.* This groundbreaking program focused on the daily lives of a stable, middle-class black family, but its tremendous popularity crossed racial, ethnic, and class boundaries.

Humble beginnings

William Henry Cosby Jr. was born on July 12, 1937, in Philadelphia, Pennsylvania. He was the oldest of four boys born to Anna Pearl

(Hite) Cosby, who worked as a housekeeper, and William Henry Cosby, who made a career in the United States Navy. Cosby's father was often away from home for long stretches of time, and his mother worked long hours. They often left Bill in charge of his younger brothers, Russell and Richard. Their other brother, James, died of rheumatic fever (a disease that causes high fever and swelling of the joints and heart) at the age of six. Even though both of Cosby's parents worked hard, the family struggled to make ends meet. They eventually had to move out of their house and into an all-black, low-income housing project in Philadelphia.

As a child, Cosby loved to listen to comedy shows on the radio. He had a good sense of humor and loved to make people laugh. In school, his good-hearted jokes and imitations made him popular among fellow students and teachers. In addition to his natural talents as a comedian, Cosby had impressive athletic skills. He served as captain of his elementary school baseball and track teams. He continued playing sports in junior high, and he also started acting in school plays.

Struggling in school

By the time he reached Philadelphia's Central High School, Cosby's grades had began to suffer. Although he was a bright young man, his many outside activities made it impossible for him to keep up with his studies. He played football, basketball, baseball, and ran track for the high school teams. In addition, Cosby worked before and after school to help support his family. During his youth, he held jobs selling produce, shining shoes, and stocking shelves at a local grocery store.

Cosby transferred to Germantown High School, but his grades did not improve. He continued to participate in sports and still struggled to complete his school work. When he was told that he would have to repeat tenth grade, Cosby dropped out of high school. He took a job as an apprentice (someone who learns a trade by helping a more experienced worker) at a shoe repair shop. But he also started working on a plan to do more with his life.

In 1956, Cosby joined the U.S. Navy. He served in the medical corps at Bethesda Naval Hospital in Maryland for the next four years. Cosby's job involved providing physical therapy to soldiers who had suffered serious injuries. He often tried to cheer up his patients by telling jokes and stories and making them laugh. During his time in the navy, Cosby also took correspondence classes to earn his high school diploma so that he could go to college. In 1961, Cosby entered Temple University in Philadelphia on a track and field scholarship. He majored in physical education in college, and he also ran track and played for Temple's football team.

Becoming a comedian

During his sophomore year at Temple, Cosby got a job as a bartender at the Underground, a nightclub in Greenwich Village in New York City. He enjoyed working behind the bar, talking to customers, and making them laugh. The Underground employed a regular comedian, but this comedian did not always show up when he was supposed to perform. Cosby was asked to fill in on a few of those days, and the crowds loved him. As more and more people saw his act, word of this funny bartender began to spread. Soon other comedy clubs sought him out to perform for their audiences. Cosby decided to drop out of college to pursue a career in comedy.

Before long, Cosby signed a contract with the William Morris Agency to manage his career. He began performing at comedy clubs around the country, and his popularity continued to grow. In 1964, Cosby recorded his first comedy album, titled *Bill Cosby Is a Very Funny Fellow . . . Right!* He won the first of eight career Grammy Awards for this effort. He went on to make other hit records throughout the 1960s, with titles such as *I Started Out as a Child; Why Is There Air?; Wonderfulness; Revenge;* and *Russell, My Brother, Whom I Slept With.*

Cosby's brand of humor was not offensive or crude. It was just funny. He counted such talented comedians as Mel Brooks, Jonathan Winters, Bob Newhart, and Lenny Bruce as his major influences. Unlike many other African American comics in the 1960s, Cosby did not focus on race issues. "Racial humor was about 35 percent of my act when I first started," he explained in *Time.* "But I realized that it was a crutch. What brought it home was when another comedian said to me, 'If you changed color tomorrow, you wouldn't have any material.' He meant it as a put-down, but I took it as a challenge." Instead, Cosby chose to tell humorous stories about his childhood and about situations he faced in everyday life. His audiences, both black and white, were able to relate to his stories. "I don't think you can bring races together by joking about the differences between them," he told *Time.* "I'd rather talk about the similarities, about what's universal in their experiences."

Cosby met his wife, Camille Hanks, while he was performing stand-up comedy in Washington, D.C. They were married in 1964 and eventually had five children. From this time on, many of the stories Cosby told in his comedy routines involved his family and the challenges of raising kids.

Breaking TV barriers with *I Spy*

In 1965, Cosby made a guest appearance on the popular late-night TV talk and variety program *The Tonight Show*. After watching Cosby's performance, television producer Sheldon Leonard invited him to co-star with actor Robert Culp (1930–) in a weekly television series called *I Spy*.

Before this time, almost all of the people who appeared on American television programs were Caucasian (white). The few minorities who did appear in TV programs tended to be presented as stereotypes (generalized, usually negative images of a group of people). This situation slowly began to change during the civil rights movement of the 1960s, when African Americans fought to end segregation (the forced separation of people by race) and gain equal rights in American society. TV news programs provided extensive coverage of civil rights protests, which helped turn public opinion in favor of the cause of racial equality. As awareness of racial discrimination increased, more social critics began complaining about the absence of minority characters on television.

Cosby's role in *I Spy* broke new ground on American television. Even though *I Spy* did not deal with racial issues directly, the show promoted equality through its portrayal of the partnership between the two main characters, who just happened to be of different races. Cosby and Culp played secret agents who traveled all over the world on spying assignments. In order to hide their true identities, Culp's character pretended to be a tennis star, and Cosby's character posed as his trainer. The action-adventure show became a hit with viewers, who enjoyed its subtle humor, its globe-trotting style, and the chemistry between Cosby and Culp.

I Spy remained on the air for three years, and Cosby earned an Emmy Award (annual honors recognizing excellence in television programming) in each of these years for his performance. By the time the show was canceled in 1968, Cosby had become famous. Afterward he returned to stand-up comedy, performing before big crowds in all the top comedy clubs across the United States.

Connecting with kids

Cosby returned to television in the early 1970s, playing high-school gym teacher Chet Kincaid in *The Bill Cosby Show*. Kincaid shared his pride in black culture with his students, as well as with TV viewers. Cosby's new-found popularity also gave him the opportunity to become a commercial spokesperson for a number of products, including Jell-O Pudding, Kodak Film, and Coca-Cola. Marketing surveys showed that he soon emerged as one of the most trusted product endorsers on television. Cosby also made several guest appearances on the PBS educational series *The Electric Company* during this time. Cosby found that he enjoyed working with kids on the show, and he decided to develop his own children's television program.

Beginning in 1972, Cosby created, hosted, and supplied the voices for an animated cartoon series called *Fat Albert and the Cosby Kids*, which aired on Saturday mornings until 1979. Based on his experiences growing up in Philadelphia, the show focused on a group of black children living in an urban neighborhood. Unlike other cartoons at that time, each humorous episode included an important lesson about life. In 1979, Cosby created *The New Fat Albert and the Cosby Kids,* an educational series that was used in many schools around the country. It was also broadcast on television until 1984.

Throughout the 1970s, Cosby worked to complete his college education. He attended the University of Massachusetts, earning a master's degree in 1972 and a doctorate in education in 1977. His doctoral thesis concerned the use of the *Fat Albert* series as a teaching aid.

Starring in *The Cosby Show*

In the early 1980s, Cosby began working to create a television series about a middle-class African-American family. Tired of situation comedies featuring sassy, disrespectful children, he decided to present a stable, traditional family led by a strong father figure. *The Cosby Show* made its debut on NBC in 1984. Cosby starred as Dr. Cliff Huxtable, a successful physician and wise and loving father. Phylicia Rashad (1948–) played his wife Clair, a respected attorney and patient mother. Their five children ranged in age from kindergarten to college.

The Cosby Show was an immediate hit with viewers. Fans enjoyed the way that the show presented the everyday aspects of family life in a humorous way. Like *I Spy, The Cosby Show* did not address racial issues directly. Instead, it helped overcome negative stereotypes by presenting the home life of a successful black family with positive values. Some critics claimed that the program was unrealistic, partly because two professional, working parents could never spend so much time at home with their children. Others complained that the show did not do enough to address issues of importance to African Americans. But many viewers found it refreshing to see the positive image of a comfortable, confident, and loving black family on TV each week.

The Cosby Show ran for eight years, won numerous Emmy Awards, and reached the top spot in the annual television ratings four times. Cosby was especially proud of the fact that the show helped create a more positive image for African Americans in the minds of many viewers. Unfortunately, many later TV comedies featuring black families were not as well received. In a speech he made upon being inducted into the Academy of Television Arts and Sciences Hall of Fame, Cosby expressed disappointment with the portrayal of African American characters on television. "I'm begging you all now. Stop this horrible massacre of images that is being put on the screen," he stated, as quoted in *Ebony*. "It isn't us. . . . I don't know where they get these people from. . . . *The Cosby Show* should have shown these writers something about our people."

Enduring tragedy and scandal

Cosby continued to appear on television shows and in commercials after *The Cosby Show* ended in 1992. He also played roles in movies and performed in comedy clubs, drawing huge crowds at every engagement. Beginning in the late 1980s, Cosby also published several best-selling books offering his humorous take on life, including *Fatherhood, Time Flies, Love and Marriage, Childhood,* and *Cosbyology: Essays and Observations from the Doctor of Comedy.* He also wrote the *Little Bill* series of children's books.

In 1997, Cosby and his family suffered a tragedy. His only son, Ennis, was shot and killed on a Los Angeles freeway after pulling over to change a flat tire. The death of his son hit Cosby extremely hard and shocked the comedian's fans across the nation. It took police over a year to solve the crime, but they finally found Ennis Cosby's murderer in 1998. The young man, a troubled teenager who had come to the United States from the Ukraine, was found guilty of murder by a Los Angeles jury and sentenced to spend the rest of his life in prison.

Around the same time that he lost his son, Cosby became entangled in a scandal. A young woman named Autumn Jackson came forward to claim that Cosby was her biological father. Before going public with her claim, Jackson had approached Cosby privately and demanded $40 million to keep the matter secret. Cosby admitted that he had a brief affair with the woman's mother in 1973, but he denied that Jackson was his daughter and offered to take a paternity test to prove it. Then he filed a lawsuit against Jackson for extortion (using force or intimidation to try to get money or property from another person). Jackson and two other people were found guilty of extortion and sentenced to spend time in prison.

In the 2000s, Cosby began speaking out about what he viewed as serious problems in the black community. In a number of widely publicized speeches and interviews, he encouraged African Americans—especially parents—to place a higher priority on education and moral values. He also stressed the need for black children to have greater respect for themselves and other people. Cosby claimed that African Americans in the twenty-first century were throwing away the accomplishments that earlier generations had worked so hard for during the civil rights movement. "These people marched and were hit in the face with rocks to get an education, and now we've got these knuckleheads walking around," he stated, as quoted by *America's Intelligence Wire*. "I can't even talk the way they talk, 'Why you ain't,' 'Where you is'... and I blamed the kid until I head the mother talk." Cosby hoped that his message, while tough to hear, would raise awareness and lead to self-improvement in the black community. But Cosby's criticism angered some people, who felt that he was unfairly blaming African Americans for the effects of discrimination.

Cosby has used some of his wealth to support various causes aimed at improving the lives of African Americans. In 1988, for instance, he and his wife donated $20 million to Spelman College, a historically black college in Atlanta, Georgia. At the time, it was the largest donation ever made to a black institution. In 1994, the Cosbys donated $1.8 million to help set up the National Center for African American Women in Washington, D.C.

For More Information

BOOKS

Adler, Bill. *The Cosby Wit: His Life and Humor.* New York: Carroll and Graf, 1986.

Smith, Ronald L. *Cosby.* New York: St. Martin's, 1986.

PERIODICALS

"Bill Cosby Exhorts Parents to Set Goals for Their Children." *America's Intelligence Wire,* October 20, 2005.

Goodgame, Dan. "'I Do Believe in Control': Cosby Is a Man Who Gets Laughs and Results—By Doing Things His Way." *Time,* September 28, 1987.

Klein, Todd. "Bill Cosby: Prime Time's Favorite Father." *Saturday Evening Post,* April 1986.

Randolph, Laura. "Life after *The Cosby Show:* Activist-Actor Celebrates 30 Years of Wedded Bliss, Continues to Fight against Black Stereotypes on TV." *Ebony,* May 1994.

WEB SITES

Merrit, Bishetta D. "Bill Cosby." *Museum of Broadcast Communications.* http://www.museum.tv/archives/etv/C/htmlC/cosbybill/cosbybill.htm (accessed on June 5, 2006).

Walter Cronkite

BORN: November 4, 1916 • St. Joseph, Missouri

*American broadcast journalist,
television anchorperson*

"[In my first news anchor job in 1950] we had slides with pictures and some film and some voice on film. But it was a very, very primitive performance compared with what we have today."

Walter Cronkite was one of the most popular and influential television journalists of the second half of the twentieth century. During his long and distinguished career in radio and then television broadcasting, he covered many important historical events, including World War II (1939–45), the civil rights movement of the 1960s, the U.S. space program, the Vietnam War (1954–75), the assassination of President John F. Kennedy (1917–1963; served 1961–63) in 1963, and the Watergate scandal that forced President Richard M. Nixon (1913–1994; served 1969–74) to resign from office in 1974.

Cronkite reported on many of these events as the anchor (main news presenter) of the *CBS Evening News*. He held this position for nearly two decades, and during that span he became America's most respected and trusted television journalist. When he finally retired from his daily news anchor duties in 1981, television scholars and viewers alike described his departure as the end of an era.

Walter Cronkite.
AP IMAGES.

Beginning a career in journalism

Walter Cronkite was born in St. Joseph, Missouri, on November 4, 1916. His father was Walter Leland Cronkite, a dentist, and his mother was Helena (Fritsch) Cronkite. According to Cronkite, both of his parents were nurturing and supportive, and they gave him strong moral values. In his autobiography *A Reporter's Life,* for example, he recalls an incident in which his family was eating dinner at the home of his father's new business partner. When his father's partner struck a black delivery boy and insulted him with racial slurs, Cronkite's father angrily marched his family out the door, refusing all apologies from his partner. Cronkite later said that the memory of that night stayed with him throughout his years of reporting on the civil rights movement in the South.

The Cronkite family moved from Missouri to Texas when Walter was still a youngster. It was after this move that he became fascinated by newspaper reporting. Cronkite viewed it as an exciting and glamorous profession. "So I took up journalism," he recalled in *American Heritage.* "I was terribly lucky: I was in a high school that, rare in that period, had a journalism course." Cronkite described the teacher who directed the course as "the inspiration for my career."

After graduating from high school in 1933, Cronkite enrolled in the University of Texas. He studied there for the next two years, while working part-time in the offices of the *Houston Post* newspaper. He left college in 1935 and spent the next several years working for newspapers and radio stations. His experiences during this time ranged from full-time work as a reporter with the *Post* to a stint as a radio sportscaster in Oklahoma City, Oklahoma.

In 1939, Cronkite's journalism career got a big boost when he was offered a position as a World War II correspondent, or field reporter, with United Press (later United Press International), a news organization that provides stories to newspapers all across the United States. One year later, he married Mary Elizabeth "Betsy" Maxwell, with whom he eventually had three children.

Reporting on World War II

World War II began in 1939, when Germany—under the control of dictator Adolf Hitler (1889–1945) and his Nazi Party—invaded neighboring Poland. The following year German forces moved across Western Europe and conquered France. Hitler also forged an alliance with Italy and

Japan that came to be known as the Axis Powers. These countries continued fighting in Europe against Great Britain and its allies. In June 1941, Germany attacked the Soviet Union, and six months later Japan attacked the United States. The Soviet Union and the United States joined forces with Great Britain to form the Allied Powers. Fighting continued in Europe, North Africa, Southeast Asia, and the Pacific Ocean until 1945, when Germany and Japan were forced to surrender to end the war.

Cronkite reported on the war in Europe for United Press. His work intensified as the war went on—and especially after the United States entered the conflict in 1941. Over the next four years, Cronkite filed stories from war zones all across Europe. He parachuted into hostile regions with airborne divisions, accompanied pilots on bombing missions over Germany, and filed reports from Normandy, France, after the important Allied invasion known as D-Day. This bloody battle on the coast of Normandy, which took place on June 6, 1944, is regarded by many historians as one of the key turning points of World War II. With each of these assignments, Cronkite's excellent work increased his reputation as one of the war's finest reporters.

Cronkite's high-quality reporting during the war even caught the eye of famous CBS Radio journalist **Edward R. Murrow** (1908–1965; see sidebar in **William S. Paley** entry). As one of the most famous American reporters of World War II, Murrow was known both for his bravery and for his high journalistic ethics. He offered Cronkite a spot on his topnotch CBS Radio crew covering the war in Europe. Cronkite was honored to receive the offer, but he reluctantly turned it down because he could not imagine getting better assignments than he already had with United Press.

After Germany and Japan surrendered in 1945, Cronkite worked as the chief correspondent for United Press at the Nuremberg war trials. These famous trials were held to judge captured Nazi officials who had been accused of various war crimes. In 1946, United Press sent Cronkite to the Soviet Union to open the agency's first-ever bureau in Moscow. Cronkite served as chief correspondent for United Press in the Soviet Union for the next two years. In this position, he filed many important stories during the early years of the Cold War (1945–91), a period of intense military and political rivalry between the United States and the Soviet Union.

Joining CBS

In 1950 Cronkite joined CBS, tripling his annual salary in the process. At that time, radio broadcasting was still the primary way in which CBS and other media networks reached American audiences. But Cronkite spent his first months with CBS serving as the anchor of the local television newscast for a CBS station in Washington, D.C. TV news was not technically advanced in those early days. "It was a studio presentation done with whatever newsreel they could purchase," Cronkite recalled in *American Heritage.* "We had slides with pictures and some film and some voice on film. But it was a very, very primitive performance compared with what we have today."

Cronkite excelled as a broadcast journalist from the outset, and within a matter of months CBS executives were looking for ways for him to have more time on television. His first major role on national television for CBS came in 1952, when he served as an anchorman for the network's coverage of the Democratic and Republican political parties' presidential nominating conventions. In 1953, he was named host of a historical re-creation series called *You Are There,* and he remained in this position for the next four years. In 1957, he began a ten-year period as narrator of the CBS documentary (fact-based film) series *Twentieth Century.*

By the late 1950s, television news broadcasting was beginning to come of age. As television technology became more sophisticated and television sets became less expensive to purchase, CBS and other media networks increasingly saw that television would dominate news in the future. With this expectation in mind, network executives began moving money, staff, and other resources away from their radio holdings and into their television operations. One of the journalists who benefited from this shift toward television was Walter Cronkite.

Becoming a famous anchorman

On April 16, 1962, Cronkite succeeded Douglas Edwards (1917–1990) as the new lead anchor for CBS's evening news program. A few months later, the show expanded from fifteen to thirty minutes. In November 1963, Cronkite became the first American anchorman to tell a stunned national audience about the assassination of President John F. Kennedy. Cronkite himself was so disturbed by the tragic event that he was unable to keep his emotions totally in check while covering the story.

Cronkite took over the *CBS Evening News* at a time when the program's ratings were far lower than the nightly news program on NBC hosted by Chet Huntley and David Brinkley. Despite Cronkite's best efforts, the show's ratings did not improve much during his first two years as lead anchor. In 1964, in fact, CBS decided to try out other anchors for the network's coverage of that year's presidential conventions. But Cronkite's absence sparked an unexpected outpouring of protests from viewers. CBS executives quickly returned Cronkite to the anchor desk, and the network's faith in him proved well deserved. By 1967, the *CBS Evening News* was the most popular nightly news program in the United States. With Cronkite as the face of the broadcast, it held this position for the next fifteen years.

The rise of Cronkite and the *CBS Evening News* has been attributed to the program's emphasis on factual news stories about important events and people, as well as Cronkite's unique blend of professionalism and personal appeal. He projected a screen image that was simultaneously reassuring and knowledgeable and attracted Americans of all political, religious, and racial backgrounds. He was widely considered to be one of the most trusted figures in America. Cronkite "became better known than most Hollywood stars," wrote Edward Bliss Jr. in *Now the News*. "Besides a zest for life—sailing, dancing, auto racing until his wife, Betsy, made him give it up—he had a respect for news that showed on camera. Viewers sensed the seasoning that came from experience. There was authority in what he said."

At the height of Cronkite's popularity, an estimated 19 million viewers tuned in to his broadcasts on a nightly basis. Cronkite, though, never stopped viewing himself as a working journalist. He retained the title of managing editor of the *CBS Evening News* throughout his years as anchor. Even after his farewell line at the end of each broadcast—"And that's the way it is"—became one of the best-known phrases in American television history, Cronkite continued to describe himself as an ordinary journalist whose main goal was to provide his audience with reliable, unbiased news.

Praising the space program and criticizing the Vietnam War

Occasionally, though, Cronkite set aside his objectivity to let viewers know his personal feelings about some issues. The Vietnam War was perhaps the best-known example of this. The United States became involved in this conflict during the Cold War, as part of its efforts to halt the spread of communism around the world. The U.S. government sent military troops to Southeast Asia in 1965 to help its ally, South Vietnam, avoid being taken over by its Communist neighbor, North Vietnam. But the

Communists enjoyed a great deal of support among the Vietnamese people. In fact, South Vietnamese Communists known as the Viet Cong joined forces with the North Vietnamese Army to fight against the American and South Vietnamese troops. Even though the United States had superior weapons and equipment, the war turned into a bloody stalemate, with neither side able to achieve victory.

During the early years of the conflict, Cronkite was privately supportive of the decision to go to war. As the war dragged on, however, Cronkite began to have doubts about the optimistic forecasts of American politicians and generals. After the 1968 Tet Offensive—a massive attack by Communist forces against cities and defensive positions held by U.S. troops and their South Vietnamese allies—CBS sent Cronkite to Vietnam to get a firsthand look at the situation. When he returned, Cronkite shared his opinions about the war in an on-air editorial. Speaking before a national audience, Cronkite contradicted positive government reports and expressed his view that the U.S.-led war effort had not made much progress. He said that the government should withdraw American troops and negotiate an end to the conflict. Cronkite's strongly worded editorial forced millions of viewers to rethink their support for U.S. involvement. It also helped convince President Lyndon B. Johnson (1908–73; served 1963–68), who had taken office following Kennedy's assassination, not to run for re-election.

Cronkite was also famous for his enthusiastic support of the American space program of the 1960s. Some observers even believe that his passion for space exploration boosted the American people's support for the National Aeronautics and Space Administration (NASA) more than any of the agency's public relations efforts. Millions of people tuned in to watch U.S. astronauts make the first manned space flight, the initial orbit of the Earth, and the first moon landing over the course of the decade. When Neil Armstrong (1930–) became the first human being to set foot on the Moon in 1969, the event drew an audience of 130 million people in the United States and 600 million around the world—or about one-fourth of the global population at that time. Cronkite was on the air for twenty-seven of the thirty hours of CBS's live coverage of this event. "I think it was just an incredible achievement of American technology and adventure and a nation's dedication to what appeared to be an impossible task," he later told *American Heritage*. "To do all of that in a decade is an exceptional performance, and the astronauts themselves were an exceptional body of men."

Walter Cronkite, right, was inducted into the Television Academy Hall of Fame in 1985 along with comedians Sid Caesar and Carol Burnett, and actor Pat Weaver. © BETTMANN/CORBIS.

Life after the CBS Evening News

On March 6, 1981, Cronkite delivered his last report from behind the anchor desk of the *CBS Evening News*. Dan Rather took over the anchor job, while Cronkite became a special correspondent for CBS News. A few months later, Cronkite received the Presidential Medal of Freedom, the highest civilian (non-military) award presented by U.S. government. This was the greatest of numerous honors Cronkite received during his career, including several Emmy Awards, two Peabody Awards for journalistic excellence, and two DuPont-Columbia University Awards in broadcast journalism. In 1985, he became the second newsman, after Edward R. Murrow, to be inducted into the Television Hall of Fame.

Cronkite delivered occasional special reports on events from around the world for CBS during the mid-1980s. But during this time, relations between the semi-retired Cronkite and his longtime employer became strained. Cronkite harshly criticized CBS for making cuts to its news division's budget and changing its focus to less important stories. CBS responded by giving the legendary newsman fewer projects to work on. These developments deeply disappointed Cronkite. "I felt I had been driven from the temple where for nineteen years, along with other believers, I had worshipped the great god News on a daily basis," he wrote in *A Reporter's Life*.

In the 1990s, Cronkite and CBS had little contact, though he remained officially under contract to the network as a special correspondent. Cronkite produced and narrated a series of critically acclaimed documentaries for PBS, the Discovery Channel, and other networks. In 1996 he published his long-awaited autobiography, *A Reporter's Life*. In 1998 CNN asked Cronkite to serve as co-anchor for its coverage of astronaut John Glenn's return to space (Glenn had been one of the astronauts Cronkite covered back in the 1960s). Cronkite's wife, Betsy, died of cancer in 2005 at their home in New York City. As of 2006, Cronkite continued to live in Manhattan, keeping busy with public speaking engagements and writing on a wide variety of subjects, from politics to sailing.

For More Information

BOOKS

Bliss, Edward J., Jr. *Now the News: The Story of Broadcast Journalism*. New York: Columbia University Press, 1991.

Cronkite, Walter. *The Challenges of Change*. Washington, DC: Public Affairs, 1971.

Cronkite, Walter. *A Reporter's Life*. New York: Knopf, 1996.

Slater, Robert. *This . . . Is CBS*. Englewood Cliffs, NJ: Prentice Hall, 1988.

PERIODICALS

"Cronkite Takes a Stand." *Newsweek,* March 11, 1968.

Snow, Richard F. "He Was There." *American Heritage,* April 23, 1984.

WEB SITES

"Cronkite, Walter." *Museum of Broadcast Communications*. http://www.museum.tv/archives/etv/C/htmlC/cronkitewal/cronkitewal.htm (accessed on May 24, 2006).

"Reporting America at War: Walter Cronkite." *PBS*. http://www.pbs.org/weta/reportingamericaatwar/reporters/Cronkite (accessed on May 12, 2006).

"Walter Cronkite on NPR." *National Public Radio*. http://www.npr.org/news/specials/cronkite (accessed on May 24, 2006).

Philo T. Farnsworth

BORN: August 19, 1906 • Beaver Creek, Utah
DIED: March 11, 1971 • Salt Lake City, Utah

American inventor

"There you are, electronic television."

Some of the most important contributions to the development of modern television technology came from a most unlikely source: a brilliant farm boy named Philo T. Farnsworth. Although he was raised in a log cabin with no electricity, Farnsworth thought up some of the key technical concepts for electronic television systems during his teen years. He used these ideas to create the first working all-electronic television camera and receiver set in 1927. Throughout the 1930s, Farnsworth successfully defended his invention against a long legal challenge by the powerful Radio Corporation of America (RCA). Nevertheless, RCA ended up taking most of the credit for the invention of television.

Growing up on a farm

Philo Taylor Farnsworth was born in Beaver Creek, Utah, on August 19, 1906. He was the first of five children born to Lewis Edwin Farnsworth, a farmer, and his wife Serena (Bastian) Farnsworth. Philo was named after his paternal grandfather, a Mormon pioneer who had helped settle Utah fifty years earlier. Farnsworth spent his boyhood living in a log

Philo T. Farnsworth.
© BETTMANN/CORBIS.

cabin with no electricity. Despite his simple lifestyle, however, he became fascinated at an early age with all kinds of technology. He loved to take things apart and use the pieces to build new gadgets.

In 1917, when Farnsworth was eleven, his family moved to Rigby, Idaho. The boy gained an interest in the science of electronics when he discovered a stash of old technical magazines, such as *Popular Science* and *Science and Invention,* in the attic of his new home. He began experimenting with electricity around this time, often fixing the power generator on the farm and finding ways to use it to help with his chores. At the age of thirteen, Farnsworth won a national invention contest with his design for an anti-theft device for automobiles.

Around 1920, Farnsworth read about some of the early attempts to transmit live, moving pictures across a distance using radio waves. Up to this time, most scientists and engineers had tried to solve the problem by creating mechanical television systems. These systems used spinning metal disks with holes in them to continuously measure the amount of light reflected off a moving image. The holes sent electrical signals, which varied in strength depending on the amount of light hitting them, across a wire to a similar device at the other end. The second device reversed the process and turned the electrical signals back into light, creating a crude representation of the moving image at the other end of the wire. From the first time he read about mechanical television, Farnsworth was convinced that the system would never be able to scan an image fast enough to make a good picture. He grew determined to use electronics to create a faster and better television system.

Inventing electronic television

Farnsworth was an excellent student at Rigby High School. As a freshman, he was so far ahead of his classmates that he begged the principal for permission to sit in on senior-level science courses. Radio broadcasting was just beginning to spread across the country at this time, so most of his classmates—and even his teachers—had never heard of television. Nevertheless, Farnsworth continued working on the problem of television during his high school years. He had a breakthrough one day while he was plowing a field on his family's farm. As he drove his horse-drawn plow back and forth in straight rows, he envisioned a television camera scanning a moving image in that same pattern, line by line.

A short time later, Farnsworth showed his high school science teacher, Justin Tolman, an original drawing of an electronic television system.

Unlike the mechanical systems that had been developed so far, Farnsworth's electronic system did not have any moving parts. Instead, the early television camera he called an Image Dissector captured the light reflected off a moving image with a glass lens. The lens focused the light onto a special plate that was coated with the element cesium, which responded to the light by giving off electrons (tiny, negatively charged particles). Farnsworth used an electrical circuit inside the camera to detect the electrons. He then amplified (increased the power of) the electronic signal and transmitted it to a television receiver set, which displayed the image.

Farnsworth's TV receiver used a picture tube he invented called a Cathode Oscillite Tube. A cathode is a filament inside a sealed glass tube, similar to those found in lightbulbs. When the filament is heated, it forms a vacuum, or an empty space that does not contain any matter. A cathode ray is a stream of electrons that pour off the cathode into the vacuum. Farnsworth's system used electrical circuits to focus these electrons into a beam and shoot them toward a flat screen at one end of the tube. The inside of the screen was coated in phosphor, a substance that emits light, or glows, when struck by a beam of radiation. The beam reproduced moving images by "painting" them onto the screen, line by line.

After completing his sophomore year of high school, Farnsworth gained early admission to Brigham Young University. In 1924, his father died, and he was forced to interrupt his education in order to help support his family. Farnsworth moved to Salt Lake City, Utah, where he got a job as a radio installer and repairman. While there, he met a group of investors who agreed to provide financial support for his television ideas. In 1926, he married Elma "Pem" Gardner. Shortly after the wedding, the young couple moved to San Francisco, California, where Farnsworth opened a research laboratory and began working to build his television system.

On September 7, 1927, Farnsworth successfully transmitted the first all-electronic television picture. His assistants held a picture of a straight line in front of the Image Dissector camera and moved it from side to side. The Cathode Oscillite Tube receiver, located in another room, picked up the signal and displayed the image. According to *Time*, when the twenty-one-year-old inventor saw the line moving on the television screen, he said simply, "There you are, electronic television."

By the end of that year, Farnsworth had applied to the U.S. government for patents (a form of legal protection that gives an inventor the exclusive right to use or make money from an invention for a period of seventeen years) on his electronic television camera and receiver. In 1928, Farnsworth demonstrated his television system to the public for the first time. He received a great deal of media attention, including a feature article in the *San Francisco Chronicle.* Newspapers across the country picked up the story of the "boy genius" who had solved the problem of electronic television.

Going to battle against RCA

One of the people who read about Farnsworth's inventions was **David Sarnoff** (1891–1971; see entry), an ambitious businessman who had recently become acting president of the Radio Corporation of America (RCA). RCA was the leading producer of radios in the United States. It also held a strong position in radio broadcasting through its ownership of the National Broadcasting Company (NBC). Sarnoff had been interested in television since the earliest mention of the potential new technology. As the head of RCA, he was also concerned that the development of television might cause people to stop buying radios. Once it appeared that TV would become a reality, Sarnoff became determined to make RCA a leader in the television industry as well.

In 1929, Sarnoff held a meeting with a Russian engineer named **Vladimir Zworykin** (1889–1982; see entry). Several years earlier, Zworykin had applied for patents on a television camera he called the Iconoscope and a television display screen he called the Kinescope. The basic idea of Zworykin's TV system was similar to Farnsworth's. Unlike Farnsworth, however, Zworykin had been unable to turn his idea into a working model. Still, Sarnoff was impressed with Zworykin's work and hired the engineer to develop an electronic television system for RCA.

In 1930, Farnsworth's application for a U.S. patent on his electronic TV system was approved. A short time later, Sarnoff sent Zworykin to San Francisco to visit Farnsworth's laboratory and check out his inventions. Farnsworth gladly gave the prominent engineer a tour and let Zworykin examine a model of the Image Dissector camera. According to Evan I. Schwartz in *Wired,* Zworykin said, "This is a beautiful instrument. I wish I had invented it myself." In 1931, Sarnoff himself visited Farnsworth's laboratory in San Francisco. Before he left, he offered to give Farnsworth a job at RCA and pay $100,000 for Farnsworth's television patents and all of his working models. But the young inventor and his business partners felt that the offer was much too low and rejected it.

Philo T. Farnsworth with some of his earliest television components. © BETTMANN/CORBIS.

At this point, RCA filed a legal challenge against Farnsworth's patents. The giant company claimed that Zworykin had invented his electronic television system first. They asked the court to throw out Farnsworth's TV patents and award the rights to the invention to Zworykin instead. The patent battles between Farnsworth and RCA continued throughout the 1930s. "They slowed the development of television, delayed its introduction to the public, squandered [wasted] Farnsworth's already thin resources, drove him to drink, and contributed to his development of a bleeding ulcer [a painful stomach problem that is often related to stress]," Schwartz wrote.

Continuing TV development

In 1931, shortly after the legal battle started, Farnsworth accepted a job with Philco—one of RCA's competitors in the manufacture of radios and electronic equipment—and moved to Philadelphia, Pennsylvania. Like RCA, Philco wanted to enter the emerging field of television, so the company hired Farnsworth to establish a TV research division. Farnsworth continued to improve upon his television system during this time. The inventor could often be found tinkering in his laboratory late at night, and he sometimes became so focused on pursuing a new idea that he forgot to eat.

In 1936, the U.S. Patent Office issued a ruling in Farnsworth's favor. After hearing testimony from his high school science teacher and seeing his early television drawings, the patent inspectors concluded that Farnsworth had indeed invented electronic television before Zworykin. But RCA appealed the decision and continued working to develop its own TV system.

In the meantime, Farnsworth built a television studio at his Philco laboratory. He and his team of engineers created a special TV transmitter and constructed a hundred-foot-tall tower that could send experimental television signals across Philadelphia. They also designed and built the world's first electronic video switcher in the studio, which allowed them to cut back and forth between the views provided by two TV cameras while a program was being broadcast. In 1937, Farnsworth received a broadcast license from the Federal Communications Commission (FCC), the U.S. government agency responsible for regulating television, and began making regular television broadcasts.

In 1939, RCA lost the final appeal in its long legal challenge and was forced to pay Farnsworth one million dollars for a license to use his television patents. This marked the first time in the history of RCA—a company known for its pioneering research and development—that it had paid for the right to use technology created by an independent inventor. But licensing his patents to RCA was only a small victory for Farnsworth. The legal battle cost him a great deal of money and took a serious toll on his health. In the end, David Sarnoff and RCA received most of the credit for inventing television.

Struggling for recognition

World War II (1939–45) temporarily halted the development of TV technology, especially after the United States entered the conflict in 1941. Farnsworth left Philco before the start of the war and formed his own company, the Farnsworth Radio and Television Corporation. During the war years, Farnsworth won government contracts to develop new technologies for military use, including radar tracking devices and electronic surveillance equipment. His business took a downturn when the war ended, however, and he was forced to sell it to the International Telephone and Telegraph Corporation (ITT) in 1949.

Around this time, Farnsworth's already poor health began to get worse. He became depressed, drank too much alcohol, and had to be hospitalized for treatment. When commercial television broadcasting took off after the war, Farnsworth was no longer involved in the industry. His long-contested television patents expired in 1947, just before the number of TV sets sold nationwide exploded from a few thousand to several million. RCA produced around 80 percent of the units sold.

As the television industry continued to grow throughout the 1950s and 1960s, Farnsworth became upset about the poor quality of programming and refused to allow his children to watch TV. "I suppose you could say that he felt he had created kind of a monster, a way for people to waste a lot of their lives," his son Kent recalled in *Time*. Late in his life, Farnsworth turned his attention to other sorts of inventions. He was awarded over 150 U.S. patents for devices ranging from an incubator for premature babies to an early air traffic control system. He also did important research in the field of atomic energy (the controlled use of nuclear reactions to create electricity).

Farnsworth died of emphysema (a disease of the lungs) on March 11, 1971, near Salt Lake City. At the time of his death, few people remembered his contributions to the development of television. But thanks to the efforts of his family and various historians of technology, his importance increasingly has been recognized in the years since then. In 1983, for instance, his image was featured on a U.S. postage stamp honoring American inventors. The following year he was inducted into the National Inventors Hall of Fame. In 1990, following a successful campaign by Utah schoolchildren, a statue of Farnsworth—with the words "Father of Television" at its base—was placed in the National Statuary Hall in Washington, D.C. In 2003, the Academy of Television Arts and Sciences named an Emmy Award (an annual honor recognizing excellence in television programming) in his honor: the Philo T. Farnsworth Award for Technical Achievement. A number of books published in the 1990s and 2000s have also told the story of Farnsworth's inventions and his long patent battle with RCA, and there was some talk of making a movie about his life. In the 2000s, it appeared that the forgotten inventor of television might finally be recognized for his contributions.

For More Information

BOOKS

Farnsworth, Elma G. *Distant Vision: Romance and Discovery on an Invisible Frontier.* Salt Lake City, UT: Pemberly Kent, 1989.

Fisher, David E., and Marshall J. Fisher. *Tube: The Invention of Television.* Washington, DC: Counterpoint, 1996.

Godfrey, Donald G., and Christopher H. Sterling. *Philo T. Farnsworth: The Father of Television.* Provo: University of Utah Press, 2001.

McPherson, Stephanie S. *TV's Forgotten Hero: The Story of Philo Farnsworth.* New York: Carolrhoda Books, 1996.

Schwartz, Evan I. *The Last Lone Inventor: A Tale of Genius, Deceit, and the Birth of Television.* Perennial, 2003.

Stashower, Daniel. *The Boy Genius and the Mogul: The Untold Story of Television.* New York: Broadway Books, 2002.

PERIODICALS

Hofer, Stephen F. "Philo Farnsworth: Television's Pioneer." *Journal of Broadcasting,* Spring 1979.

Postman, Neil. "*Time* 100 Most Important Scientists and Thinkers of the Century: Philo Farnsworth." *Time,* March 29, 1999.

Schwartz, Evan I. "Televisionary." *Wired,* April 2002.

WEB SITES

Arrington, Leonard J. "Philo T. Farnsworth." *Museum of Broadcast Communications.* http://www.museum.tv/archives/etv/F/htmlF/farnsworthp/farnsworthp. htm (accessed on June 5, 2006).

"Elma Farnsworth Passes at 98: Widow of TV Pioneer." *Academy of Television Arts and Sciences,* April 28, 2006. http://www.emmys.org/news/2006/april/farnsworth.php (accessed on June 5, 2006).

"Farnsworth's Image Dissector" and "Electronic Television." *IEEE Virtual Museum.* http://www.ieee-virtual-museum.org/collection/tech.php?id=2345850&lid=1 (accessed on June 5, 2006).

Schatzkin, Paul. "The Farnsworth Chronicles." *Farnovision.* http://www.farnovision.com/chronicles (accessed on June 5, 2006).

Larry Gelbart

BORN: February 25, 1928 • Chicago, Illinois

American comedy writer

Larry Gelbart.
© KATY WINN/CORBIS.

"After years of writing material that would conform with a performer's image, I was able to try molding one to my own."

arry Gelbart began his professional comedy writing career in high school. From that time on, he has enjoyed tremendous success as a writer of jokes for comedians, dialogue for radio and television programs, and scripts for Broadway plays and Hollywood films. In his long and varied career, however, Gelbart is probably best known as the creator of the innovative 1970s television series $M^*A^*S^*H$. Set in a U.S. Army hospital on the front lines of the Korean War, the show was one of the first to feature the unusual combination of drama and comedy that became known as "dramedy." The $M^*A^*S^*H$ series finale in 1983 was the most-watched program in television history up to that time.

Writing comedy in high school

Larry Simon Gelbart was born on February 25, 1928, in Chicago, Illinois. He was the oldest child of Harry Gelbart, a barber, and Freida (Sturner) Gelbart. In 1942, Harry Gelbart moved his family to Los Angeles, where he began cutting the hair of some of Hollywood's biggest stars, such as Gregory Peck (1916–2003) and Edward G. Robinson (1893–1973). One day, while he was shaving Danny Thomas (a comedian and actor who was then the host of a popular radio show), the elder Gelbart began telling Thomas about his son Larry, who had a gift for writing comedy. Up to that point, sixteen-year-old Larry Gelbart had only written for small high school productions. But Thomas gave a sample of the young man's work to the head writer for his radio show, who liked it so much that he invited Gelbart to come to his office every day after school to suggest jokes.

Pitching jokes to a big radio show enabled Gelbart to sign a contract with an agent. In 1945, when Gelbart was a seventeen-year-old high school student, the agent got him a job as a junior writer on a big radio show called *Duffy's Tavern*. "I wouldn't say I was writing at this point in my life," Gelbart recalled in his autobiography, *Laughing Matters*. "What I was doing was exercising a particular knack that some people have for making up funny lines. . . . On *Duffy's* we would create story lines, loose situations to hook the show's continuing cast of characters together for the half hour, and that was instructive."

After graduating from high school, Gelbart was drafted into the U.S. Army. When he completed his military service, he began writing for various radio comedians, such as Jack Paar (1918–2004) and Eddie Cantor (1892–1964). In 1948, he joined the writing staff of one of the greatest comedians in history, Bob Hope (1903–2003). As part of his job, Gelbart traveled with Hope as the entertainer performed for U.S. military personnel at bases all over the world. Gelbart was also with Hope when he did his first special in the still very young medium of television, on Easter Sunday in 1950.

Although Bob Hope specials were to become a staple of television for the next four decades, this first effort was not an example of the success that would follow. Gelbart blamed himself and the other writers for the show's failure to take advantage of TV. "In terms of freshness, the writing team came up empty," he admitted in *Laughing Matters*, "writing more of a static [motionless] radio show with cameras aimed at it rather than tapping into the potential of an exciting new medium."

Working on *Caesar's Hour*

With that initial television experience to learn from, Gelbart left Hope's staff and began writing for a few more television shows. In 1955, he joined the writing staff of *Caesar's Hour*, a variety show featuring comedian Sid Caesar (1922–). Caesar had previously served as the host of *Your Show of Shows* (1950–1954), which helped set the standard for comedy in the early days of television. The talented staff of his new show featured a number of young writers who would go on to become comedy legends, such as Mel Brooks, Neil Simon, and Carl Reiner.

Caesar's Hour was a tremendous learning experience for Gelbart, because the show's talented and outrageous host encouraged his group of writers to try anything. "Everything, every subject, was fair game," Gelbart wrote in his autobiography. "Nothing was too hip for the [writer's] room. . . . We had total freedom."

After two years of working on *Caesar's Hour,* and another season writing for singer Pat Boone's variety series, Gelbart turned his attention to writing plays. His first play appeared on Broadway in 1961. Unfortunately, *Hail the Conquering Hero* closed after only seven performances. But Gelbart's next effort was much more successful. The following year, he and Bert Shevelove wrote *A Funny Thing Happened on the Way to the Forum,* with music and lyrics by Stephen Sondheim. The production won a coveted Tony Award as Best Musical of the Year. Gelbart and Shevelove also collected Tony Awards for their writing, while Zero Mostel claimed the honor for Best Lead Actor in a Musical. The show became a classic, and it was revived in 1979 and again in 1997.

In 1963, Gelbart followed the original production of *Forum* to London, and he ended up living in England for nine years. While there, he worked on a few movie scripts and television shows, but he spent most of his time watching, and learning from, British television. "The best of it is very fine indeed," he noted to Michael Winship in *Television*. "I think what I learned mostly was that you could use language. . . . They're much more playful with words."

Creating M*A*S*H

While he was in London, Gelbart got a call from producer Gene Reynolds, who was working with the CBS network to develop a television series based on Robert Altman's 1970 movie M*A*S*H. Set during the Korean War (1950–53), the film (and the novel on which it is based) tells the story of a team of U.S. Army doctors working in a M*A*S*H (Mobile Army Surgical Hospital) unit near the battle lines. At a time when the American people were deeply divided over U.S. military involvement in the Vietnam War (1954–75), the movie received a great deal of attention for providing a realistic, darkly funny view of soldiers at war.

Alan Alda, left, and Mike Farrell starred as Hawkeye Pierce and B.J. Hunnicutt on the CBS dramedy M*A*S*H. © BETTMANN/ CORBIS.

Reynolds wanted to develop a TV show that would capture the essence of the film: its bold commentary on current events, as well as its sarcastic humor. The producer asked Gelbart to write a script for the pilot (initial test) episode of the series. CBS accepted Gelbart's script, and the TV version of M*A*S*H made its debut on September 17, 1972.

During its first season, the show received a mixed response from TV critics and failed to find an audience. In fact, it ranked in forty-sixth place among all network series at the end of its first season, and Gelbart was surprised when CBS renewed it for a second season. But the network made a key decision to change the time slot for $M^*A^*S^*H$ so that it followed the hit situation comedy *All in the Family*. This change allowed many people to discover the show for the first time. As viewers got to know the characters of Hawkeye Pierce, Trapper John, Henry Blake, Radar O'Reilly, Frank Burns, and Margaret Hoolihan, the show began to attract a devoted audience.

More so than any previous sitcom (situation comedy), $M^*A^*S^*H$ combined comedy with serious and sad moments that often made it seem like a drama. Reviewers even coined a new term, dramedy, to describe its unusually downbeat style of humor. Gelbart explained that he gave the series a dark side in order to comment on the senselessness of war. "We all felt very keenly that inasmuch as an actual war was going on [in Vietnam], we owed it to the . . . audience to take cognizance [show awareness] of the fact that Americans were really being killed every week," he told the *New York Times*.

As the principal writer for the series, Gelbart chose to focus on the character of Hawkeye Pierce (played by Alan Alda [1936–]). He modeled the character—a talented surgeon and practical joker who made frequent observations about the absurdities of war—on himself. "It was the first time that I ever tried writing a character who would speak as I do, act as I do," Gelbart noted in *Classic Sitcoms*. "After years of writing material that would conform with a performer's image, I was able to try molding one to my own." The character became a favorite of viewers and made Alda a huge star.

Gelbart left $M^*A^*S^*H$ in 1976. Although the series was one of the most popular programs on television at that time, its creator felt that he had run out of original story ideas and wanted to spend time on other projects. $M^*A^*S^*H$ remained on the air for six more seasons, winning fourteen Emmy Awards and enjoying steady popularity. The series finale in 1983 drew more than 125 million viewers, making the episode the most-watched single TV program up to that time.

Writing successful screenplays

Gelbart's first project after leaving $M^*A^*S^*H$ involved writing the script of the movie *Oh, God!*, which was directed by his old associate from *Caesar's Hour*, Carl Reiner (1922–). The film told the story of a supermarket manager (played by John Denver) who receives a visit from God

(George Burns). The comedy was a hit upon its release in 1977, and Gelbart earned an Academy Award nomination for his screenplay.

Gelbart followed that success with two lesser comedies, *Movie, Movie* in 1978 and *Neighbors* in 1981. In 1982, however, he scored another Academy Award nomination for best screenplay for *Tootsie*. This film starred Dustin Hoffman as an out-of-work actor who dresses as a woman to get a part on a television show. *Tootsie* was one of the most successful films of 1982, and it received additional Academy Award nominations for Best Picture, Best Actor (Hoffman), Best Supporting Actress (Jessica Lange and Teri Garr), and Best Director (Sidney Pollack).

Despite the box-office success of *Tootsie,* Gelbart did not enjoy working on the movie, because his script was constantly being rewritten by others. Afterward, he returned to the theater and had two plays produced on Broadway in 1989: *Mastergate,* a political comedy; and *City of Angels,* a musical-comedy set in Los Angeles in the 1940s. *City of Angels* went on to win six Tony Awards, including one for Gelbart's script.

Gelbart attempted to return to television writing in the 1980s with the situation comedy series *United States,* which provided a realistic view of married life. The show received critical acclaim (some TV critics called it one of the best comedies ever produced) but failed to find an audience, and it was canceled after only eight episodes due to low ratings. Since the rise of cable TV, Gelbart has written the screenplays for several critically acclaimed movies that aired on HBO, including *Barbarians at the Gate* in 1993, *Weapons of Mass Distraction* in 1997, and *And Starring Pancho Villa as Himself* in 2003. Gelbart also wrote a memoir about his life as a comedy writer, called *Laughing Matters: On Writing M*A*S*H, Tootsie, Oh, God!, and a Few Other Things.*

For More Information

BOOKS

Gelbart, Larry. *Laughing Matters: On Writing M*A*S*H, Tootsie, Oh, God!, and a Few Other Funny Things.* New York: Random House, 1998.

Waldron, Vince. *Classic Sitcoms: A Celebration of the Best in Prime-Time Comedy.* Los Angeles: Silman James Press, 1997.

Winship, Michael. *Television.* New York: Random House, 1988.

PERIODICALS

Daly, Steve. "Laughing Matters." *Entertainment Weekly,* March 6, 1998.

Isenberg, Barbara. "Nonstop Laughs: At 75, Larry Gelbart Could Rest Easy. Instead He's Still Churning Out Screenplays and Lots of Yuks." *New York Times,* December 12, 1989.

Kaufman, Joanne. "Larry Gelbart: For the Man Who Wrote M*A*S*H, Comedy Comes with an Edge." *People Weekly,* April 13, 1998.

Rich, Frank. "40s Hollywood Doubly Mocked in Gelbart's *City of Angels.*" *Time,* June 30, 2003.

WEB SITES

"Gelbart, Larry." *Museum of Broadcast Communications.* http://www.museum.tv/archives/etv/G/htmlG/gelbartlarr/gelbartlarr.htm (accessed on May 22, 2006).

Merv Griffin

BORN: July 6, 1925 • San Mateo, California

American television producer, talk show host

Merv Griffin.
AP IMAGES.

"I've never lost the thrill of reinventing myself, turning an idea into reality, and discovering new talents."

The versatile Merv Griffin has made an impact in many different areas of the entertainment field, first as a popular singer, then as a long-running television talk show host, and finally as the creator of the two most popular TV game shows in the world: *Jeopardy!* and *Wheel of Fortune.*

Seeking success as a singer

Mervyn Edward Griffin Jr. was born on July 6, 1925, in San Mateo, California, to Mervyn Edward Griffin and Rita (Robinson) Griffin. Griffin's father was a stockbroker who suffered great financial losses when the U.S. stock market crashed in 1929. This rapid decline in the value of American businesses launched the country into a long period of economic downturn known as the Great Depression (1929–41). The Griffin family lost their home during this time, and this early experience with hardship left young Merv determined to achieve financial security. While still a child, he began mowing lawns and selling Christmas wreaths to help support his family.

Griffin learned to play the piano at the age of four and began singing in the church choir when he was ten. By the time he was fourteen, he began to earn money by playing music at dances and other local events. Griffin longed to break into show business. He performed wherever he could and often participated in talent shows in the hope of being discovered by a talent scout who could help his career. In 1945, he got a job as a singer on the KFRC radio station in San Francisco. It was there that bandleader Freddy Martin heard his pleasant baritone voice and hired him as a vocalist for his orchestra. Griffin toured with Martin's band from 1948 to 1951, visiting all fifty U.S. states, often playing in a different city every night, and singing on six of the band's record albums.

In 1950, Griffin began to make his own name in the music business, when he and the band recorded the lighthearted song "I've Got a Lovely Bunch of Coconuts." The song sold over three million copies to become the number one hit in the country. It also launched Griffin on a solo singing career during which he produced eight albums full of songs.

In the early 1950s, Griffin was singing in a nightclub when he met the actress Doris Day, who helped him get work in Hollywood movies. Between 1953 and 1954, he appeared in several Warner Brothers films. He even landed a starring role in the forgettable movie *So This Is Love.* When Griffin's career as a film actor failed to develop, he went to New York to sign a recording contract with the Radio Corporation of America (RCA) and to try his luck on stage in the Broadway musical *Finian's Rainbow.* But he left these career paths behind when he became involved in the new medium of television.

Shaping the early days of television

Television was still in the early stages of its development when Griffin went to work on such shows as the inspirational series *Look Up and Live* in 1955 and *Morning Show* in 1956. He was hired as the host of a Miami-based talk show called *Going Places* in 1957. The following year he began hosting his first game show, *Play Your Hunch,* which stayed on the air until 1961. His handsome face and smooth manner soon became familiar to television viewers, both during the day and at night. He became a regular substitute for late-night talk-show host Jack Paar, and in 1962 the NBC network gave him his own daytime talk show, called *The Merv Griffin Show.* In 1965 *The Merv Griffin Show* moved to the evening hours as a syndicated program (one that a producer distributes independently to TV stations in various markets, instead of selling it to a major broadcast network).

The 1960s was a turbulent decade. African Americans fought for equal rights and opportunities in society through the civil rights movement, for instance, and an increasing number of Americans protested against the U.S. involvement in the Vietnam War. Recognizing these important trends, Griffin tried to feature interesting and politically controversial guests on his show. Though he never allowed his show to become confrontational, Griffin did not shy away from guests with strong opinions. He interviewed many entertainers rarely seen on television, such as the classical British actor Laurence Olivier and the radical comedians Dick Gregory and Richard Pryor. He also featured many famous people from outside Hollywood, such as artist Salvador Dali (1904–1989) and writer Norman Mailer (1923–).

In 1969, the CBS network signed Griffin to host a late-night talk show. In this role, Griffin competed with other popular late-night hosts, such as Johnny Carson, Joey Bishop, and David Frost. This version of *The Merv Griffin Show* was not a success, partly because the network objected to Griffin's unconventional choices of guests. In a famous 1970 episode, Griffin featured the controversial antiwar activist Abbie Hoffman (1936–1989). As part of his protest against the U.S. government's policies, Hoffman wore a shirt made from an American flag. CBS censors (people who review programs airing on the network and delete any material that might be considered offensive) blurred his image throughout the interview, so that the television audience could not see his shirt or his face.

When CBS canceled his show in 1972, Griffin made a syndication deal with the TV station group Metromedia. "I just couldn't do the show right on the networks," he explained in the *Miami Herald*. "You had to submit the names of anybody you wanted to have on the show. And anybody who wasn't a friend of the company, or had insulted the friend of a president of the company, or even a friend of a friend of the president, was eliminated." *The Merv Griffin Show* aired in syndication from 1972 to 1986. It could be seen every afternoon on dozens of stations throughout the United States. Griffin became known for conducting respectful and engaging interviews with a wide variety of celebrities, from Grace Kelly (1928–1982) to Jerry Seinfeld. His program drew a large daily audience and became one of the standards by which other talk shows were measured. Over the course of his twenty-four years as a talk-show host, Griffin appeared in 7,000 episodes and interviewed an amazing 25,000 guests.

Producing game shows

At the same time that Griffin was developing his career as a talk show host, he was also actively involved in producing TV game shows. Some of his earliest jobs in television had included substituting for host Bill Cullen on *The Price Is Right* and hosting *Play Your Hunch* from 1958 to 1961. He also hosted several game shows that he created, beginning with *Word for Word* in 1963.

In 1964 Griffin founded his own production company, Merv Griffin Productions, to produce his game shows. That same year, he introduced a new game show called *Jeopardy!,* which went on to become one of the longest-running and most popular game shows of all time. *Jeopardy!* grew out of the quiz show scandals of the late 1950s, when several producers got in trouble for fixing the outcome of shows by giving favored contestants the answers in advance. "I wanted to get a game show on the air, but the networks wouldn't touch them," Griffin recalled in the *Miami Herald*. "My wife said, 'Why don't you do a show where you give contestants the answers?' I said, 'How do you think all those people just got sent to jail?'" After she explained the concept further, he adopted it for the show. The unique twist to *Jeopardy!* is that the answers appear on a screen, and the contestants are asked to come up with the correct questions. Griffin himself wrote the bouncy tune that became the memorable theme song for *Jeopardy!*

Most of Griffin's game shows grew out of one basic principle—that the viewing audience at home likes to play along and to feel smart. He designed *Jeopardy!* to be fun to watch but also engaging enough for viewers to play along with at home. Many fans of the show enjoy impressing their friends and family members with their knowledge of various answer categories. The original version of *Jeopardy!* aired on NBC from 1964 to 1975, when NBC replaced it with another Griffin creation: *Wheel of Fortune.*

Griffin told the *Miami Herald* that he got the idea for *Wheel of Fortune* from "a game my sister and I used to play in the back seat of the car while the family was driving somewhere—Hangman, we called it." The game show combined Hangman, in which contestants try to solve a word puzzle by guessing letters, with a popular carnival game where participants spin a wheel for a chance to win a prize.

Wheel of Fortune aired on NBC until 1983, when Griffin moved it into syndication. The following year he syndicated a new version of *Jeopardy!*

Created by Merv Griffin in 1975, Wheel of Fortune *remains one of the most popular game shows of all time.* THE KOBAL COLLECTION.

The pair of shows, most often shown in the early evening, have been numbers one and two in the ratings since their debuts. Unlike some modern game shows, *Wheel of Fortune* and *Jeopardy!* do not humiliate their contestants, but maintain a respectful, if playful, atmosphere.

Griffin retired from running his television production business in 1986, when he sold Merv Griffin Productions to Coca-Cola for $250 million. He remained involved with his game shows as executive producer, but he also began to look outside the entertainment industry for business opportunities. Griffin bought and developed several hotels and vacation resorts, purchased a vineyard and started his own winery, and also became involved in horse racing. He negotiated many high-end real estate deals, including a plan for a luxurious equestrian center in the wealthy resort town of Palm Springs, California. "I've never lost the thrill of reinventing myself, turning an idea into reality, and discovering new talents," Griffin stated on his Web site, www.merv.com.

In 1994, Griffin was inducted into the Broadcasting and Cable Hall of Fame. He has also published books about his career and videotapes of some of his most memorable interviews from *The Merv Griffin Show*. In 2001, he released a new music album entitled *It's Like a Dream*. Griffin was married to Julann Wright for nearly twenty years before they divorced in 1976. They had one son, Anthony Patrick Griffin.

For More Information

BOOKS

Druxman, Michael B. *Merv*. New York: Leisure Books, 1980.

Griffin, Merv, and Peter Barsocchini. *Merv: An Autobiography*. New York: Simon and Schuster, 1980.

Griffin, Merv, and David Bender. *Merv: Making the Good Life Last*. New York: Simon and Schuster, 2003.

PERIODICALS

Friedman, Wayne. "Talk Opens Doors to Kingdom." *Daily Variety,* May 20, 2005.

Garvin, Glenn. "Merv over Miami: TV Host Merv Griffin Returns to Where It All Began." *Miami Herald,* April 16, 2006.

WEB SITES

"About Merv." *Merv.com*. http://www.merv.com (accessed on May 24, 2006).

Timberg, Bernard M. "Merv Griffin." *Museum of Broadcast Communications*. http://www.museum.tv/archives/etv/G/htmlG/griffinmerv/griffinmerv.htm (accessed on May 24, 2006).

Don Hewitt

BORN: December 14, 1922 • New York, New York

American television producer

"Confrontation is not a dirty word. Sometimes it's the best kind of journalism as long as you don't confront people just for the sake of confrontation."

Don Hewitt is probably best known as the founding producer of television's most acclaimed investigative news program, the long-running CBS series *60 Minutes*. He is also a pioneering and influential journalist and television news producer. Highlights of his long career include working with such TV news legends as **Edward R. Murrow** (1908–1965; see sidebar in **William S. Paley** entry) and **Walter Cronkite** (1916–; see entry), and serving as the producer-director of the first presidential debates ever to appear on television, the 1960 contests between Republican Richard Nixon (1913–1994) and Democrat John F. Kennedy (1917–1963; served 1961–63).

A newsman from an early age

Don Hewitt.
AP IMAGES.

Don Hewitt was born on December 14, 1922, in New York City. He was the son of Ely S. Hewitt, an advertising salesman for Hearst newspapers,

87

and Frieda Pike Hewitt. Don knew that he wanted to be a journalist from an early age. In fact, his childhood idol was Hildy Johnson, the sarcastic, hard-hitting reporter in the 1931 movie *The Front Page.* In 1941 he attended New York University on an athletic scholarship, but he dropped out after his freshman year to start his career in journalism as a copy boy at the *New York Herald Tribune.* (A copy boy carries copies of articles and runs errands in a newspaper company.)

During World War II (1939–45), Hewitt worked as a front-line reporter in Europe for the War Shipping Administration. While there, he got the chance to work with two young journalists, Andy Rooney (1919–) and Walter Cronkite. Once the war was over, Hewitt worked at a number of short-term jobs in journalism. In one of these positions, as a night editor at the Associated Press in Memphis, Tennessee, he met his first wife, Mary Weaver. They would eventually have three children: Jeffrey, Steven, and Jilian. Hewitt returned to New York City in 1947, where he worked on the suburban paper *Pelham Sun* and then as a photo editor for Acme News Pictures. In 1948, he got a job offer from Edmund Chester, the head of the CBS TV network's news division. Hewitt jumped at the chance to work in the emerging field of television news.

At CBS, Hewitt was put to work in the control room on a news show hosted by Douglas Edwards (1917–1990). At that time, newscasts did not have videotape of major stories, on-screen graphics, or filmed reports from the field. In fact, most of the programs consisted of the anchor (host) reading the news from a script. Hewitt immediately began to think of ways to make the nightly news broadcasts more interesting. He came up with several new ideas, including the use of a lineup (a list detailing what stories would be covered and what resources would be needed for each night's broadcast). He also thought up a technique for superimposing letters on the screen, or making words appear along with the image of the newscaster. It soon became apparent that Hewitt had a flair for the visual presentation of the news.

In 1956 Hewitt made history when he flew over the sinking Italian luxury liner *Andrea Doria* with Edwards and a cameraman to film the story for CBS News. The ship, which carried 1,700 passengers and crew members, had collided with another ship in heavy fog off the coast of Massachusetts. The dramatic news footage, which showed the crippled vessel lying on its side as survivors struggled to board lifeboats, had a profound emotional effect on viewers and illustrated the power of televised news events.

Don Hewitt, center, pictured with Senator John F. Kennedy, left, and Vice President Richard M. Nixon just before the first-ever televised presidential debate in September 1960. CBS PHOTO ARCHIVE/GETTY IMAGES.

In 1960 Hewitt directed the first-ever televised presidential debates. A debate is a discussion that gives each person a chance to voice his or her thoughts on various issues. Vice President Richard M. Nixon entered the first debate with a comfortable lead in the polls over his relatively unknown opponent, Massachusetts senator John F. Kennedy. As the two candidates answered questions on stage, however, Kennedy seemed calm and confident, while Nixon sweated visibly and appeared uncomfortable. Kennedy's strong performance on television helped convince television viewers that he had the experience and maturity to be president, and he ended up winning the election a few months later. "That night I learned TV was a very dangerous medium," Hewitt recalled in *Zap! A Brief History of Television.* "We elected a president that night and we didn't have to wait to vote."

In 1962 Edwards was fired because of poor ratings (measures of the number of viewers watching a particular program), and Hewitt became executive producer of *The CBS Evening News with Walter Cronkite*. When the ratings of the newscast remained in second place behind NBC, Hewitt was replaced by Ernie Leiser, who was regarded as a more traditional and serious news producer. In his personal life, Hewitt divorced his first wife and married Frankie Teague Childers, a public relations advisor to the U.S. delegation to the United Nations. In 1967 the couple had a daughter, Lisa.

Creating *60 Minutes*

From 1965 through 1968, Hewitt produced documentaries (fact-based films) for CBS. He produced a highly regarded profile of singer Frank Sinatra in 1965, for instance, as well as aggressive investigations of poverty and race relations in America. Throughout this period, though, he wanted to get back into producing news broadcasts. He eventually came up with an innovative format for a new show—an hour-long news magazine that would provide both investigative reports and feature stories, similar to the mix of articles in a print magazine. The show would use several reporters, with each focusing on a separate story. Unlike the nightly news, the show would be able to devote enough time to cover various sides of a story, providing in-depth analysis of political, social, and cultural issues that appealed to viewers.

Hewitt filmed a pilot (initial test) episode of the show, which would become *60 Minutes,* with reporters Harry Reasoner (1923–1991) and Mike Wallace (1918–). It began airing on television on September 24, 1968. Critics immediately recognized that the show represented a new kind of broadcast journalism. Over the first few seasons, however, *60 Minutes* struggled to find the right mix of aggressive investigative pieces and softer entertainment stories. Although it received poor ratings in its initial Tuesday-night time slot, CBS was willing to stick with it because the news magazine cost far less to produce than a situation comedy or drama.

Under Hewitt's guidance, *60 Minutes* soon gained a reputation for covering difficult and controversial stories. In 1969, the show caused an intense debate when it aired an interview with Paul Meadlo, an American veteran of the Vietnam War who claimed that U.S. soldiers had massacred Vietnamese civilians (people not involved in a war, including women and children). Later that season, reporter Mike Wallace conducted a controversial interview with Eldridge Cleaver, a leader of the Black Panther Party who encouraged people to overthrow the U.S. government. This interview attracted the attention of the U.S. Justice Department, which filed a lawsuit to force CBS to turn over its interview footage and outtakes. The legal argument over the case put *60 Minutes* on the front page of every newspaper in the country. As the show itself became news, more viewers began watching it.

By the early 1970s, *60 Minutes* had also earned a reputation for having a highly competitive atmosphere behind the scenes. Hewitt upset many colleagues with his aggressive, argumentative style. Meanwhile, reporters such as Mike Wallace and Morley Safer (1931–) developed a bitter personal rivalry. Finally, some producers complained that the star power of the main reporters overshadowed their in-depth research and reporting work. Somehow, though, the on-camera result emerged as one of the best shows in television news.

Finding a home on Sunday nights

In 1971, CBS moved *60 Minutes* to a new weekly time slot on Sunday nights. The program continued to air a mix of entertaining and investigative stories. Many people felt that it provided a voice for the average citizen in disputes with powerful corporate and government interests. Despite the growing critical praise for the show and its popular stories, however, *60 Minutes* still pulled in low ratings.

In 1975, *60 Minutes* moved from 6 PM to 7 PM and added another news reporter, Dan Rather (1931–). His addition meant more competition for airtime, as well as more aggressive stories. The rivalry that developed between Rather, Reasoner, Safer, and Wallace resulted in positive reviews and increased ratings. Stories from the mid-1970s covered such issues as safety concerns at the nation's nuclear power plants and the mystery surrounding the disappearance of union leader Jimmy Hoffa.

Becoming a star in the news business

With the growing success of *60 Minutes,* Hewitt became a star in the news business. In 1976, he was asked to produce a new, gossip-driven entertainment news magazine called *Who's Who.* Unfortunately, the show premiered against two of ABC's biggest hits, the sitcoms *Happy Days* and *Laverne and Shirley,* and it was canceled quickly despite good reviews. Hewitt was also asked to move to ABC and take over the production of the network's morning news program, *Good Morning America.* But ABC withdrew the offer when Hewitt demanded to own half the show. In 1979 Hewitt got married for the third time, to reporter Marilyn Berger.

By the late 1970s, *60 Minutes* had grown into one of the most popular shows on television. In September 1978, it hit the top spot in the weekly TV ratings, marking the first time that a regularly scheduled nonfiction program ranked number one in the history of television.

By the 2000s, *60 Minutes* was considered one of the most successful news programs of all time. It spent twenty years among the top ten prime-time series, and it was the only show to hold the number one position in the annual TV ratings in three different decades. Although the reporters varied throughout the decades it appeared on the air, the format essentially remained the same. Hewitt was regarded as the creative thinker behind the show, and he received widespread praise for his innovations to the field of television news.

In 2004 Hewitt stepped down from his role as executive producer of *60 Minutes,* but he remained at CBS with the title of executive producer. Over the years, Hewitt has received numerous awards for his work. In 1980 he received the Broadcaster of the Year Award, and a decade later he was named to the National Academy of Television Arts and Sciences Hall of Fame. He also received numerous Emmy Awards, the President's Award for Lifetime Achievement from the Overseas Press Club, and a Lifetime Achievement Award from the Producers Guild of America.

For More Information

BOOKS

Blum, David. *Tick, Tick, Tick: The Long Life and Turbulent Times of "60 Minutes."* New York: HarperCollins, 2004.

Calabro, Marian. *Zap! A Brief History of Television.* New York: Four Winds Press, 1992.

Hewitt, Don. *Minute by Minute.* New York: Random House, 1985.

Madsen, Axel. *"60 Minutes": The Power and the Politics of America's Most Popular TV News Show.* New York: Dodd, Mead, 1984.

WEB SITES

"Don Hewitt." *Museum of Broadcast Communications.* http://www.museum.tv/archives/etv/H/htmlH/hewittdon/hewittdon.htm (accessed on May 22, 2006).

Robert L. Johnson

BORN: April 8, 1946 • Hickory, Mississippi

American television executive, founder of Black Entertainment Television

Robert L. Johnson.
AP IMAGES.

"Treat racism like rain. Racism exists, but put up an [emotional] umbrella and go to work. Don't stand out there and get drenched."

Cable television pioneer Robert L. Johnson is the founder of Black Entertainment Television (BET), the first cable network specifically targeted at African American viewers. He built upon the success of BET to create a diverse business empire that made him one of the wealthiest people in the United States.

Growing up poor

Robert L. Johnson was born on April 8, 1946, in the small, rural town of Hickory, Mississippi. He was the ninth of ten children born to Archie and Edna Johnson. When he was a boy, his family moved to Freeport, Illinois, where his parents took jobs in factories. Johnson worked odd jobs to help support the family. He delivered newspapers, mowed lawns, cleaned up at the local fairs, and worked in a battery factory.

Johnson was a well-rounded student. He did well academically, and he participated in sports. Even at a young age, Johnson was ambitious and knew that he did not want to work as a common laborer when he grew up. His first career goal was to be a fighter pilot in the United States Air Force. Unfortunately for Johnson, he could not meet the Air Force's requirement that all fighter pilots have perfect eyesight. After ruling out this career path, he hoped to represent the United States as an ambassador to foreign countries.

Johnson graduated from high school with honors and went on to attend the University of Illinois on an academic scholarship. In 1968, he earned his bachelor's degree in history, thus becoming the first member of his family to graduate from college. But Johnson had no intention of stopping there. He went on to attend graduate school at Princeton University's Woodrow Wilson School of Public and International Affairs, which had established a program to attract minorities to careers in international relations. In 1972, Johnson graduated sixth in his class with a master's degree in international relations.

Making connections

After completing his graduate degree, Johnson took a job as a public affairs officer for the Corporation for Public Broadcasting (CPB). Established by an act of Congress in 1967, the CPB is a national nonprofit organization that raises funds to support public radio and television broadcasting in the United States. Throughout his college years and in his early business career, Johnson worked hard to meet people with important political connections. "All business is personal, so make your friends before you need them," he told Robert G. Miller in the *Black Collegian*.

Johnson's next job was as the director of communications for the National Urban League office in Washington, D.C. The Urban League is a nonprofit social service and civil rights organization that was founded in 1910 to help African Americans achieve social and economic equality. Johnson soon changed jobs again, becoming the press secretary for Walter Fauntroy, a member of the U.S. House of Representatives from the District of Columbia. Johnson made many powerful political connections during his years in the nation's capital.

Founding Black Entertainment Television (BET)

In 1976, Johnson went to work for the National Cable Television Association (NCTA) as the vice president of governmental relations. The

NCTA is a trade organization for cable television service providers, with approximately 1,500 members. Johnson's job involved lobbying, or using his political connections to encourage the government to pursue policies that would be favorable to the cable TV industry. In his work for the NCTA, Johnson learned a lot about cable television, its programming, and its viewers. Perhaps the most important thing he learned was that African Americans watched a lot of cable television programs, but none of the cable networks focused specifically on them as an audience group.

Johnson soon came up with the idea of creating a cable TV channel that would provide programs targeted at African Americans. He spent a great deal of time conducting research to see whether it would be profitable for him to pursue this idea. He created with a business plan and presented it to his boss, who loaned him $15,000. He was able to use his other connections to raise enough money to start his own cable network: Black Entertainment Television (BET). "I started it because I was a lobbyist for the cable industry," he said in the *Black Collegian*. "I realized there was an opportunity to start a niche service for the black community using cable television technology."

BET made its first broadcast on January 25, 1980, reaching 3.8 million American homes. In the beginning, BET was only on the air from 11:00 P.M. until 2:00 A.M. on Friday nights. BET's programming was limited because Johnson had trouble finding television shows that featured black characters in leading roles. He mostly had to settle for broadcasting low-budget movies from the 1940s and 1950s, as well as "blaxploitation" films from the 1970s (urban crime dramas with African American directors and actors).

By 1982, BET had increased its broadcasting time to six hours a day, seven days a week. The network showed music videos, black-oriented talk shows, college sporting events featuring African American athletes, and reruns of black situation comedies. In 1984, BET expanded to a full broadcast schedule, remaining on the air twenty-four hours a day, seven days a week. By 1987, Johnson's network boasted over 15 million subscribers.

Branching out

With the success of Black Entertainment Television, Johnson realized that there were other business opportunities to be found in reaching out to African American consumers. "When I see BET, I don't see a

MTV Networks Chairman Judy McGrath

Judy McGrath. BLOOMBERG NEWS/LANDOV.

Judy McGrath is one of the most powerful executives in cable television. As the chairman and chief executive officer (CEO) of MTV Networks, she oversaw a global business that generated $7 billion per year in 2006.

McGrath was born in 1955 in Scranton, Pennsylvania. Her parents encouraged her to express her opinions and pursue her dreams. McGrath always loved rock 'n roll music. By her teen years, she dreamed of becoming a writer for *Rolling Stone* magazine and hanging out with famous musicians. "I had this idea that I could write about music," she told Tom Lowry in a 2006 *Business Week* cover story. "That would be the ideal job for me."

McGrath earned a bachelor's degree in English from Cedar Crest College in 1974. She started her writing career at a Scranton radio station. In 1978 she moved to New York City, where she initially shared a cramped apartment with seven other women. She wrote articles for several women's magazines over the next three years, including *Mademoiselle* and *Glamour*.

cable network. I see a black media conglomerate," he explained in *Essence.* "I want to be a communications giant." In 1991, Johnson established BET Holdings, Inc. to operate his various media businesses. He offered shares of ownership in the company to the public by listing it on the New York Stock Exchange (NYSE), one of the world's largest markets for trading stocks and bonds. BET Holdings became the first primarily black-owned company to be listed on the NYSE.

Also in 1991, BET Holdings entered the field of magazine publishing with *Young Sisters and Brothers,* which was aimed at black youth. The magazine included articles on subjects of interest and relevance to African American teenagers, such as education, careers, sex, drugs, family relationships, popular music, art, movies, and sports. Over the next few years, BET Holdings continued to diversify its business interests. Johnson added several more cable channels, such as BET Gospel,

In 1981 McGrath got a job at MTV—Music Television, a new cable TV network that focused on music. Record companies often produced short videos to accompany songs by the artists they wanted to promote, and MTV aired these promotional videos. Even though there were a limited number of videos available at first, ratings for the network soared. It proved to be especially popular among teenagers and young adults, and before long it became a cultural phenomenon. The music industry realized that MTV had the power to make or break musical groups, and music videos became essential tools for artists seeking to attract and connect with fans.

In the early 1980s, McGrath wrote on-air promotions for MTV and helped design the channel's logo. She moved up through the ranks quickly, and in 1991 she took on all responsibility for programming at the cable network. One of her first moves involved pushing MTV into politics. During the presidential election of 1992, MTV encouraged young people to take an interest in politics with its Rock the Vote campaign. McGrath also began moving MTV programming beyond music videos. In 1992 she started one of the network's most successful series, *The Real World*. Among the earliest of the type of programs that became known as reality TV, it brought together seven young people from different backgrounds to live in the same house, while a film crew followed their daily interactions.

In 2002 McGrath became president of MTV Networks, which had grown to include other popular cable channels, such as Video Hits 1 (VH1) and Country Music Television (CMT). In 2004 Viacom, the large media company that owned MTV Networks, named McGrath chairman and CEO of all of its cable operations. She took charge of a business that owned 94 cable channels—including Nickelodeon, TV Land, and Comedy Central—which reached 400 million viewers in 164 countries around the world.

BET Jazz, BET Action Pay-Per-View, and BET Movies. He also launched more magazines, including *Emerge, Heart and Soul,* and *BET Weekend.* Some of his other business investments included a line of romance books written by African Americans, a home-shopping network called BET Shop, a nightclub at Walt Disney World, and the BET Sound-Stage Casino in Las Vegas, Nevada.

One of Johnson's last major business ventures as the head of BET Holdings was launching the Web site BET.com in 1999. The site was designed to provide news, other kinds of information, entertainment, and online shopping to the black community. "Among African Americans, the Internet is not seen as something you have to have yet, and we're going to change that mind-set," he told *Investor's Business Daily.* "Nobody has been talking to the [black] community about why it's important. The Internet is the platform for the powerful new digital economy and

Though the deal fell through, Robert Johnson, center, was poised to be the first African American to own an airline when plans were announced in May 2000. Here, Johnson shakes hands with James Goodwin, CEO of United Airlines, left, and Stephen Wolf, CEO of U.S. Airways. © MARC ASNIN/CORBIS SABA.

connected society. The failure of any community to avail itself of the resources of the Internet will limit its ability to succeed in the new millennium."

In 2000, Johnson sold BET Holdings for $3 billion to Viacom, a large media corporation that also owned cable channels such as MTV and Nickelodeon. By this time, BET Holdings employed over 500 people and had annual sales of approximately $170 million, while the BET cable network reached more than 62 million homes. The transaction made Johnson the first black billionaire in the United States. Under the terms of the sale, Johnson continued to serve as the chief executive officer of BET until the end of 2005. But he gave up many of his business responsibilities at BET, which gave him the opportunity to pursue other interests.

Flying high

In May 2000, Johnson attempted to form a new airline called DC Air, which was to offer service from the Ronald Reagan International Airport in Washington, D.C., to forty-four cities around the United States.

Johnson was a member of the board of directors for U.S. Airways at the time, so he knew something about the airline industry. DC Air would have been the first major airline in the United States to be owned by an African American. Unfortunately for Johnson, the $141 million business deal fell through.

In 2001, Johnson formed another company, called RLJ Development, to pursue opportunities in commercial real estate. His new company bought several Homewood Suites hotels in Washington, D.C., Massachusetts, Tennessee, Minnesota, Texas, Connecticut, and Florida. Johnson decided to enter the hotel management business after serving on the board of directors of Hilton Hotels Corporation for five years. "There is no long-term game plan here," he told *Black Enterprise*. "This is no winding-down strategy. It's just that I'm fortunate enough to be in a position to see good deals when they come across the table [are presented]." In 2002, Johnson purchased a majority interest in the Charlotte Bobcats of the National Basketball Association (NBA). He thus became the first African American owner of a men's professional basketball team.

Sharing the secrets of success

As one of the most successful African American business leaders in U.S. history, Johnson has often been asked to give advice to young people. "You've got to start with a fundamental belief that you can do just about anything you set your mind to," he stated in *Black Collegian*. "Second, you have to know how to communicate with people whom you need to help you achieve your goal. I don't just mean speaking or writing. It's everything from how you carry yourself, to how you arrange a meeting, to whether or not you show up on time."

Johnson has always stressed the importance of education. "Education is essential for anyone," he declared to Miller. "It's not just degree-oriented. It's the exposure of your mind to every idea and how to process information that you're exposed to in validating whatever you're trying to accomplish. Going to college is a statement of your determination to get engaged in being exposed to information and how important knowledge is."

Johnson has also encouraged minorities in business to work hard to counteract the effects of racial discrimination. "Treat racism like rain. Racism exists, but put up an [emotional] umbrella and go to work. Don't stand out there and get drenched in it," he said in *Black Collegian*.

"I liken it to playing in the NFL. You know you're going to get hit, so get up and keep on playing. Get on with your life and do what needs to be done."

For More Information

BOOKS

Pulley, Brett. *The Billion Dollar BET: Robert Johnson and the Inside Story of Black Entertainment Television.* Hoboken, NJ: Wiley, 2005.

PERIODICALS

"BET.com." *Investor's Business Daily,* February 29, 2000.

Little, Benilde. "Robert Johnson: The Eyes behind BET." *Essence,* November 1990.

Lowry, Tom. "Can MTV Stay Cool? How CEO Judy McGrath Must Remake Her TV Empire for a Digital World." *Business Week,* February 20, 2006.

Miller, Robert G. "Robert L. Johnson: A Business Titan." *Black Collegian,* October 2000.

Scott, Matthew S. "Robert L. Johnson: The Captain of Capitalism." *Black Enterprise,* November 1, 2005.

WEB SITES

"2004 Global Business Influentials: Judy McGrath, MTV Networks." *CNN.com.* http://www.cnn.com/SPECIALS/2004/global.influentials/stories/mcgrath (accessed on June 19, 2006).

Norman Lear

BORN: July 27, 1922 • New Haven, Connecticut

American television producer

"By changing the way television looked, *All in the Family* changed forever the way we look at television."

— Vince Waldron, *Classic Sitcoms.*

Norman Lear is one of the most successful producers in television history. Every year from 1972 to 1983, at least two shows that he created ranked among the top twenty in the annual TV ratings (a measure of the number of viewers who watched various programs). During this period, Lear changed American television by introducing situation comedies that dealt with real social issues, from racial prejudice to abortion. "These were not new subjects to the American people," Lear told *People.* "They just happened to be subjects that television had not touched." Some of his most influential programs were *All in the Family, Maude, Good Times, The Jeffersons,* and *One Day at a Time.*

An early talent for comedy

Norman Lear.
© LAURA FARR/
ZUMA/CORBIS.

Norman Milton Lear was born in New Haven, Connecticut, on July 27, 1922. His mother, Jeanette (Scicol) Lear, was a homemaker. His father,

101

TV Writer and Producer Sherwood Schwartz

Sherwood Schwartz. FREDERICK M. BROWN/GETTY IMAGES.

Sherwood Schwartz created two of the most beloved television comedy series of all time,

Gilligan's Island and *The Brady Bunch*. Although both shows failed to impress TV critics, they were popular during their initial runs in the 1970s and they attracted even larger audiences in reruns (repeat showings of programs that aired earlier).

Sherwood Charles Schwartz was born on November 14, 1916, in Passaic, New Jersey. He started his career in 1939 as a professional writer, by working on a radio show hosted by the comedian Bob Hope. During World War II (1939–45) he wrote comedy programs for the Armed Forces Radio Service. After the war ended, he worked on the popular radio comedy series *The Adventures of Ozzie and Harriet*.

In the early 1950s Schwartz turned his attention to television. Over the next fifty years, he wrote, produced, or contributed to more than seven hundred television shows. One of his first successful programs was *My Favorite Martian*, a comedy about a family that must come to terms with a very strange uncle who turns out to be a visitor from another planet.

Herman Lear, was a securities broker who served as a model for one of Lear's most enduring characters, Archie Bunker of *All in the Family*. Throughout his youth, Lear and his father would engage in heated discussions about the issues of the day. "I'd accuse him of making racial slurs [referring to people of other races in negative terms]," Lear recounted in *Classic Sitcoms,* "and we'd get into real . . . shouting matches. And we were a nice Jewish family."

Lear studied communications at Emerson College in Boston, but he left school to join the U.S. Air Force during World War II. As a Jew, Lear felt compelled to help the Allied war effort against Nazi Germany, which was responsible for systematically murdering millions of Jews in Europe. After returning from his military service,

In 1963 Schwartz created *Gilligan's Island,* which ran on CBS from 1964 through 1967. This situation comedy (sitcom) follows the wacky adventures of a group of people shipwrecked on a deserted island. The seven castaways, who come from a variety of backgrounds, struggle to find a way to live together. New generations of fans discovered the appeal of *Gilligan's Island* in the 1980s, 1990s, and beyond. In fact, it has been rerun more than any other series in TV history.

Another Schwartz creation that has enjoyed lasting popularity is *The Brady Bunch,* which originally ran on ABC from 1969 to 1974. *The Brady Bunch* tells the story of a family that is formed when a widower (a husband whose wife has died) with three sons marries a widow (a wife whose husband has died) with three daughters.

The Brady Bunch appealed to a broad range of kids—both boys and girls, of various ages—by giving them six different young characters with whom they could identify. At a time when a growing number of young people had to deal with divorce and the creation of new families,

the Bradys provided a model of a highly functional blended family. The show also appealed to kids of the 1980s, 1990s, and beyond who enjoyed its portrayal of family life during a pleasant, innocent time.

Schwartz co-wrote the theme songs for *Gilligan's Island* and *The Brady Bunch,* both of which are often mentioned among the favorite TV theme songs of all time. The lyrics of the songs provide viewers with background about the characters and their situations. Schwartz said that he used this approach in order to avoid having to explain the story during each weekly episode.

Schwartz used his two most popular TV series as the basis for books, cartoons, movies, and plays. In 1988, for example, he published the book *Inside Gilligan's Island,* which describes the creation of the show and also provides an inside look at the television industry. In 1994 he produced the comedy film *The Brady Bunch Movie.* Using a new cast of actors to portray the familiar characters, the movie poked gentle fun at the TV series by moving the Bradys into the fast-paced world of the 1990s.

Lear married his first wife and took a job in public relations in New York City.

In 1949, Lear moved to Los Angeles, where he sought work as a writer in the new medium of television. By 1951, he was writing comedy sketches for the NBC variety program *Ford Star Revue.* His work impressed comedian Jerry Lewis (1926–), who hired Lear to write material for *The Colgate Comedy Hour,* which featured Lewis and his partner Dean Martin (1917–1995). During the early 1950s, Lear also directed and wrote for TV variety shows starring comedians such as George Gobel, Don Rickles, and Martha Raye.

After a decade of working in television, though, Lear became dissatisfied with the medium. He felt that the commercial and political pressures facing the television industry made it difficult for producers to take risks and develop artistically. In 1959, Lear joined forces with Bud Yorkin to form Tandem Productions, a company that developed and produced movies. Over the next twelve years, Lear wrote and produced a series of light comedy films, including *Come Blow Your Horn* (1963); *Divorce, American Style* (1967); *The Night They Raided Minsky's* (1968); and *Cold Turkey* (1971), which he also directed.

Creating *All in the Family*

In 1968, Lear read about a hit television comedy show in England called *Till Death Us Do Part*. The show focused on a bigoted dockworker and his family. Tandem Productions quickly bought the legal rights to do a version of the show for American television. After watching a few episodes of *Till Death Us Do Part,* however, Lear found it too abrasive. He then decided to model the lead character of the American version, originally named Archie Justice, after his father. He also drew from his own experience in writing about Archie's family and their frequent arguments about politics, race, and gender roles.

Lear initially called the new show *Those Were the Days*. He set the family in Queens, New York, and cast Carroll O'Connor (1924–2001) as Archie and Jean Stapleton (1923–) as his kind-hearted wife, Edith. The ABC network agreed to finance the production of a pilot (initial test) episode. In the pilot, Lear made it clear that Archie was a prejudiced man who distrusted blacks, Jews, feminists, hippies, and others who did not share his working-class values. Archie also engaged in loud arguments and name-calling with his family. ABC found the subject matter too controversial and decided to pass on turning the pilot into a series.

Those Were the Days languished for the next two years. Even though the 1960s saw a great deal of social upheaval in the United States— with the civil rights movement, the women's liberation movement, and protests over the Vietnam War—most prime-time TV series did not address the various changes taking place in American society. Fearful of offending the audience with social commentary, the major television networks instead offered viewers an assortment of goofy comedies and light-hearted adventures. By the 1970s, however, some bold network executives began to think that the American people might be ready to watch more realistic shows that dealt openly with current events and social issues.

In 1970, CBS president Robert Wood canceled several unsophisticated, escapist comedies, such as *The Beverly Hillbillies,* and began searching for shows that would appeal to a more mature audience. Wood heard about Lear's show, and CBS ordered thirteen episodes. The network suggested changing the name of the series from *Those Were the Days* to *All in the Family*. Lear agreed, and he also changed the last name of the family from Justice to Bunker.

A new kind of TV comedy

All in the Family made its debut on January 12, 1971. CBS executives knew that some viewers might be shocked by the program, since it was so different from most shows of that era. Immediately before the series premiere, according to Joe Garner in *Stay Tuned,* the network aired a message explaining that the show "seeks to throw a humorous spotlight on our frailties, prejudices, and concerns. By making them a source of laughter, we hope to show—in a mature fashion—just how absurd they are." CBS also set up a special telephone switchboard to respond to calls from viewers who found the program upsetting. As it turned out, though, the few people who called in offered mostly positive comments.

As the first TV series to deal with the daily struggles of a working-class family, *All in the Family* received a great deal of attention from TV critics. It was not an immediate hit with viewers, but Lear felt confident that the show would soon find an audience. In May 1971, only five months after it premiered, *All in the Family* collected Emmy Awards as Outstanding New Series and Outstanding Comedy Series. Jean Stapleton was also honored as Outstanding Lead Actress in a Comedy for her portrayal of Edith Bunker.

From that point on, *All in the Family* enjoyed tremendous success. Each week, millions of Americans tuned in to see how the groundbreaking situation comedy (sitcom) would deal with issues of race, religion, sexuality, politics, and family. It aired on CBS for a dozen years and was the top-rated show on television for five consecutive seasons. It also claimed nineteen Emmy Awards, including three more selections as Outstanding Comedy Series.

Influencing development of the sitcom format

All in the Family influenced the development of TV comedy in a number of ways. For instance, it started a trend toward more realistic sitcoms that tackled a broader range of social concerns. *All in the Family* also focused on wordplay and verbal sparring more than previous sitcoms. Many later

TV shows adopted this approach, from sitcoms such as *Seinfeld* to news programs such as *Crossfire*.

In addition, *All in the Family* was the first major American TV series to be videotaped in front of a live studio audience. Before it aired, most sitcoms were either shot on film in front of an audience, or filmed without an audience but using a recorded laugh track (a recording of an audience laughing) to reproduce an audience response. With the success of *All in the Family*, the crisp appearance of videotape and spontaneous live response from a studio audience became the standard for situation comedies.

Finally, *All in the Family* was one of the first programs to generate successful spin-off series, or new programs featuring members of the original program's cast. Lear built several new shows around characters from *All in the Family*, including *Maude* and *The Jeffersons*. Analysts of popular culture claim that spin-offs help viewers forge a closer connection to television, because they are able to watch familiar characters adjust to new situations and grow.

Vince Waldron summed up the show's lasting influence in *Classic Sitcoms:* "By breaking down every established notion of how TV comedy should be written, performed, edited, and scored, the series almost single-handedly revolutionized the creative community's attitude toward the medium. By changing the way television looked, *All in the Family* changed forever the way we look at television."

Continuing success with other new programs

Lear followed the success of *All in the Family* by introducing two new series in 1972, *Maude* and *Sanford and Son*. The character of Maude, played by Bea Arthur, had appeared on *All in the Family* as Edith's cousin. She was a successful, liberal, divorced woman in her forties who had some memorable clashes with Archie. In the spin-off series *Maude*, Lear and his staff of writers addressed such topical issues as women's rights, alcoholism, and abortion. *Sanford and Son* was a more straightforward comedy that starred African American comedian Redd Foxx as a junk dealer named Fred Sanford who lived with his son in the Watts section of Los Angeles. Both series were top-ten hits in the 1970s.

With his next two series, *Good Times* and *The Jeffersons*, Lear introduced a new format known as the black situation comedy. *Good Times* revolved around an African American woman, Florida Evans, who had

Norman Lear, center, celebrates the 200th episode of his show The Jeffersons *with its stars Sherman Hemsley and Isabel Sanford in 1983.* AP IMAGES.

appeared as a maid on *Maude.* Evans and her family lived in a public housing project in Chicago. Lear used the series to address such issues as poverty, unemployment, and crime. *The Jeffersons* centered on George and Louise Jefferson, who were the Bunkers' African American neighbors on *All in the Family.* In the spin-off series, George's successful business allows the family to move into a luxury high-rise apartment on the Upper East Side of Manhattan. These shows were some of the earliest to make black families the focus of a weekly TV series.

Not every television show Lear touched in the seventies turned into a hit. In fact, he helped develop more than twenty series during the 1970s, and most of them lasted one season or less. Lear did find success with *One Day at a Time,* a sitcom about a divorced mother struggling to raise two teenaged daughters. The show premiered in 1975 and lasted eight years. In the late 1970s, Lear created two new comedies that received a great deal of critical attention and remained popular in reruns into the early 2000s: *Mary Hartman, Mary Hartman,* which provided a humorous take on soap operas; and *Fernwood 2-Nite,* which provided a funny view of talk shows.

Although Lear continued to dabble in television in the 1980s and 1990s, his work focused less on creating new shows and more on arranging behind-the-scenes business deals. After ending his partnership with Bud Yorkin, Lear founded TAT Communications with another partner, Jerry Perenchio. This company, which later became Embassy Communications, produced such popular 1980s shows as *Diff'rent Strokes* and *The Facts of Life.* In 1986, Lear and his partner sold Embassy to the Coca-Cola Company for $485 million.

With his share of the proceeds, Lear started a new company, Act III, which formed the basis of a communications business consisting of magazines, television stations, and movie theaters. Lear's company also invested in several hit motion pictures, including *Stand By Me* and *The Princess Bride,* both directed by former *All in the Family* star Rob Reiner. In 2005, Lear announced a $115 million investment in Village Roadshow Pictures, a film production and distribution company.

Over the years, Lear has also emerged as an active supporter of liberal social and political causes. In the 1980s, he founded People for the American Way, an organization dedicated to defending civil liberties and promoting tolerance in American media and culture. Lear has also supported various organizations that promote free speech and encourage young people to vote. As part of this mission, he sponsored a nationwide tour of one of the original signed copies of the Declaration of Independence.

For More Information

BOOKS

Garner, Joe. *Stay Tuned: Television's Unforgettable Moments.* Kansas City, MO: Andrews McMeel Publishing, 2002.

Marc, David, and Robert Thompson. *Prime Time, Prime Movers.* Syracuse, NY: Syracuse University Press, 1995.

McCrohan, Donna. *Archie and Edith, Mike and Gloria.* New York: Workman, 1987.

McNeil, Alex. *Total Television: The Comprehensive Guide to Programming from 1948 to the Present.* New York: Penguin, 1996.

Newcomb, Horace, and Robert S. Alley. *The Producer's Medium: Conversations with Creators of American TV.* New York: Oxford University Press, 1983.

Waldron, Vince. *Classic Sitcoms: A Celebration of the Best in Prime-Time Comedy.* Los Angeles: Silman James Press, 1997.

PERIODICALS

Bellafante, Gina. "The Inventor of Bad TV: What Would the '70s Have Been without Sherwood Schwartz?" *Time,* March 13, 1995.

"King Lear: Witty and Brave, Norman Lear Toppled Taboos by Getting Us to Laugh at Our Foibles." *People Weekly,* March 15, 1999.

WEB SITES

"Norman Lear." *Museum of Broadcast Communications.* http://www.museum.tv/archives/etv/L/htmlL/learnorman/learnorman.htm (accessed on May 22, 2006).

Schwartz, Sherwood. "How It All Began," 1998. *BradyWorld.com.* http://www.bradyworld.com/cover/begin.htm (accessed on June 19, 2006).

Schwartz, Sherwood. "Professional Biography," 1998. *BradyWorld.com.* http://www.bradyworld.com/cover/schwartz.htm (accessed on June 19, 2006).

Lorne Michaels

BORN: November 17, 1944 • Toronto, Ontario, Canada

Canadian television and movie producer

"I just did a show that I would watch if I were the audience."

B est known as the creator and longtime producer of the late-night, sketch-comedy series *Saturday Night Live* (SNL), Lorne Michaels is considered one of the most influential names in television comedy. In its thirty-year run on the NBC network, SNL shaped American popular culture and launched the careers of countless comedians, including Bill Murray, John Belushi, Eddie Murphy, Mike Myers, Will Ferrell, and Adam Sandler. "*Saturday Night Live* is more than a television show. Since its premiere in 1975, it has served as a trendsetter in American humor, and had a remarkable effect on American mores, manners, music, politics, and even fashion," Tom Shales and James Andrew Miller wrote in *Live from New York: An Uncensored History of "Saturday Night Live."* "Though the basic form wasn't entirely new, the content was, and so were the show's attitude and collective mind-set."

Training in comedy

Lorne Michaels.
PETER KRAMER/
GETTY IMAGES.

Lorne Michaels was born Lorne David Lipowitz on November 17, 1944, in Toronto, Canada. He changed his last name to Michaels at the time he

111

launched his comedy career. The son of Abraham and Florence (Becker) Lipowitz, young Michaels was always interested in show business, and especially the relatively new medium of television. "As I was growing up, we had a mixture of Canadian television, American television, and . . . the best of English television. I watched everything," he recounted to Michael Winship in *Television*. "I remember television sort of being a miracle."

In his teen years, Michaels began staging shows at summer camp. His partners in this venture were Rosie Shuster, who later became his first wife and a writer on SNL, and Howard Shore, who became SNL's original musical director. "We did comedy, we did sketches, we had kind of a repertory company and some musicians," Shore recalled in *Live from New York*. "If you think about it, it was truly the beginning of *Saturday Night Live,* because it was a show we put on every Saturday night, it was a live show, and it was somewhat improvisational [spur-of-the-moment], with comedy and music."

Rosie Shuster's father was Frank Shuster, one-half of the comedy team of Wayne and Shuster. This duo had great success in Canada and also appeared on television programs in the United States, such as *The Ed Sullivan Show*. After Michaels lost his father at age fourteen, Frank Shuster played an important role in the teenager's development. "My dad really mentored Lorne in terms of comedy," Rosie Shuster told Shales and Miller. "Lorne was a very avid, eager sponge for all of it." Frank Shuster was also the person who suggested Lorne change his last name from Lipowitz to something with more show-business appeal.

Early work

Michaels attended University College in Toronto, where he became involved in stage work. He co-wrote and directed the 1964 *UC Follies,* a student production of songs and satirical skits. While working on the *Follies,* Michaels met Hart Pomerantz, and the two students developed a comedy act. They initially wrote for a comedy radio show on the Canadian Broadcasting Company (CBC) called *Five Nights a Week at This Time,* and they also submitted jokes to famous comedians they liked, such as Woody Allen (1935–). Some of these jokes made their way around comedy circles, and in 1968 Michaels and Pomerantz were offered a job in Hollywood as writers for a television series starring comedian Phyllis Diller (1917–). But the series, *The Beautiful Phyllis Diller Show,* lasted only nine weeks before it was canceled.

Though their first job in California did not work out, Michaels and Pomerantz were quickly hired as junior writers for *Rowan and Martin's Laugh-In*. One of the most popular comedy shows on TV at that time, it featured future stars such as Lily Tomlin (1939–) and Goldie Hawn (1945–). Michaels and Pomerantz mostly wrote monologues (humorous introductory speeches) for the show's hosts, Dan Rowan (1922–1987) and Dick Martin (1922–). But they grew disillusioned when all of their jokes were extensively rewritten by other people. The duo decided that if they were to continue to work in television, they would have to produce their own shows in order to protect their material.

In 1969, Michaels and Pomerantz returned to Canada after the CBC offered them the opportunity to write, produce, and star in their own television specials. Over the next three years they created four comedy specials a year, including *Today Makes Me Nervous* and *The Hart and Lorne Terrific Hour*. Like Michaels's earlier efforts at camp and in college, these shows used the same format as the future SNL, with an opening monologue, sketch comedy by a repertory company, and musical guests. Michaels used the show to develop his skills in television production. "I learned how to do television mostly because the CBC was this tremendous training ground," he told Winship. "I began to feel very comfortable in a television studio. . . . I was able to learn an enormous amount in a very short time."

Intrigued by producing, confident of his newly acquired skills, and no longer content to play the straight man for Pomerantz's jokes, Michaels returned to Hollywood alone determined to become a success in television. His first project, a series for the comedy team of Burns and Schreiber, was only on the air for a short time before being dropped by the network. His fortunes changed, however, when he met up with Lily Tomlin in 1973.

Tomlin's fame had increased steadily since she appeared on *Laugh-In*, until by 1973 she was one of the most successful comedians in the country. Tomlin and Michaels clashed on occasion, but she still hired him as a writer for her 1973 CBS special, *Lily,* and as a co-producer and writer for two later specials on ABC. Though the shows were well received and earned Michaels two Emmy Awards (annual honors recognizing excellence in television), the networks chose not to expand them into series.

"Live from New York . . . It's Saturday Night"

In 1974 Johnny Carson, host of *The Tonight Show* on NBC, decided that he no longer wanted repeats of his show to air at 11:30 P.M. on Saturday

The 1976–77 cast of Saturday Night Live, *also known as the Not Ready for Prime Time Players.* AP IMAGES.

nights, as they had for ten years. Executives at the network decided to create a new show for that time slot and enlisted Dick Ebersol, the head of weekend late-night programming, to come up with a program. Ebersol had recently met Michaels and been impressed with his talent. Michaels had pitched an idea for a new kind of television show that would "speak the language of the time," as Ebersol told Shales and Miller. "He wanted the show to be the first show in the history of television to talk the same language being talked on college campuses and streets and everywhere else."

Ebersol liked the idea and agreed to have Michaels produce it. The first episode of *NBC's Saturday Night* aired on October 11, 1975 (it would not be called *Saturday Night Live* until two years later, due to a conflict with a show airing on another network). The show featured a relatively unknown group of young comedians called the Not Ready for Prime Time Players, including Dan Ackroyd (1952–), John Belushi (1949–1982),

Chevy Chase (1943–), Jane Curtin, Garrett Morris, Laraine Newman, and Gilda Radner (1946–1989). From the very start, it was unlike anything else on television. "I just did a show that I would watch if I were the audience," Michaels explained to Winship. "Everyone else I assembled in the first year really had just sprung from the audience. With one or two exceptions, they [the cast] weren't people with very long résumés."

Though not a runaway success from the beginning, SNL was immediately recognized for its innovative style and its influence on popular culture. After the fourth episode, for instance, *Washington Post* TV critic Tom Shales wrote, "NBC's *Saturday Night* can boast the freshest satire on commercial TV, but it is more than that. It is probably the first network series produced by and for the television generation—those late-[World War II] and post-war babies who were the first to have TV as a sitter."

As the first season progressed, SNL attracted more and more media attention, its ratings improved, and several of the cast members (especially Chevy Chase) became big stars. In the spring of 1976, SNL received five Emmy Award nominations. It ended up winning three awards—for Outstanding Comedy-Variety Series, Outstanding Writing in a Comedy-Variety Series, and Outstanding Supporting Player for Chase—which ensured that the show would be renewed for a second season.

Chase left the show during that second season to pursue a movie career. But his successor, Bill Murray (1950–), turned out to be equally popular, and SNL's exceptional success continued. The show was honored with another Emmy as Outstanding Comedy-Variety Series, and Michaels and the cast were rewarded with pay increases. As SNL's influence grew, Michael proved to be a tough negotiator in contract talks with the network. He ended up signing a deal that gave him money to set up his own production company (Broadway Video), a 50 percent share of all future syndication (rerun) and video rights, and an estimated $1.5 million per year in salary.

Leaving and returning to *Saturday Night Live*

The pressures of producing a live show, coming up with funny and topical material week after week, and managing the personalities of various cast members took a toll on Michaels and others involved in *Saturday Night Live*. In fact, the situation became so bad that the entire cast and crew, including Michaels, left the show after the fifth season in 1980. "I'd given so much energy to holding things together for all those years," Michaels explained in *Live from New York*. "I was truly drained, just spent. . . . It was very hard for me."

Despite the changes, however, SNL continued running on NBC. Between 1980 and 1985, the show had two different producers and a constantly changing cast. A few notable comedians got their starts on SNL during this period, including Eddie Murphy and Julia Louis-Dreyfus (who later played Elaine on the hit sitcom *Seinfeld*). For the most part, though, SNL failed to maintain its place on the cutting-edge of TV comedy, and its ratings suffered as a result.

In the meantime, Michaels built up his production company and produced various television specials and concert events, such as Paul Simon and Art Garfunkel's 1982 reunion concert in New York City's Central Park. He made a return to television in 1984 with a sketch-comedy program called *The New Show,* but it was canceled after three months.

By the spring of 1985, SNL was on the verge of being canceled as well. NBC approached Michaels and asked if he would be interested in returning to the helm of the show he had created a decade earlier. Although he was in the midst of filming *Three Amigos,* a movie he wrote with Steve Martin and Randy Newman, Michaels agreed. He was eager to see SNL once again become a cultural force on television.

Finding a new groove

After an uncertain first year back, SNL improved in its second season following Michaels's return. The show entered the 1990s with great writers and a stellar cast that included Dana Carvey, Dennis Miller, Jan Hooks, and Phil Hartman. The next decade saw new stars emerge, such as Chris Rock, Mike Myers, Adam Sandler, and Will Ferrell. As SNL regained its audience, Michaels became more confident of the show's place in the history of comedy. He then branched out and began producing movies—many of which starred current or former SNL cast members—such as *Wayne's World* (1992), *Tommy Boy* (1995), *Ladies' Man* (2000), and *Mean Girls* (2004).

In 1993, NBC asked Michaels to produce a new late-night talk show to replace the celebrated *Late Night with David Letterman,* after Letterman moved to another network. Michaels picked a relative unknown named Conan O'Brien, who had worked as a writer for SNL and *The Simpsons,* to be the host of the revamped program. To the surprise of many industry insiders, *Late Night with Conan O'Brien* became a hit. In 1997, Michaels became chairman of SNL Studios, a new production company that was formed to create programming for NBC and also develop feature films in partnership with Paramount Pictures.

Whatever the future may hold for Michaels, he will always be closely associated with *Saturday Night Live,* which was the longest-running and highest-rated late-night TV program as of 2006. During his twenty-five years of guiding SNL, the show was nominated for an amazing 85 Emmy Awards. It won 17, as well as earning a 1990 George Foster Peabody Award as an "American institution." Michaels has collected a number of individual honors, as well. In 1994, he received the Kennedy Center's Mark Twain Prize for American Humor, for instance, and in 1999, he was inducted into the Television Hall of Fame and also received the Order of Canada, his native country's highest honor for lifetime achievement.

For More Information

BOOKS

Hill, Doug, and Jeff Weingrad. *Saturday Night: A Backstage History of "Saturday Night Live."* New York: Morrow, 1987.

Shales, Tom, and James Andrew Miller. *Live from New York: An Uncensored History of "Saturday Night Live."* Boston: Little, Brown, 2003.

Winship, Michael. *Television.* New York: Random House, 1988.

WEB SITES

"Lorne Michaels Biography." http://www.lornemichaels.com (accessed on May 22, 2006).

"Lorne Michaels Biography." http://www.nbc.com/Saturday_Night_Live/bios/Lorne_Michaels.html (accessed on May 22, 2006).

"Saturday Night Live." *Museum of Broadcast Communications.* http://www.museum.tv/archives/etv/S/htmlS/saturdaynigh/saturdaynigh.htm (accessed on May 22, 2006).

Mary Tyler Moore

BORN: December 29, 1936 • Brooklyn, New York

American actress, television executive

"Take chances. Make mistakes. That's how you grow. You have to fail in order to practice being brave."

M ary Tyler Moore is best known as one of the stars of the beloved 1960s and 1970s television comedy series *The Dick Van Dyke Show* and *The Mary Tyler Moore Show.* Her portrayal of the independent, spunky television news producer Mary Richards on *The Mary Tyler Moore Show* made her a hero to many American women, who were beginning to break out of traditional feminine roles at that time. Moore also inspired feminists with her real-life success as the chairman of the board of MTM Enterprises, a television production company that created a number of successful shows in the 1970s and 1980s.

Performing at an early age

Mary Tyler Moore.
© GLENN WEINER/
ZUMA/CORBIS.

Mary Tyler Moore was born on December 29, 1936, in Brooklyn, New York. Her father, George, was an auditor for a utility company. Her mother, Marjorie, was a homemaker who suffered from alcoholism, a disease that Moore herself developed later in life. In 1945, the family moved to Los Angeles, California, where her father got a job with the Southern California Gas Company.

The move to Los Angeles was not easy for Moore. She fell behind in school, and she became anxious about growing troubles in her parents' marriage. Since she had always enjoyed singing and dancing for her family, Moore began to direct her energy toward performing. She started training as a dancer, and she was excited when it turned out that she had found something at which she excelled.

When she was seventeen, Moore met Dick Meeker, a 27-year-old salesman living next door to her family. They were married the following year. Around the same time, Moore landed her first professional acting job. She played Happy Hotpoint, a tiny elf who danced on appliances, in a series of television commercials. That job came to an end in 1955, when Moore gave birth to her son, Richard.

Becoming a comic actress

Moore's dance training helped her land roles in the chorus on two different television variety shows, *The Eddie Fisher Show* and *The George Gobel Show*. Although she loved dancing, Moore was determined to become an actress. She got her first break in 1957 playing Sam, the sultry secretary on the TV detective series *Richard Diamond*. An unsuccessful audition for the popular Danny Thomas series *Make Room for Daddy* led to a tryout for a new show in 1961. Moore won the part of Laura Petrie on *The Dick Van Dyke Show*, which was produced by Danny Thomas (1914–1991) and Carl Reiner (1922–).

The Dick Van Dyke Show appeared on CBS for five years beginning in 1961. Actor Dick Van Dyke (1925–) starred as Rob Petrie, a successful television writer, and Moore played his wife. Although Laura Petrie stays home to take care of the couple's young son, Ritchie, she does not always fit into the traditional housewife role. In fact, Moore's character generated controversy by wearing cropped pants and flat shoes at a time when other TV wives wore dresses and high heels. She also participated in household decisions more than many female television characters. *The Dick Van Dyke Show* featured strong writing and won more than a dozen Emmy Awards (annual honors recognizing excellence in television programming), including two for Moore as Best Actress in a Comedy Series.

Moore's real-life marriage was less successful than her TV relationship, however, and she divorced Dick Meeker in 1962. A year later she married Grant Tinker, who at that time was an account executive at an advertising agency. Tinker later became president and chief executive officer of the NBC television network.

When *The Dick Van Dyke Show* went off the air in 1966, Moore acted in Broadway plays and motion pictures. After suffering a miscarriage, she was shocked to learn that she had diabetes, a disease in which the body loses the ability to process the sugar in food. Left untreated, diabetes can cause kidney failure, heart disease, circulation problems, or stroke. After her diagnosis, Moore monitored her diet carefully and injected herself with insulin in order to regulate the level of sugar in her blood. Moore also became an activist on behalf of diabetics, helping to raise money to fight the disease. She even served as the international chairman of the Juvenile Diabetes Foundation.

Starring in *The Mary Tyler Moore Show*

In 1969, Moore reunited with the cast of *The Dick Van Dyke Show* for a musical-variety special called *Dick Van Dyke and the Other Woman*. The show was such a hit that CBS offered Moore a chance to develop her own half-hour sitcom. Along with her husband, Grant Tinker, Moore established an independent television production company called MTM Productions. The couple hired talented producers and writers, such as Jim Brooks and Allan Burns, and the creative team worked together to develop the concept for *The Mary Tyler Moore Show*. Moore played the role of Mary Richards, a young woman who gets dumped by her boyfriend, moves to Minneapolis, and finds a job as a television news producer in a newsroom filled with eccentric characters.

The Mary Tyler Moore Show first appeared on CBS in 1970 and was a big hit with both critics and viewers. "The show played better than any of us had imagined . . . and surpassed even the well-wishing we'd heaped on each other," Moore recalled in her autobiography, *After All*. "Everyone who was present for the filming, as well as those who saw the episode, agreed that it was a winner, the cast had the easy chemistry that usually evolves after years of working together."

Moore's character, Mary Richards, introduced a new type of female role on TV as a happy, successful, independent, single working woman. She struck a chord at a time when many American women were staying single longer and building successful careers. Mary Richards became a role model in the growing women's liberation or feminist movement of the 1970s, which worked to secure equal right and opportunities for

The cast of **The Mary Tyler Moore Show** *gathers for the series finale in 1977, after seven successful years of doing the show.* CBS PHOTO ARCHIVE/GETTY IMAGES.

women in the United States. Moore earned three Emmy Awards as Outstanding Actress in a Comedy Series for her spunky portrayal of the beloved character.

The Mary Tyler Moore Show ran for seven years, airing its last episode in 1977. In the meantime, Moore's company, MTM Productions, also experienced tremendous success in developing other television shows. MTM created two spin-off series revolving around popular characters from *The Mary Tyler Moore Show, Rhoda* and *Phyllis.* In later years, the company also developed such television hits as *The Bob Newhart Show, Hill Street Blues, WKRP in Cincinnati, The White Shadow,* and *St. Elsewhere.*

Moore took a long break after her namesake series went off the air. When she returned to television, she decided that a variety show would be the best follow-up to her successful sitcom. Her producers assembled a cast of talented co-stars who would eventually become stars in their own right, including Michael Keaton (1951–), David Letterman (1947–), and Swoosie Kurtz. But with the variety show format losing popularity among viewers, *The Mary Tyler Moore Hour* lasted only eight episodes.

In 1978, Moore drew critical attention for her performance in a serious role for a television movie, *First You Cry,* about a woman suffering from breast cancer. In 1980, she received more praise for her performance in the play *Whose Life Is It Anyway* on Broadway. In 1981, she landed one of the biggest roles of her career in the film *Ordinary People,* directed by Robert Redford. Moore played Beth Jarrett, the rigid, demanding mother of a sensitive son who is full with guilt over his brother's death. *Ordinary People* earned four Academy Awards, including Best Picture of the Year, and Moore received an Oscar nomination for her performance in the film.

Facing tragedy

Although Moore's professional life was soaring, her personal life was beset by tragedy and personal setbacks. In 1978, her sister Elizabeth died of a drug overdose at the age of twenty-one. In 1980, her son Richard accidentally shot himself to death. A year later, Moore and her second husband, Grant Tinker, were divorced.

Following the end of her marriage, Moore settled in New York City. In 1983, she married Dr. Robert Levine, a cardiologist who was seventeen years younger than she. With her husband's support, Moore finally decided to confront a problem that had been growing for years—her alcoholism. Realizing that her constant drinking complicated her diabetes and caused other health issues, she checked herself into a famous therapy center, the Betty Ford Clinic. With the help of the counselors there, as well as her own inner strength, she was able to get sober.

In 1984, Moore returned to work, and she appeared in a number of theatrical films and TV movies throughout the remainder of the decade. She also made a workout video, played Mary Todd Lincoln in the TV miniseries *Gore Vidal's Lincoln,* and played the title role in a short-lived comedy series *Mary,* set in a Chicago newsroom. One of the high points of her professional career came in 1985, when she was inducted into the Television Hall of Fame.

Moore continued to work steadily during the 1990s and 2000s, appearing in television shows, made-for-TV movies, and theatrical films. In 1995, for instance, she starred in another short-lived television series, *New York News*. The following year she earned critical praise for her sassy role in *Flirting with Disaster,* a motion picture starring Ben Stiller, Patricia Arquette, and George Segal. In 2001, she once again garnered critical praise for her portrayal of con artist Sante Kimes in the television movie *Like Mother, Like Son*. Moore also appeared in several reunion projects with her friends from her popular 1970s series, including *Mary and Rhoda* (2000) and *The Dick Van Dyke Show Revisited* (2004).

For More Information

BOOKS

Bonderoff, Jason. *Mary Tyler Moore: A Biography*. New York: St. Martin's Press, 1986.

Moore, Mary Tyler. *After All*. New York: G. P. Putnam's Sons, 1995.

WEB SITES

"Mary Tyler Moore." *Internet Movie Database*. http://www.imdb.com/name/nm0001546/ (accessed on May 22, 2006).

Agnes Nixon

BORN: December 10, 1927 • Chicago, Illinois

American television producer, television writer

"I am a storyteller and I like the dramatic form. To me it's just the thing I love to do. Seeing it come to life on the air by actors is just a great thrill for me."

Agnes Nixon is frequently called the queen of the contemporary soap opera. During a career that has spanned over fifty years, she wrote for and created some of television's best-loved daytime dramas, such as *All My Children* and *One Life to Live*. She also received praise from television critics and viewers alike for addressing current events and controversial issues in her work.

Becoming a soap opera writer

Agnes Eckhardt Nixon was born on December 10, 1927, in Chicago, Illinois. Her father, Harry Eckhardt, manufactured burial garments (clothing for the dead). Her mother, Agnes Eckhardt, was a treasurer for an insurance company. They divorced when Agnes was young. An only child, Agnes was raised mostly in Nashville, Tennessee. She turned to writing at an early age as a means to escape the controlling ways of her grandmother.

Agnes Nixon.
BRYAN BEDDER/
GETTY IMAGES.

125

Nixon attended Northwestern University in Evanston, Illinois, where she studied drama. Her classmates included actors Charlton Heston (1924–), Patricia Neal (1926–), and Cloris Leachman (1926–). Nixon received her bachelor's degree in 1948. Since she was determined to become a writer, her father set up a meeting with Irna Philips, one of the leading writers of serial dramas at that time.

Serial dramas were a popular form of entertainment on the radio beginning in the 1920s. In the late 1940s and early 1950s, sponsors adapted these programs to the new medium of TV. The early television serials were aimed at women, who were expected to be home during the day taking care of the house and children. Most of the shows were sponsored by the makers of household cleaning products, packaged foods, and cosmetic items, so they became known as soap operas.

Soap operas tell complicated, ongoing stories that continue over weeks, months, or even years. Instead of reaching a conclusion, each episode is open-ended, with some unresolved issue or problem remaining to be handled in future episodes. Soap operas feature large casts of characters who change over time, get older, and sometimes die. The characters also face many problems and crises as the show's writers try to advance the story and keep it interesting. Since the stories are so complex, viewers must watch regularly in order to keep up with new developments. As a result, serial dramas develop the most loyal audience of any type of television program, and many fans form deep emotional connections with their favorite shows.

Nixon impressed Irna Philips with her talent, and the veteran soap opera writer hired the young college graduate to work on her radio serials, *The Woman in White* and *Guiding Light*. The two women worked together to develop *Guiding Light* into a relevant, entertaining program.

During the first few years of her career, Nixon also worked as a self-employed, independent writer for various early television programs, including *Philco Playhouse, Hallmark Hall of Fame, Studio One,* and *Somerset Maugham Theatre.* She moved to New York City at the age of twenty-four, determined to further her writing career.

Emerging as the queen of modern soap operas

In 1951, Nixon created her first serial drama for television, *Search for Tomorrow,* and she worked as a writer on that show until 1957. In 1953, she became co-creator and head writer of another soap opera, *As the World*

Turns, which continued to run on television into the 2000s. In 1959, Nixon was hired to be the head writer of the TV version of *Guiding Light,* a position she held for six years.

During the early years of her television career, Nixon married Bob Nixon, an executive with Chrysler Corporation. The marriage lasted until his death in 1997, and the couple had four children together. Nixon was determined to spend time at home raising her children as well as continuing to write for soaps such as *Search for Tomorrow, As the World Turns, Another World,* and *Guiding Light.* She arranged to work from her Philadelphia home, writing scripts for the shows while also raising her kids.

For several years, Nixon wrote for both *Guiding Light* and *Another World.* Trying to keep up with two complicated story lines led to a few minor script problems. For example, Nixon once set a scene for *Another World* in a coffee house that really belonged in *Guiding Light.*

Nixon realized early on that the continuing story lines of soap operas provided her with a unique opportunity to explore important, yet much-debated, social issues. She felt that her job gave her a responsibility to educate and inform as well as entertain her viewers. Although it was a hectic time in her career, Nixon began to introduce a variety of new issues to daytime drama, such as racism, women's health, child abuse, and teenage pregnancy.

When one of her friends died from cancer, for instance, Nixon incorporated a story line in *Guiding Light* in which a key character, Bert Bauer, is diagnosed with cancer. The story emphasizes the importance of women getting an annual Pap smear (a test for cervical cancer). Studies showed that after the story line aired, the number of Pap smears performed in the United States that year rose significantly. In 2002, Nixon was awarded a special Sentinel for Health award for her pioneering work in exploring women's health issues on *Guiding Light.*

Making daytime dramas explore controversial issues

During the 1960s and 1970s, American society experienced a number of important changes. For instance, African Americans began seeking equal rights and opportunities through the civil rights movement. Women began breaking out of the traditional roles of wife and mother and became more independent; they remained unmarried longer and established successful careers. In 1968, Nixon created the daytime drama *One Life to Live* for the ABC network (it continued to air on ABC into the 2000s). This

Agnes Nixon, right, with All My Children *actress Susan Lucci as Lucci receives a star on the Hollywood Walk of Fame in 2005.* © CHRIS FARINA/CORBIS.

program emphasized the differences in ethnic background and social class among the residents of a fictional town. The show also reflected some of the changes taking place in American society at that time. It dealt with such issues as gender roles, sexuality, class conflict, and race relations, and it encouraged viewers to think about and discuss these topics.

In 1970, Nixon created another serial daytime drama for ABC, *All My Children*. As head writer and executive producer of the show, she once again explored social and cultural issues of interest to women. For example, the show addressed the much-debated subject of abortion (the termination of a pregnancy) in one story line. *All My Children* was also the first fictional TV series to deal with the effects of the Vietnam War (1954–75). Nixon wrote a story line in which the son of a major character is killed in the conflict. She showed the character's reaction to the news, then traced her development into a person who actively protested against the war. Nixon always made sure to provide viewers who found themselves affected by similar problems with information and resources for getting help. During a story line about child abuse, for instance, the show offered viewers the phone numbers of organizations that provide help for abused children.

Many viewers appreciated Nixon's willingness to address difficult issues, and *All My Children* became very successful as a result. In fact, it remained one of the top-rated daytime dramas on television into the 2000s. The most popular character on the show was the scheming model and businesswoman Erica Kane, played by Susan Lucci (1946–). Fans loved watching Erica grow and change over time, have exciting adventures, and become romantically attached to many interesting men.

Receiving honors for her work

In 1981, Nixon tried her hand at writing for a prime-time miniseries drama. Running almost five hours, *The Manions of America* followed the story of an Irish family as they immigrated to the United States and found success. In 1983, Nixon introduced a half-hour daytime drama, *Loving,* with co-creator Douglas Marland. The title of the show was later changed to *The City,* and it ran in this form until 1995.

In 1992, Nixon stepped back from day-to-day writing responsibilities on *All My Children,* though she continued to be involved with the show as a story consultant. In 1999, she was asked to return to the show as head writer. Shortly after resuming her former job, Nixon introduced a story line in which a main character, Bianca Montgomery, publicly reveals that she is a lesbian. This story line attracted new interest to the show, and it also earned praise from gay and lesbian groups. In fact, Nixon's sensitive and compelling treatment of the subject helped *All My Children* win a media award from the Gay and Lesbian Alliance Against Defamation

(GLAAD), an organization that promotes positive treatment of homosexuals in the media. In 2000, Nixon became ABC-TV's overall consultant for daytime programming.

Throughout her long career, Nixon and her shows received a number of prestigious awards, including four Daytime Emmy Awards for writing, five Writer's Guild of America Awards, and a Soap Opera Digest Award. Nixon also received numerous citations for public service and for outstanding contributions to daytime television. In 1993 she was admitted into the Television Hall of Fame, and a year later she became a member of the Soap Opera Hall of Fame.

In a 1999 interview with *Broadcasting and Cable,* Nixon shared some thoughts about her career. She noted that soaps hold a strong appeal for TV viewers because "it's the form of entertainment nearest to real life. Every day is a new episode, there's that appeal, as well as the fact that it's never repeated. I think there's something about a continued story." She claimed that the most difficult aspect of being a soap writer is "the discipline you have to have because of the time pressure. It takes five days a week, fifty-two weeks a year, and that's pretty grueling." Despite the challenges, Nixon explained that she enjoyed writing serials dramas because "I am a storyteller and I like the dramatic form. To me it's just the thing I love to do. You take something in life that generates an idea and then it grows and one embellishes it. Seeing it come to life on the air by actors is just a great thrill for me."

For More Information

BOOKS

Current Biography. New York: H. W. Wilson, 2001.

PERIODICALS

"The Scheherazade of Soaps." *Broadcasting and Cable,* May 31, 1999.

Stengel, Richard. "Doyenne of Daytime." *Time,* August 15, 1983.

WEB SITES

"Agnes Nixon." *Museum of Broadcast Communications.* http://www.museum.tv/archives/etv/N/htmlN/nixonagnes/nixonagnes.htm (accessed on May 22, 2006).

"*All My Children:* Agnes Nixon." *ABC.* http://www.abcmedianet.com/showpage/showpage.html?program_id=000259&type=producers (accessed on May 22, 2006).

William S. Paley

BORN: September 28, 1901 • Chicago, Illinois
DIED: October 26, 1990 • New York, New York

American radio and television executive

"I always say we have to give most of the people what they want most of the time. That's what they expect from us."

William S. Paley ranks among the giants of American television executives. During his long reign as president and chairman of the Columbia Broadcasting System (CBS), he helped establish it as the most popular and respected of the three major U.S. broadcast networks (ABC and NBC are the other two). He gave the CBS News division the resources and direction it needed to become a major force in American journalism. He also encouraged the development of legendary CBS entertainment programs such as *All in the Family* and *M*A*S*H*. Once CBS reached the number one spot among the broadcast networks, the colorful executive was criticized at times for being too protective of CBS's profits and reputation. Even so, Paley's contributions to the development of network television are unquestioned.

Developing the CBS radio network

William S. Paley.
CARL MYDANS/TIME LIFE
PICTURES/GETTY IMAGES.

William Samuel Paley was born on September 28, 1901, in Chicago, Illinois. His father, Samuel Paley, a Jewish immigrant from the Eastern

European nation of Ukraine, built a successful cigar-making company in the United States. His mother was Goldie (Drell) Paley. William had one younger sister, Blanche.

Paley grew up in a Jewish neighborhood of Chicago. He attended public schools in the city until his senior year of high school, when his parents enrolled him in the Western Military Academy in Alton, Illinois. After graduating from the academy in 1918, Paley attended the University of Chicago. After one year of study there, his family moved to Philadelphia, so Paley transferred to the Wharton School of Finance at the University of Pennsylvania. He graduated from Wharton with a bachelor of science degree in 1922.

Paley had worked for his father's Congress Cigar Company throughout his youth, sweeping floors and running errands. After graduating from Wharton, Paley immediately took a management position with his father's company. During the next several years, Paley showed an impressive grasp of business principles and an instinct for making smart business decisions.

During the mid-1920s, Paley also became interested in the new medium of commercial radio. In 1928, he convinced his father to buy the Columbia Broadcasting System (CBS), a struggling radio network consisting of sixteen stations. Paley was named president of the network at the young age of twenty-seven. He quickly began working to build CBS into a respectable challenger to the National Broadcasting Company (NBC), which was the largest radio network in the United States at that time.

Over the next few years, Paley gradually turned CBS into a competitor. One key to his success was his ability to lure other radio stations to join the CBS network. He did this by ending a policy that required affiliate stations (those grouped together into one system) to pay for all non-sponsored programming (programs that were not sponsored by a company for advertising purposes) supplied by the network. Under the new arrangements offered by Paley, CBS radio stations would receive these programs free of charge in return for keeping other blocks of time available for the network to broadcast sponsored programs. This scheme gave CBS a big competitive advantage over NBC, and the number of stations that chose to join the CBS network grew rapidly. Meanwhile, Paley took a number of steps to make advertising on CBS both easy and profitable. He also married Dorothy Hart Hearst in 1932. They raised two children together before divorcing in 1947.

Building an empire

During the 1930s, Paley continued to build CBS Radio into a major force in the industry. One key to his success was his ability to find new talent to feature on CBS stations. Legendary singers such as Kate Smith (1907–1986), Bing Crosby (1903–1977), and Frank Sinatra (1915–1998) launched their careers on CBS Radio during this time. Another factor in CBS's rise was Paley's ability to lure already popular musicians and comedians away from NBC. These so-called "Paley Raids" of the 1930s and 1940s brought such popular entertainers as Jack Benny (1894–1974), George Burns (1896–1996), and Gracie Allen (1895–1964) into the group of performers managed by CBS.

Paley handled complex and controversial management issues on a case-by-case basis during this time. For example, in 1931, Paley directed CBS Radio to drop its broadcasts of Father Charles Coughlin (1891–1979), a Catholic priest based in Michigan who had become notorious for his anti-Jewish statements. CBS reportedly received hundreds of thousands of letters from listeners protesting this decision, but Paley refused to change his mind. Coughlin was forced to mount a fundraising campaign so that he could continue making his broadcasts on independent radio stations.

Paley also established a strong news division that emphasized balanced coverage and objectivity (reporting both sides of controversial issues in a fair manner, without being influenced by one's own opinion). This investment in journalistic talent and resources paid off during World War II (1939–45), when CBS Radio journalists provided some of the best news coverage of the entire war. Paley, meanwhile, served on the staff of U.S. general Dwight Eisenhower (1890–1969) during the war. It was also during the war years that Paley struck up a friendship with legendary CBS newsman Edward R. Murrow (1908–1965).

Life among the rich and famous

In 1946, Paley became chairman of the board of CBS, turning the presidency of the company over to Frank Stanton, a trusted executive. Stanton would serve Paley loyally in that position for the next twenty-seven years.

Over the next few years, Paley joined various CBS entertainers to become a well-known figure in the circles of the rich and famous. He divorced his first wife after several years of separation, and in 1947 he married Barbara "Babe" Cushing Mortimer, a wealthy socialite from

Edward R. Murrow

Legendary broadcast journalist Edward R. Murrow was born as Egbert Roscoe Murrow on April 25, 1908, near Greensboro, North Carolina. He started using the nickname "Ed" during his teen years and changed his first name to "Edward" when he launched his broadcasting career. He was the youngest of three sons born to Roscoe and Ethel (Lamb) Murrow, who made a living by farming corn and hay. For the first five years of his life, Murrow lived in a log cabin with no electricity or running water. Then his family moved to northern Washington State, just thirty miles from the Canadian border, and his father became a locomotive engineer.

Murrow attended Edison High School in Washington, where he was an excellent student and also showed strong leadership qualities. He played in the school orchestra, sang in the glee club, participated in sports, and served as president of the student body in his senior year. But Murrow showed the greatest skill as a member

of the debate team. Crafting arguments about current events helped the young man gain a lifelong interest in political and social issues.

Murrow worked in the timber industry in order to earn enough money to attend Washington State College, where he once again served as president of the student body. In this position, he was invited to attend the annual convention of the National Student Federation of America (NSFA), the largest student organization in the United States. At the convention, Murrow gave a speech in which he encouraged his fellow students to devote more of their attention to national and world affairs. The group found his message so inspiring that they elected him president of the NSFA.

Murrow graduated from Washington State College in 1930. That same year, the NSFA held its annual convention in Atlanta, Georgia. At a time when schools in the South were segregated

Boston. Paley and his second wife gained a reputation as world travelers who socialized with wealthy and famous friends all across North America and Europe. Paley also established himself as a generous and knowledgeable patron of the arts. He served as president and chairman of the famous Museum of Modern Art in New York for many years, and he personally built one of the world's most valuable collections of modern art. Paley also provided a financial gift that laid the foundation for the establishment of the Museum of Television and Radio in New York.

Entering television broadcasting

As commercial television broadcasting got started after World War II, CBS spent a great deal of time and money developing a color television system. This system, developed by CBS engineer Peter Goldmark (1906–1977), was the national standard for a few years in the early 1950s. But the Federal Communications Commission (FCC) eventually replaced it (divided by race), Murrow made a point of inviting representatives of African American colleges to attend the meeting. When the convention center refused to serve dinner to the black students, Murrow encouraged white students to pass down their plates full of food. In 1934 Murrow married Janet Huntington Brewster. They had a son, Charles.

During his college years, Murrow had created an educational series called *University of the Air* for the new CBS radio network. In 1935 he accepted a full-time job with CBS. The network was just starting to build a news division at that time, so Murrow lined up experts to appear on the air and talk about various topics in the news. In 1937 he moved to London, England, to become director of the network's European news bureau.

Murrow remained in Europe throughout World War II (1939–45). He became famous for standing on London rooftops to provide American radio audiences with live descriptions of German bombing raids. Murrow also hired and trained a staff of talented young war correspondents to give similar reports from other cities in Europe. Murrow returned to the United States after the war ended, and in 1946 he was promoted to vice president and director of public affairs at CBS. In 1950 he launched a popular radio news program called *Hear It Now.* The following year he brought the series to the new medium of television as *See It Now.*

During its seven-year run, *See It Now* tackled a number of controversial issues, earned four Emmy Awards as Best News or Public Affairs Program, and helped change history on several occasions. Murrow also hosted a popular celebrity-interview series called *Person to Person* for CBS during the 1950s. Ongoing conflicts with management convinced him to leave the network in 1960. President John F. Kennedy then appointed Murrow director of the U.S. Information Office, but poor health forced him to leave this position in 1964. He died of lung cancer on April 28, 1965.

with an all-electronic color system developed by the Radio Corporation of America (RCA), which owned the competing NBC radio and television networks. Paley was disappointed by the FCC decision, but he wasted little time complaining about it. Instead, he set about building a strong group of local affiliate television stations and luring big radio stars to appear on CBS television programs.

Meanwhile, Goldmark helped Paley expand his business empire in another way. Goldmark was instrumental in the development of the long-playing (LP) record, introduced in 1948. The LP enabled recording artists and record companies to achieve a dramatic increase in the amount of music that fit on a single record. It revolutionized the recording industry and made CBS Records the leading record company in America for many years (the company was sold to Sony in 1987 for $2 billion).

Paley and CBS also diversified into other industries during the 1950s and 1960s. CBS became involved in such widely different industries as television set manufacturing, book and magazine publishing, and toy distribution. CBS even owned baseball's New York Yankees from 1964 to 1973, when Paley arranged the sale of the team to a group of investors led by George Steinbrenner.

Television, though, remained the most important part of the growing CBS empire. Under Paley's visionary leadership, the CBS network made a very successful transition from radio to television. CBS News, for instance, was able to maintain its reputation as a leading broadcast news organization when television emerged as the American people's main source of news and information. Paley skillfully directed the careers of some of his top radio journalists, including Edward R. Murrow, Howard K. Smith (1914–2003), and **Walter Cronkite** (1916–; see entry), as they entered the new medium of television.

Working with Edward R. Murrow

Paley also increased the reputation of CBS Television by being willing to invest in hard-hitting news and public affairs shows such as *See It Now*, which aired from 1951 to 1958. Hosted by Murrow, this program was presented as a series of documentaries (fact-based films) that investigated serious issues affecting American society, such as the relationship between cigarette smoking and lung cancer and the unfair treatment of migrant farm workers.

See It Now is probably best known for a 1954 program about Joseph McCarthy (1908–1957), a U.S. senator from Wisconsin who had ruined the careers of many American politicians and entertainers by falsely accusing them of being Communists. McCarthy used the tensions of the Cold War (1945–91; a period of intense military and political rivalry that pitted the United States and its democratic system of government against the Soviet Union and its Communist system of government) to hurt his enemies and advance his own career. Murrow's show helped turn public opinion against McCarthy, and the senator soon fell from power. Before the episode went on the air, however, Paley and other top CBS executives felt so nervous about the subject matter that they did not promote it. Tensions over this and other controversial episodes of *See It Now* badly strained the relationship between Paley and Murrow.

Many television historians believe that Paley's concerns about the public reaction to such controversial programming was a major factor in the eventual cancellation of *See It Now*. Some scholars have also criticized Paley for other actions he took during the McCarthy era,

CBS President Frank Stanton, left, presents CBS Chairman William S. Paley with a silver gavel in appreciation of his decades of leadership at the network. © BETTMANN/CORBIS.

including his cooperation in establishing a blacklist of entertainers and writers suspected of being Communists. Americans who were blacklisted during this era found it nearly impossible to work in their chosen careers, often for years at a time, because companies would simply refuse to hire them.

CBS becomes the industry leader

From 1955 through 1976, CBS television consistently led the other two major broadcast networks (ABC and NBC) in creating prime-time programs that attracted large audiences and high ratings. Much of this success has been credited to Paley, who had an exceptional ability to figure

Television in American Society: Biographies

out which new program proposals were worth pursuing. Under Paley's direction, CBS broke new ground with such innovative programs as *60 Minutes, M*A*S*H,* and *All in the Family.* Other classic television programs that appeared on CBS during these decades were *The Mary Tyler Moore Show, The Waltons,* and *The Andy Griffith Show.* These legendary shows were complemented by dozens of less memorable but still popular shows.

By the early 1970s, it was clear that Paley believed the CBS policy of forcing employees to retire at the age of sixty-five did not apply to him. He tried out a number of potential replacements over the years, but he did not step down as the company's chief executive officer (CEO) until 1977, and he remained its chairman until 1983. When Paley finally gave up control of CBS, the network was earning more than $4 billion per year.

Paley's departure paved the way for Thomas H. Wyman to take over as the head of CBS. But Paley soon became very unhappy with Wyman's leadership. In 1985, only two years after his retirement, Paley joined forces with Lawrence Tisch (CBS's largest stockholder) to remove Wyman and install Tisch as CEO of the CBS media empire. Determined to make CBS more profitable, Tisch launched a variety of cost-cutting programs, which included making major budget cuts in the company's news division. These moves brought harsh criticism from legendary CBS newsman Walter Cronkite and others. The critics argued that reducing the money spent on news showed that CBS no longer valued its history or understood its responsibilities to its viewers.

When Tisch replaced Wyman in the mid-1980s, Paley reclaimed his place as chairman of the board. But he was not very involved in actual decision making at CBS during the late 1980s. He died of a heart attack on October 26, 1990, in New York City. In his will, he donated one of the world's most significant private collections of twentieth-century art to New York's Museum of Modern Art. He also left behind a legacy as one of the true shapers of American radio and television of the twentieth century.

For More Information

BOOKS

Edwards, Bob. *Edward R. Murrow and the Birth of Broadcast Journalism.* New York: Wiley, 2004.

Paley, William S. *As It Happened: A Memoir.* Garden City, NY: Doubleday, 1979.

Paper, Lewis J. *Empire: William S. Paley and the Making of CBS*. New York: St. Martin's, 1987.

Smith, Sally Bedell. *In All His Glory: The Life of William S. Paley, the Legendary Tycoon and His Brilliant Circle*. New York: Simon and Schuster, 1990.

WEB SITES

Sterling, Christopher H. "William S. Paley." *Museum of Broadcast Communications*. http://www.museum.tv/archives/etv/P/htmlP/paleywillia/paleywillia.htm (accessed on June 5, 2006).

David Sarnoff

BORN: February 27, 1891 • Uzlian, Russia
DIED: December 12, 1971 • New York, New York

Russian American television executive

"This miracle of engineering skill which one day will bring the world to the home also brings a new American industry to serve man's material welfare."

David Sarnoff is one of the most famous business leaders in U.S. history. He arrived in the United States as a poor child from Russia in 1900. Over the next thirty years, he worked his way up through the ranks of the communications industry to become president of the Radio Corporation of America (RCA). In his four decades at the head of RCA, Sarnoff combined a strong understanding of technology with a clear vision of the future to play a major role in the early development of radio and television broadcasting.

Arriving as a poor immigrant

David Sarnoff was born on February 27, 1891, in Uzlian, a Jewish community near Minsk, Russia. His father, Abraham Sarnoff, painted houses and hung wallpaper for a living. His mother, Leah (Privin) Sarnoff, came from a long line of rabbis (Jewish religious leaders). As the oldest of five

David Sarnoff.
© BETTMANN/CORBIS.

141

children in his family, David was expected to continue this tradition. During his boyhood, he followed a strict schedule of religious study and prayer.

In 1900, when David was nine years old, his family immigrated to the United States. Following a difficult month-long journey across the Atlantic Ocean, they settled in a poor Jewish neighborhood on the Lower East Side of New York City. They lived in a tiny, three-room apartment, and they had to share a single bathroom with several other families who lived on their floor.

Sarnoff's father suffered from tuberculosis (a bacterial infection of the lungs), which left him too weak to support the family. Shortly after arriving in New York, young David had to go to work selling newspapers. The hardworking boy also attended public schools and studied English in his free time. Before long, he was operating his own newspaper stand. By the age of fifteen, Sarnoff had completed the eighth grade and qualified to attend college preparatory school. But his father's health continued to decline, so he was forced to get a full-time job instead.

Getting ahead through hard work and ambition

Sarnoff's experience selling newspapers gave him an interest in journalism, so he went to the offices of the *New York Herald* to ask for a job. Without realizing it, he walked into the nearby offices of the Commercial Cable Company by mistake. As it turned out, they were looking for a messenger boy, and Sarnoff accepted the position. He earned five dollars per week riding a bicycle around the city delivering messages from Europe that had been carried across the ocean through underwater cables.

Spending time in the cable company's offices, Sarnoff became fascinated by the wireless telegraph machines in use there. He bought his own telegraph key (a device used to tap out telegraph messages) and learned Morse code (a system of telegraph communication using a series of dots and dashes to represent letters and words). Sarnoff's interest in telegraphy soon led him to take a job in the offices of the Marconi Wireless Telegraph Company of America. He introduced himself to Guglielmo Marconi (1874–1937)—the great Italian engineer who had invented wireless radio and founded the company—and served as his personal assistant whenever he visited New York.

When Sarnoff was sixteen, Marconi helped him get a job as a junior wireless telegraph operator. Although his father had recently died, Sarnoff's salary in this job enabled him to move his family into a larger apartment in a nicer neighborhood. Over the next few years, he agreed to serve in several remote Marconi telegraph offices in order to earn extra pay. During the hours whenl he was not working, he studied the technical manuals in the office libraries and took high-school courses through the mail.

Reinventing himself

A bright, hardworking, and ambitious young man, Sarnoff moved up quickly in rank and responsibility at the telegraph company. In 1912, he became the manager of a new Marconi wireless station in the John Wanamaker department store in New York City. That April, the luxury ocean liner *Titanic* hit an iceberg in the northern Atlantic Ocean and sank, resulting in the deaths of more than 1,500 people on board. Sarnoff attracted a great deal of publicity by claiming that he was the sole telegraph operator to receive distress calls from the *Titanic*. He said that he had remained at his post for three straight days relaying messages about the tragedy. In reality, however, a number of wireless operators had received the distress signals and informed authorities about the sinking ship. Historians have found evidence that suggests Sarnoff either greatly exaggerated or completely made up the story about his role in the incident.

In any case, the *Titanic* story proved helpful to Sarnoff's career. The incident convinced the U.S. Congress to pass a law requiring all ships to carry wireless radio equipment. Sarnoff then received a promotion to a position in which he installed and inspected Marconi equipment on board ships. The increase in pay allowed him to move his family to an even nicer apartment in the Bronx area of New York City.

Sarnoff continued to develop a reputation for having strong technical knowledge and marketing skills. In 1914, he was promoted to the position of contract manager, which allowed him to investigate new technologies and negotiate business deals. He soon became interested in the idea of using wireless radio transmission technology to broadcast music and entertainment programs to American homes. Sarnoff claimed that he sent a memo to his bosses at Marconi in 1915 encouraging them to pursue commercial radio broadcasting. "I have in mind a plan of development which would make radio a household utility in the same sense as the piano or phonograph. The idea is to bring music into the house by wireless," he wrote, as quoted in *Tube*. "The receiver can be designed in the form of a simple 'Radio Music Box.'" If he really composed this famous memo in 1915, Sarnoff would have been among of the first people to envision radio as a medium of mass communication. But some historians believe that he actually sent the memo in 1920, when a number of other people were pursuing the same idea.

Joining RCA

During World War I (1914–1918), the U.S. Navy controlled all American wireless radio facilities for the purposes of national security and defense. Once the war ended, the U.S. government decided to take steps to ensure that this important technology remained under American control. It forced the Marconi company, which was based in England, to sell its American operations to General Electric (GE). In 1919, GE turned American Marconi into a new division called the Radio Corporation of America (RCA). A short time later, GE formed a partnership with two other powerful electronic equipment companies, Westinghouse and American Telephone and Telegraph (AT&T). These companies received part ownership in RCA in exchange for giving RCA control over all of their major communications inventions.

By 1917, Sarnoff had become the head of a department at American Marconi, overseeing the work of more than seven hundred employees. He also married Lizette Hermant that year, and they eventually had three sons. When American Marconi became RCA, Sarnoff was promoted to commercial manager of the new company. In this position, he continued to push his bosses to enter commercial radio broadcasting. He also came up with an idea to make radio more appealing to the American people. Sarnoff suggested that RCA broadcast entertainment programs nationally by linking hundreds of local radio stations together to form a network.

In 1926, RCA followed through on Sarnoff's plan and formed a commercial broadcasting division called the National Broadcasting Company (NBC). NBC built and operated two radio networks, Red and Blue. NBC's first commercial broadcast included live coverage of a star-studded event in the grand ballroom of the Waldorf-Astoria Hotel in New York City. Featuring leading singers, orchestras, and humorists of the day, the program was heard by millions of people in the city and surrounding areas. In 1927, Sarnoff joined the RCA board of directors, and the following year he became acting president of the company. In this position, he oversaw the creation of the RKO (Radio-Keith-Orpheum) motion picture company and helped introduce radio receivers as standard features in automobiles.

Investing in television

Sarnoff had been interested in television since the first time he heard mention of the possibility of using radio waves to transmit live, moving images across a distance. By the time he took charge of RCA, he was convinced that television represented the future of mass communications. In 1929, Sarnoff invited a Westinghouse engineer named **Vladimir Zworykin** (1889–1982; see entry) to RCA headquarters for a meeting. A few years earlier, Zworykin had applied for patents (a form of legal protection for an invention) on a television camera he called the Iconoscope and a television display screen he called the Kinescope. In a famous exchange, Sarnoff asked the engineer what it would take to develop an electronic television system that could be sold to the public. Zworykin estimated that he would need a year and a half and $100,000 to perfect the system. Instead, it ended up taking a decade and costing RCA $50 million before the company made TV available to the public.

In 1930, at the age of thirty-nine, Sarnoff became the president of RCA. A few months later, the U.S. Department of Justice filed a lawsuit against the company. The government charged that RCA was a monopoly (a powerful company that holds complete control over a business or industry) that unfairly limited competition in the communications industry. Sarnoff made a deal with the government that resulted in RCA being separated from GE, Westinghouse, and AT&T. As an independent company, RCA kept its radio manufacturing plants and broadcasting stations, as well as its communications inventions. The deal also gave Sarnoff greater freedom to pursue his interest in television technology without worrying about how anyone else would view his plans.

Determined to make RCA the leader in the new technology, Sarnoff hired Zworykin to develop an electronic television system for RCA. He also purchased the patents for TV technology held by several other inventors over the next few years. In 1935, Sarnoff established a three-part plan for RCA to follow in order to increase public demand for TV technology. This plan involved mass-producing TV sets to make them more affordable for consumers, expanding entertainment programming on NBC to make TV ownership more appealing, and organizing public demonstrations of television to expose more people to the possibilities of the exciting new technology.

Before Sarnoff could follow through on his plans, however, RCA had to clear up some legal issues. The U.S. Patent Office had granted an important patent to an independent inventor named **Philo T.**

David Sarnoff makes the first TV news broadcast by dedicating the RCA pavilion at the 1939 World's Fair, thus introducing television to the public. © BETTMANN/CORBIS.

Farnsworth (1906–1971; see entry), giving him the exclusive legal rights to produce and market several key components of electronic television systems. After losing a long legal challenge against Farnsworth's patents, RCA was forced to pay Farnsworth a licensing fee, or royalty, in order to use his patented components in its TV sets. This marked the first time that RCA, which was famous for its own research and development, had ever paid to use someone else's technology since the company's founding in 1919.

Once RCA gained access to Farnsworth's patents, Sarnoff finally introduced television to the public at the 1939 World's Fair in New York. He marked this historic occasion with a televised speech called

"The Birth of an Industry." As quoted in *Time,* Sarnoff announced that "now we add radio sight to sound. It is with a feeling of humbleness that I come to this moment of announcing the birth in this country of a new art so important in its implications that it is bound to affect all of society. It is an art which shines like a torch of hope in the troubled world. It is a creative force which we must learn to utilize for the benefit of all mankind. This miracle of engineering skill which one day will bring the world to the home also brings a new American industry to serve man's material welfare."

Becoming "The General"

Despite Sarnoff's efforts, television technology did not catch on immediately. By the time the United States entered World War II in 1941, only twenty-three television stations existed nationwide, and only a few thousand TV sets had been sold. During the war, both the production of television sets and most TV broadcasting came to a halt. The U.S. government needed a large supply of electronic parts and communications equipment for the war effort, so many television and radio assembly plants were converted in order to produce materials for national defense.

Sarnoff made RCA's manufacturing facilities available for military purposes during the war. He also contributed to the war effort by serving as a special assistant for communications under U.S. general Dwight Eisenhower (1890–1969). In this position, Sarnoff helped build a radio broadcast station that could reach all American forces in Europe. In appreciation for his wartime service, Sarnoff received the rank of brigadier general. From this time on, he preferred to be called "General Sarnoff."

Television finally fulfilled Sarnoff's predictions in the postwar years. According to the *TV History* Web site, annual sales of television sets increased from around 200,000 units in 1947 to 7.4 million units in 1950, and RCA controlled 80 percent of the market. The company employed 54,000 people and earned a profit of $46 million in 1950.

Around this time, Sarnoff engaged in competitive battles with the Columbia Broadcasting System (CBS), a rival television network. Consistently more interested in technology than programming, Sarnoff was not always popular among the entertainers who appeared on NBC radio and television shows. In the late 1940s and early 1950s, CBS president **William S. Paley** (1901–1990; see entry) managed to lure away a number of NBC's most talented performers. Paley's ability to recognize and reward talent helped CBS overtake NBC to become the most-watched television network.

CBS Engineer Peter Goldmark

Inventor Peter Goldmark worked as an engineer for the Columbia Broadcasting System (CBS) for thirty-five years, from 1936 to 1971. During this time, he invented the first working color television system, the long-playing (LP) record album, and an early type of videocassette recorder (VCR).

Peter Carl Goldmark was born on December 2, 1906, in Budapest, Hungary. He showed an interest in science and technology from an early age. He built a laboratory in the bathroom of his family's home, for instance, and he experimented with various new technologies, including radio sets and motion picture projectors.

Goldmark received a doctorate in physics from the University of Vienna, Austria, in 1931. After graduating, Goldmark spent two years working as a television engineer for a British radio company before immigrating to the United States in 1933. In 1936 he got a job as the chief engineer of the newly formed television research department at CBS. The following year, he became a U.S. citizen.

Goldmark first became interested in adding color to television in early 1940, when he saw the movie *Gone with the Wind* and was amazed by the brilliant color in the film. Upon returning to his lab at CBS, Goldmark spent the next six months working hard to develop a color television system. The method he came up with became known as a field-sequential color system. It involved two mechanical spinning wheels with red, blue, and green filters—one behind the lens of a TV camera, and one in front of the picture tube inside a TV set. The spinning wheel in the camera scanned the image in color, and the spinning wheel in the receiver set reproduced the colors in sequence as they appeared in the original scene.

Goldmark's color system was a hybrid, or combination, of the two main types of TV systems that had been developed up to that time (mechanical and electronic). It used a mechanical spinning wheel to insert color into an electronic television system. By the 1940s, most experts viewed mechanical TV systems as a less advanced form of technology than electronic TV

During the 1950s, RCA entered a race against CBS to develop color television technology. CBS produced the first working system, but it was not compatible with existing black-and-white TV sets, which meant that anyone who had already purchased a black-and-white TV set would see only static during color broadcasts using the CBS system. Nevertheless, the Federal Communications Commission (FCC) approved the CBS system in 1951, over Sarnoff's strong objections. Two years later, however, the FCC reversed its earlier decision and approved a newly developed RCA color TV system that was compatible with existing black-and-white sets.

During the 1960s, RCA entered such diverse lines of business as computers and book publishing. Sarnoff stepped down as chief executive systems. In addition, the CBS color system faced strong opposition from the powerful Radio Corporation of America (RCA), which had invested a great deal of time and money in the development of black-and-white TV sets. For these reasons, Goldmark's early color TV system never became available to the public.

One of Goldmark's other inventions, however, had a tremendous impact on American popular culture. A big fan of classical music, Goldmark grew frustrated by the methods that were available in the 1940s for people to play recorded music at home. Phonographs of that time played ten-inch-wide vinyl records that spun on a turntable at 78 revolutions per minute (RPM). These records could only hold a few minutes' worth of music. In order to listen to an entire symphony, Goldmark had to flip over or change records many times. He became determined to develop a new technology that could hold more recorded music.

In 1948 he introduced the long-playing (LP) record album—a twelve-inch-wide vinyl disk that spun at 33 RPM and could hold forty minutes' worth of music. In addition to holding

more music, the LP also provided listeners with improved sound quality. The technology contributed to the popularity of rock 'n' roll music in the 1950s and 1960s and remained the main system of home audio until the introduction of the compact disc (CD) in 1982.

Goldmark also invented a number of other important technologies over the years. During World War II (1939–45), for instance, he developed a device that allowed U.S. troops to disrupt enemy radar tracking systems. Goldmark also came up with one of the earliest types of videocassette recorder (VCR) technology. His device, called an Electronic Video Recorder, could record a television program on film enclosed in a small plastic cartridge.

In 1971 Goldmark left CBS to form his own company, Goldmark Communications. In 1973 he published a book about his long career with the company, called *Maverick Inventor: My Turbulent Years at CBS*. Goldmark was killed in an automobile accident on December 7, 1977, just two weeks after he received the prestigious National Medal of Science from President Jimmy Carter.

officer of RCA in 1965, but he retained his position as chairman of the board of directors. His son Robert became president of the company at this time. Following a serious illness in 1968, Sarnoff no longer participated in the daily management of RCA. He retired as chairman in 1970, and he died in his sleep of a heart attack the following year. RCA continued to diversify its business interests after the death of its legendary leader. In 1986, the company was taken over by GE, the company that had formed RCA six decades earlier.

Sarnoff is remembered as a leading supporter of research in the field of electronic communications. The technologies developed at RCA under his guidance led to countless innovations in related fields, including computers. Sarnoff is also credited with the idea of organizing radio and later television broadcast stations into networks. "The uniqueness of David Sarnoff lies in his combination of a visionary and determined builder and hardheaded industrial leader," Jerome B. Wiesner noted in his foreword to *Looking Ahead: The Papers of David Sarnoff*. "He was among the first to recognize the role that science could play in modern industry and to stake his future entirely on its promise."

For More Information

BOOKS

Bilby, Kenneth. *The General: David Sarnoff and the Rise of the Communications Industry.* New York: Harper and Row, 1986.

"David Sarnoff." *Dictionary of American Biography,* Supplement 9: 1971–1975. New York: Charles Scribner's Sons, 1994.

Fisher, David E., and Marshall J. Fisher. *Tube: The Invention of Television.* Washington, DC: Counterpoint, 2002.

Goldmark, Peter, with Lee Edson. *Maverick Inventor: My Turbulent Years at CBS.* New York: Saturday Review Press, 1973.

Lewis, Thomas S. W. *Empire of the Air: The Men Who Made Radio.* New York: Edward Burlingame Books, 1991.

Sobel, Robert. *RCA.* New York: Stein and Day, 1984.

Wiesner, Jerome B., ed. *Looking Ahead: The Papers of David Sarnoff.* Princeton, NJ: David Sarnoff Research Center, 1968.

PERIODICALS

Brewster, Mike J. "Peter Goldmark: CBS's In-House Genius." *Business Week,* August 25, 2004.

Carsey, Marcy, and Tom Werner. "*Time* 100 Most Important Builders and Titans of the Century: David Sarnoff." *Time,* March 29, 1999.

"David Sarnoff of RCA Is Dead: Visionary Broadcast Pioneer." *New York Times,* December 13, 1971.

WEB SITES

"David Sarnoff." *Museum of Broadcast Communications.* http://www.museum.tv/archives/etv/S/htmlS/sarnoffdavi/sarnoffdavi.htm (accessed on June 5, 2006).

Donnelly, David. "Radio Corporation of America." *Museum of Broadcast Communications.* http://www.museum.tv/archives/etv/R/htmlR/radiocorpora/radiocorpora.htm (accessed on June 5, 2006).

"History of Television: The First 75 Years." *TV History.* http://www.tvhistory.tv/facts-stats.htm (accessed on June 5, 2006).

Fred Silverman

BORN: September 13, 1937 • New York, New York

American television producer

Fred Silverman.
KEVIN WINTER/
GETTY IMAGES.

"I think that the most distinguished series programming has been in the hour form...I just don't think that TV comedy has progressed. If anything, it's taken several steps backward."

Television executive Fred Silverman is the only person ever to have held top programming positions at all three major American television networks (ABC, CBS, and NBC). His prominent role in developing prime-time TV content made him a very influential figure in the broadcast industry. Among his many innovations, Silverman is known for introducing the program format known as jiggle TV during the 1970s, when he produced a number of shows that featured beautiful women in skimpy clothing. Although many of these shows enjoyed great popularity, they also generated controversy among critics, who complained that the shows exploited women and promoted immoral behavior. In his later career, Silverman became an independent television producer and served as a programming consultant for ABC.

Rising to power

Fred Silverman was born on September 13, 1937, in New York City. He attended Syracuse University and then went on to earn his master's degree in television and theater arts from Ohio State University. Silverman knew all along that he was interested in working for a television network. In fact, his master's thesis provided an analysis of ABC's television programming.

After graduating from Ohio State in 1961, Silverman got a job overseeing the children's programming at a Chicago TV station, WGN. He was so successful in that position that he was offered a job at the CBS network in 1962. Silverman took charge of daytime programming for the network, and he quickly improved its Saturday morning cartoon lineup. The ratings for CBS on Saturday mornings soon climbed from third place to first.

After that initial success, Silverman became vice president of programming at the network in 1963. At this time, CBS's prime-time lineup consisted mainly of silly, escapist comedies. Silverman was one of the leading executives who pushed to develop more realistic shows that dealt with current social and political issues. Based on his recommendations, CBS canceled a number of country-themed comedies, such as *Green Acres,* in a programming move that became known as the rural purge. The network replaced these shows with more realistic sitcoms (situation comedies) that featured a darker brand of humor and addressed many of the important issues of the day. Some of the hit shows that premiered over the next few years were *All in the Family, Maude, The Jeffersons, M*A*S*H,* and *The Mary Tyler Moore Show.*

During Silverman's twelve-year tenure at CBS, viewers increasingly tuned in to the programs he had supported, and ratings for the network's prime-time schedule increased steadily. With Silverman's success, however, came attention from other networks. In 1975, he accepted an offer from ABC to become the head of ABC Entertainment. This position gave him control over all programming decisions on the network, which was the lowest-rated among the Big Three networks (ABC, CBS, and NBC) at that time.

Bringing jiggle to TV

As head of programming at ABC, Silverman immediately set to work trying to craft a schedule that would increase the network's ratings. He

Charlie's Angels *was one of many successful shows developed for ABC during Fred Silverman's 1975 to 1978 turn as head of programming.* AP IMAGES.

approved the development of several shows that turned out to be very popular with viewers, including the miniseries (a program that continues over several episodes) *Roots*. Based on a historical novel by Alex Haley, *Roots* followed an African American family through four generations, beginning when the first member was brought to America as a slave. When ABC broadcast episodes of *Roots* on eight consecutive nights in 1977, it became one of the most-watched television events in history.

Silverman also had a hand in developing successful dramatic series such as *Starsky and Hutch* and *Charlie's Angels,* as well as hit sitcoms such as *Happy Days, Laverne and Shirley,* and *Three's Company.* Although these shows attracted large audiences, some of them were attacked by critics for featuring attractive women in minimal clothing. The critics referred to the trend in programming launched by *Charlie's Angels* and *Three's Company* as jiggle TV. Feminists argued that such shows exploited women by treating them as little more than sex objects. Other critics complained that TV's growing emphasis on sex and violence would have a negative effect on morality and family values.

Despite such criticisms, however, jiggle TV proved to be a winner in the ratings for Silverman and ABC. It was clear that Silverman had an instinct for what the public wanted to see on television at a particular time. A 1977 *Time* magazine cover story called Silverman "the man with the golden gut," in reference to the remarkable success of his bold programming moves. Within a short time of his arrival at ABC, Silverman managed to improve the network's overall ratings from third place to first place.

A rocky tenure at NBC

In 1978, Silverman decided to leave ABC to become president and chief operating officer of rival network NBC. Thanks to his successful tenures at the two other major networks, he faced very high expectations in his new job. "The announcement of Fred Silverman's jump from ABC to NBC not only sent shock waves through [surprised] the broadcast industry but also attracted a great deal of coverage by the general news media," Harry Castleman and Walter J. Podrazik wrote in *Watching TV*. "Once again, Silverman was leaving a number one television network and taking his tremendous programming expertise to the last place competition. In 1975 that had marked the beginning of a changed television world that soon found ABC at the top of the heap. Comparisons and speculation were inevitable: Could 'Freddie' work his magic once again?"

But the instincts that had launched Silverman to the top of his profession at CBS and ABC abandoned him during his short stay at NBC, and he faced disappointment after disappointment. In fact, most of the shows that were conceived and produced during his reign were failures. The network lost ratings ground in all programming areas—including prime time, daytime, late night, and morning and evening news—and profits fell sharply. The network was also negatively affected by writers' and actors' strikes during this time. (A strike is when workers walk off the job with the hope of gaining better pay and/or working conditions.) When Silverman lost his programming touch, his unpredictable and demanding behavior became less acceptable. A number of his colleagues spoke out against him in the press, and his reputation suffered severe damage as a result.

In 1981, Silverman resigned as president and chief operating officer of NBC and was replaced by Grant Tinker. His string of failures outweighed his previous successes in the minds of many people in the TV industry, so there was little chance of his getting a job offer from another television network.

In the 2000s, most critics still consider Silverman's time at NBC to be a spectacular failure. But they do give him credit for rescuing a high-quality, innovative program that might otherwise have been canceled. Shortly before he resigned from NBC, Silverman renewed the critically acclaimed police drama *Hill Street Blues* for a second season, despite the fact that the show had received terrible ratings. Silverman recognized that the series had great potential, and he decided to give it more time to gain an audience. It ended up running for six years, winning numerous awards, and revolutionizing television drama.

Hill Street Blues was an intense, realistic police drama that featured well-developed characters and complex plots. Each episode presented a single day in the lives of the people who worked at an urban police station. But unlike other cop shows that had come before, *Hill Street Blues* also included elements of a workplace comedy and a soap opera. The series was shot with a shaky, handheld camera, which gave it a distinctive, edgy look. The innovative aspects of *Hill Street Blues* influenced many later programs and helped NBC attract educated viewers who wanted TV to provide a source of engagement rather than escape.

Embarking on a new venture

After resigning from NBC in 1981, Silverman became an independent television producer. He formed his own production company, the Fred Silverman Company, and began to develop programs for larger entertainment firms, such as Viacom International, MGM/UA Communications, and Columbia Pictures Entertainment. The first few years, however, were very difficult for Silverman. During his career in network television, he had made many enemies among rival executives. Despite the bad feelings, though, Silverman believed that if he created quality programs, the networks would buy them.

Silverman had his first major success as an independent producer in 1985, when he developed a two-hour movie special around the popular TV character Perry Mason, starring Raymond Burr in the title role. The movie attracted a large audience and placed first in the ratings on the night it aired. Silverman went on to use that formula—putting identifiable and well-loved stars in familiar, comfortable situations—to create other successful programs.

The formula produced several successful shows for Silverman in the 1980s and 1990s. In 1986, he cast Andy Griffith, star of the beloved 1960s comedy *The Andy Griffith Show,* as a Georgia lawyer in *Matlock.* The series was a hit and ran until 1995. In 1993, Silverman gave another popular older star, Dick Van Dyke, a starring role in the detective series *Diagnosis Murder,* which ran until 2001. In 1998, Silverman cast Carroll O'Connor, the actor who had played Archie Bunker on the hit 1970s sit-com *All in the Family,* in the long-running police drama *In the Heat of the Night.*

All of these series proved very popular among viewers older than age fifty-five. Silverman believed that he could create profitable shows by targeting these viewers, since there were few programs designed to appeal to an older audience at that time. His vision proved successful, and these shows did very well in the ratings and ran for several years.

In 1989, Silverman teamed with a former network television colleague, Fred Pierce, to form PierceSilverman, a production company that created original programming for the broadcast networks, cable systems, and home video market. In the following years, Silverman served as a programming advisor to ABC, helping to plan the network's prime-time schedule. Silverman also bought a stake in the Pax network, which airs programs targeted toward families and older viewers. In 2002, he became an adjunct professor at the University of Southern California's School of Cinema and Television.

For More Information

BOOKS

Castleman, Harry, and Walter J. Podrazik. *Watching TV: Four Decades of American Television.* New York: McGraw-Hill Books, 1982.

PERIODICALS

"I'm Not Rumpled Anymore." *Forbes,* March 6, 1989.

"Silverman: Nets Need Aunt Nellie." *MediaWeek,* July 27, 1998.

"Where Are They Now." *Time,* May 27, 1996.

WEB SITES

"Fred Silverman." *Museum of Broadcast Communications.* http://www.museum.tv/archives/etv/S/htmlS/silvermanfr/silvermanfr.htm (accessed on May 22, 2006).

Aaron Spelling

BORN: April 22, 1923 • Dallas, Texas

DIED: June 23, 2006 • Los Angeles, California

American television producer

"You can't predict if a show is going to work out or not until it's on the air."

During his fifty years in the television industry, producer Aaron Spelling created over 4,300 hours of network TV programming—more than anyone else in history. He is probably best known for introducing soap opera-style dramas to prime-time TV, including *Dynasty, The Love Boat, Beverly Hills, 90210,* and *Melrose Place.* While some of Spelling's programs have been dismissed by critics as lightweight entertainment with no lasting value, the veteran producer also won a number of awards for addressing difficult social problems and issues in his work.

Becoming an actor and writer

Born April 22, 1923, Aaron Spelling grew up in a poor area of Dallas, Texas, as the son of Russian-Jewish immigrants. Aaron's father worked as a tailor, and his family, which included five children, lived humbly. As the only Jewish kid in his primary and secondary schools, Spelling was teased a lot by his peers. This social rejection caused him so

Aaron Spelling.
AP IMAGES.

157

much anxiety that he developed a psychosomatic reaction (physical symptoms caused by an emotional disturbance) and lost the use of his legs for a year. While bedridden, Spelling spent much time reading. Authors Mark Twain and O. Henry were among his favorites.

After serving the Army Air Force, Spelling enrolled in Southern Methodist University. He studied theater and received the Eugene O'Neill and Harvard Awards for plays he wrote during his undergraduate years. In an era when many schools in the South were segregated by race, Spelling angered many people by agreeing to serve as the director of an African American high school play. His courageous decision had negative consequences, though: Spelling was forced to leave Texas, and his father very nearly lost his job.

Spelling then moved to New York, where he found some work as an actor but had little success as a writer. In 1953, Spelling married Carolyn Jones, an actress best known for her role as Morticia in the television series *The Addams Family*. The couple moved to Hollywood, where Spelling acted in several small roles in movies and television shows, including *I Love Lucy, Dragnet,* and *Gunsmoke*. Within three years of his arrival in California, Spelling had also sold several scripts for TV series, including *Playhouse 90*.

Finding success as a television producer

Spelling began working as a television producer in the early 1960s. Although he eventually became the most successful producer in the history of television, his first series, *The Lloyd Bridges Show,* was a failure in 1962 and was canceled after only one season. His next effort, *Burke's Law,* fared better, running from 1963 to 1966. In 1967, Spelling joined forces with comedian and actor Danny Thomas (1914–1991) to create Thomas-Spelling Productions. Their most successful TV series, a detective show called *The Mod Squad,* featuring teenage detectives, received numerous Emmy Award nominations. (Emmy Awards are annual honors recognizing excellence in television programming.) Spelling divorced his first wife in 1965, and three years later he married socialite Carol Jean (Candy) Marer. They had two children, Randy and Tori.

Spelling's career took off in 1973, when he formed a partnership with fellow producer Leonard Goldberg. Spelling and Goldberg produced a number of hit drama series in the 1970s, including *Charlie's Angels,* about three attractive female private detectives; *Starsky and Hutch,* about a pair of tough city cops; and *Fantasy Island,* about a magical place where troubled

The Job of a Television Producer

The role of a television producer varies greatly, depending on the individual and the project. Some producers control every creative and technical aspect of a show. They come up with the original concept, write the script, arrange for financing, oversee the building of a set, hire a director and cast, and participate in network scheduling decisions. On the other hand, some celebrity producers might lend their name to a project and have very little hands-on participation in its development. In general, television producers tend to have a higher level of involvement in their projects than film producers. As Muriel G. Cantor noted in *The Hollywood TV Producer: His Work and His Audience,* film is a "director's medium," while television is a "producer's medium."

Many successful TV producers, like Aaron Spelling, start out as writers for a particular network. Even as his success increased, Spelling continued to collaborate with other writers on the shows that he produced. "The producer hires the writers to do one or more scripts during a season, and often works with them, directing the tone and content of the script," Cantor explained. Casting is often a collaborative effort between the director and producer of a TV show, although the producer usually has the final say. Spelling has often been recognized for his brilliant casting choices.

Even the most powerful television producers, however, must answer to big production studios and networks. A producer may write, own, cast, and produce a show, but final approval for all of these decisions must be granted by the network that ultimately airs the program. Spelling found the work of a television producer to be both busy and rewarding. "Right now I'm doing four shows at a time, trying to read four outlines every week, four scripts every week, and watching four rough cuts," he told Anna Carugati of *Worldscreen.com* in 2003. "It's a lot of good work."

people could go to solve their problems and make their dreams come true. Spelling and Goldberg also produced a popular made-for-TV movie, *The Boy in the Plastic Bubble,* starring a young John Travolta.

One of Spelling's most highly regarded shows from this era was *Family.* This series—an hour-long, realistic drama about a middle-class family— premiered on ABC in 1976. "When we did *Family,* everybody said, 'You can't do a family show,'" Spelling told Anna Carugati of Worldscreen.com. "I don't know who said that but I think he doesn't have a family." The show proved to be very popular, earned four Emmy Awards, and is still considered to be one of Spelling's best works.

Creating his own production company

In 1977, Spelling formed his own company, Aaron Spelling Productions (later called Spelling Entertainment). The company's first series, *The Love*

Boat, was hugely popular and ran for nine years. Set aboard a cruise ship, the show was unusual in that each episode introduced viewers to a new set of passengers—and their romantic entanglements. A number of big-name celebrities made one-time appearances on the show as passengers. The only recurring characters were a few members of the ship's crew, who helped to advance the story.

In 1981, Spelling produced *Dynasty,* a prime-time soap opera about the conflicts between wealthy and powerful families. The show was a tremendous success, ranking among the top shows on television for most of its eight-year run. Spelling oversaw every detail of production on *Dynasty,* from casting to costumes and hairstyles to dialogue. Some critics claimed that *Dynasty* stood out among the many similar shows of that era because of Spelling's brilliant casting decisions. His best move was hiring Joan Collins to play the rich and beautiful villain, Alexis Carrington Colby. "Joan Collins is . . . the archetype [example for all similar characters in the future]," E. Duke Vincent, vice chairman of Spelling Entertainment, told the *Sydney Morning Herald.* "How do you get that? You get it in the storytelling, obviously, but the actress herself, her personality, brought something to that role which I don't think anybody else could have done."

By 1984, Spelling had seven different series running on ABC. In fact, some people jokingly referred to the network as Aaron's Broadcasting Company. Spelling also branched out into producing full-length feature films during the 1980s, including *'Night Mother,* an intimate drama starring Sissy Spacek; and *Mr. Mom,* a comedy starring Michael Keaton.

Continuing to reach television audiences

Spelling helped launch a major television trend in the 1990s when he created several popular programs aimed at teenagers, beginning with the drama *Beverly Hills, 90210.* The story follows a group of students at West Beverly Hills High School. It revolves around twins Brandon and Brenda Walsh (played by Jason Priestly and Shannen Doherty), whose family has recently moved to the glitzy area of southern California from Minnesota. The cast also featured Spelling's daughter, Tori, in a prominent role.

Although *90210* used some of the conventions of the prime-time soap opera, it treated the concerns of its youthful audience more seriously than most teen dramas. For instance, one of the main characters, Dylan, struggles with drug and alcohol abuse. Several other characters

Following the success of Beverly Hills 90210, *Aaron Spelling launched another youthful soap,* Melrose Place *(pictured), in 1992.* 20TH CENTURY FOX/FOTOS INTERNATIONAL/GETTY IMAGES.

cope with the divorce and remarriage of their parents or face the decision of whether or not to become sexually active. Although some critics complained that the show focused exclusively on upper-class white kids, many teenaged viewers recognized themselves and their problems in the characters. *90210* became a pop culture phenomenon, launching books and fan clubs and setting clothing and hairstyle trends across the country. It also started a trend in which the television industry increasingly targeted younger viewers.

Following the success of *90210,* Spelling launched another youthful soap, *Melrose Place,* in 1992. Also set in southern California, this show revolves around a group of attractive people in their twenties. Most of the characters are at a point in their lives when they are concerned about starting careers or getting married. *Melrose Place* tended to be less serious and more sensational than *90210.* The show's wild story lines, dark humor, and cynical outlook gained a huge following among college students, who enjoyed watching the show in large groups. *Melrose Place* also became one of the first programs to build a presence on the Internet, as fans gathered online to discuss plot developments and predict the fate of various characters.

In 1993, Spelling showed his serious side by producing the Emmy Award-winning HBO movie *And the Band Played On,* which challenges viewers' assumptions about homosexuality and AIDS. Based on the book by Randy Shilts, the movie took four years to complete. As soon as he read the book, Spelling invited the author to Hollywood and began negotiating with various TV networks. The broadcast networks shied away from the controversial subject matter, but Spelling eventually found a home for the project with the pay-cable network HBO.

And the Band Played On demonstrated Spelling's long-standing commitment to increasing diversity in TV programming. "I love giving time to gay actors, gay characters; I think it's wrong to say, 'You don't exist,'" he told Carugati. "I like diversity in shows." Over the years, Spelling also received six Image Awards from the National Association for the Advancement of Colored People (NAACP) for his contributions to improving the representation of African Americans on television.

Michael Idato of the *Sydney Morning Herald* noted that throughout his career, Spelling's productions have "successfully tapped the sensibility of their audience at the time, whether they were looking for challenging television or pure escapist candy to take them out of their ordinary lives." In order to stay in touch with TV viewers, Spelling often asked for opinions from a wide variety of people—from fellow passengers on trains and airplanes to his colleagues at Spelling Entertainment.

Diagnosed with oral cancer in 2001, Spelling underwent successful treatment. In June 2006 Spelling suffered a stroke and died a few days later. Just prior to his death, the veteran producer had two hit shows running on prime-time television, the family drama *7th Heaven,* which had ended its ten-year run but was picked up by the new CW network, and the teen-oriented supernatural series *Charmed,* which ended its successful eight-year run in May 2006.

For More Information

BOOKS

Cantor, Muriel G. *The Hollywood TV Producer: His Work and His Audience.* New Brunswick: Transaction Books, 1988.

PERIODICALS

Idato, Michael. "The Great Escape." *Sydney Morning Herald,* September 19, 2005.

Rauch, Melissa. "Who Will Be Next Survivor of New Fall Programs?" *Observer,* September 20, 2000.

Stein, Joel. "Aaron Spelling." *Time,* August 13, 2001.

WEB SITES

"Aaron Spelling: Prime Time Patriarch." *Oralcancerfoundation.org.* http://www.oralcancerfoundation.org/people/aaron_spelling.htm (accessed on May 22, 2006).

Carugati, Anna. "Spelling Television's Aaron Spelling." *Worldscreen.com,* April 2003. http://www.worldscreen.com/print.php?filename=0403spelling.txt (accessed on May 22, 2006).

"Frequently Asked Questions." *Producers Guild of America.* http://www.producersguild.org/pg/about_a/faq.asp (accessed on May 22, 2006).

Brandon Tartikoff

BORN: January 13, 1949 • Long Island, New York

DIED: August 27, 1997 • Los Angeles, California

American television executive

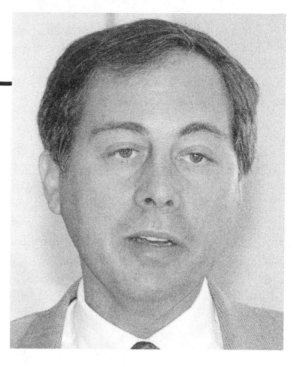

"Brandon wasn't impatient. If he believed in a show, he gave it time to find its audience. Brandon understood what viewers wanted. He loved making television because he loved watching television."

— PBS president Pat Mitchell

Brandon Tartikoff.
AP IMAGES.

When Brandon Tartikoff was only thirty-one years old, he became the president of programming for the NBC television network. During the ten years that Tartikoff remained in this position, his choices helped make NBC the highest-rated network in the United States. The secret to the young businessman's success lay in his belief that American viewers wanted to see innovative, well-written shows. Instead of canceling critically praised series that received low ratings (measures of the number of viewers watching a particular program), Tartikoff waited for the television audience to discover the virtues of these shows. Some of the programs that he kept despite low ratings were *Family Ties, Cheers,* and *St. Elsewhere.* Tartikoff was also responsible for introducing viewers to such new programs as *The Cosby Show, Miami Vice, Hill Street Blues, L.A. Law,* and *Seinfeld.*

Building a career in television

Brandon Tartikoff was born on January 13, 1949, in the town of Freeport on Long Island, New York. His parents, Jordan and Enid Tartikoff, noticed early on that their son had a different relationship to television than most kids. Instead of just watching television shows, Tartikoff always viewed the entertainment critically. After watching the premiere of the situation comedy *Dennis the Menace,* according to *The Last Great Ride,* the young boy remarked, "They could have made that show much better."

After completing boarding school, Tartikoff went on to study broadcasting at Yale University. He graduated from Yale with honors in 1970 and then got a job as the director of advertising and promotion for WTNH, a television station in New Haven, Connecticut. Tartikoff had only been out of Yale three years when ABC affiliate WLS-TV in Chicago, Illinois, hired him as its executive in charge of dramatic programming. Tartikoff improved the station's ratings by writing a comedy-variety show and coming up with creative promotions. For example, Tartikoff originated programming stunts such as "Not for the Weak Week," when the station broadcast lots of horror films.

While working in Chicago, Tartikoff was diagnosed with Hodgkin's disease, a type of cancer that affects the lymph nodes (part of the immune system). Although he underwent a difficult series of treatments that caused him to lose fifty pounds, Tartikoff did not take any sick leave. Once his cancer went into remission (stopped growing and became inactive), the young executive became determined to use the experience as motivation. "When I got cancer and was faced with at least an understanding of my mortality, nothing was a given anymore," he explained to *People.* "It helped me channel my energies."

Turning around a failing network

Tartikoff's career really started to take off in 1976, when the president of ABC, **Fred Silverman** (1937–; see entry), saw a WLS promotion called *Gorilla My Dreams.* When Silverman learned that Tartikoff had come up with the idea, he hired the young programmer to be the manager of dramatic development for ABC. Within a year, Tartikoff had earned a promotion to the position of program executive for current dramatic programming at the network.

In 1978, Silverman took a job as the president of rival network NBC. Tartikoff followed him to NBC and immediately began climbing through the executive ranks of the network. By 1980, at the age of thirty-one, Tartikoff had been named NBC's president of programming. At this time, NBC ranked a distant third among the three major broadcast networks in terms of overall audience. The network had a number of unpopular programs and faced financial difficulties. Many people in the television industry wondered whether the new management team could lead NBC out of its slump.

Unfortunately, NBC continued to struggle under Silverman, and he resigned as head of the network in 1981. But Tartikoff remained on as president of programming under new network president Grant Tinker, a former television producer with MTM Productions. Tinker gave Tartikoff a great deal of freedom to make programming choices, and the young executive soon found a formula for success. Tartikoff decided to support solidly written, critically well-received programs even if they failed to attract strong ratings at first. Some of the shows he saved from cancellation were *Family Ties, Cheers, Hill Street Blues,* and *St. Elsewhere*. All of these shows went on to find an enthusiastic audience and become hits.

Tartikoff also participated in the creation of several new shows as president of programming at NBC. In 1984, for instance, he saw the African American actor and comedian **Bill Cosby** (1937–; see entry) perform on *The Tonight Show* and decided to work with Cosby to develop a family comedy series. Tartikoff brought in producers Tom Werner and Marcy Carsey to help create *The Cosby Show,* which aired from 1984 to 1992 and reached the top spot in the annual TV ratings for four seasons. The success of *The Cosby Show* led to increased opportunities for African Americans on television and helped energize the sitcom format.

Tartikoff's programming choices, although sometimes risky, paid off for NBC by enhancing its reputation as a high-quality network. Of course, Tartikoff promoted some forgettable shows during his tenure at NBC, such as *The Bay City Blues* and *Jennifer Slept Here,* but he also helped develop some tremendously successful programs, such as *Miami Vice, L.A. Law,* and *Seinfeld*.

During his years at NBC, Tartikoff not only became one of the most powerful figures in television, but he also emerged as a sort of celebrity.

Brandon Tartikoff developed a number of huge hits for NBC, including L.A. Law, *pictured,* Miami Vice, *and* Seinfeld. THE KOBAL COLLECTION.

He made several guest appearances on TV programs, gave interviews on talk shows, and even hosted *Saturday Night Live*. "So much of what NBC is about today is due to Brandon," Dick Ebersol, president of NBC Sports, told *People*. "He was the most competitive person I ever knew, and for the first time in history NBC cared about winning. He always won with style, grace, and most of all humor." By the time Tartikoff left NBC in 1991, the network had been ranked number one for six seasons in a row.

Taking over Paramount Pictures and AOL Entertainment

After leaving NBC, Tartikoff spent one year as the chairman of a major motion picture studio, Paramount Pictures. Despite facing budget limitations, he managed to turn out several box-office successes, including *The Addams Family, Wayne's World,* and *Indecent Proposal.* Tartikoff also wrote a memoir, *The Last Great Ride,* about his years at NBC.

In 1992, Tartikoff and one of his two daughters were involved in a serious car accident. His daughter suffered a traumatic head injury, and Tartikoff resigned from his job at Paramount in order to help out during her recovery. Afterward he became head of New World Entertainment, but he left a short time later when it was purchased by another company. Then Tartikoff started his own production company, which he called H. Beale after a character in the movie *Network.* In 1997, Tartikoff took a job with the Internet services company America Online (AOL) to help develop online entertainment programs.

Tartikoff's cancer returned shortly after he embarked on this new venture. Once again, he continued to work while he underwent treatment, frustrating his doctors by ignoring their orders to rest. On August 27, 1997, Tartikoff finally lost his twenty-five-year battle against Hodgkin's disease and died at the UCLA Medical Center. His funeral was attended by hundreds of notable figures from the world of television, including Ted Danson, Jerry Seinfeld, Fred Silverman, Grant Tinker, and Danny De Vito.

In 2004, the National Association of Television Programming Executives (NATPE) honored Tartikoff by presenting the first annual Brandon Tartikoff Legacy Awards. "In the spirit of Tartikoff's generosity of spirit and creative leadership, the awards will celebrate a select group of television professionals who exhibit extraordinary passion, leadership, independence, and vision in the process of creating television programming," the organization explained in a press release quoted by *PR Newswire.*

Upon winning one of the awards, PBS president Pat Mitchell provided her recollections of Tartikoff to *Variety:* "Brandon Tartikoff's legacy can be seen in some of television's biggest hits of the moment, whether it's *Desperate Housewives, Lost, The Sopranos,* or *The Shield.* They're examples of his legacy because he showed quality programming can succeed in commercial television. Brandon wasn't impatient. If he believed in a show, he gave it time to find its audience. Brandon understood what viewers wanted. He loved making television because he loved watching television."

For More Information

BOOKS

Tartikoff, Brandon, with Charles Leerhsen. *The Last Great Ride.* New York: Random House, 1992.

PERIODICALS

Aucoin, Don. "Tartikoff Never Muted His Own Audio." *Milwaukee Journal Sentinel,* October 27, 1997.

Gliatto, Tom. "Televisionary." *People,* September 15, 1997.

Levine, Stuart. "Brandon Tartikoff Legacy Awards." *Variety,* January 22, 2003.

WEB SITES

Goodman, Tim. "Brandon Tartikoff Dead of Cancer." *SFGate.com,* August 28, 1997. http://www.sfgate.com/cgi-bin/article.cgi?f=/e/a/1997/08/28/STY-LE1231.dtl&hw=brandon+tartikoff&sn=002&sc=796 (accessed on May 22, 2006).

Hatton, Steve. "NBC Celebrates 75 Years of Broadcasting: The Brandon Tartikoff Era." *Suite101.com,* April 1, 2002. http://www.suite101.com/article.cfm/television_review/90650 (accessed on May 22, 2006).

"NATPE Unveils the Brandon Tartikoff Legacy Awards." *NATPE.org,* October 22, 2003. http://www.prnewswire.com/cgi-bin/stories.pl?ACCT=104&STORY=/www/story/10-22-2003/0002041815&EDATE= (accessed on May 22, 2006).

"Tartikoff, Brandon." *Museum of Broadcast Communications.* http://www. museum. tv/archives/etv/T/htmlT/tartikoffbr/tartikoffbr.htm (accessed on May 22, 2006).

"The Two-Edged Legacy of Brandon Tartikoff." *TeeVee.org,* August 29, 1997. http://www.teevee.org/archive/1997/08/29/index.html (accessed on May 22, 2006).

Ted Turner

BORN: November 19, 1938 • Cincinnati, Ohio

American television executive

"All my big competitors were like a pack of wolves, and they were all chasing me, but I was fast enough to be out in front of them."

Ted Turner is one of the most influential forces in the development of modern cable television. Between the 1960s and the 1980s, Turner went from being the head of a failing billboard company to being one of the best-known television executives in the world. He founded the first cable superstation to broadcast programs across the country via satellite. He also pioneered the concept of a twenty-four-hour, all-news cable network. His creation, CNN, completely changed U.S. news broadcasting. Turner's bold willingness to invest in his own vision in the face of doubt and ridicule made him a billionaire and secured his place in television history.

A rebellious childhood

Ted Turner.
WIREIMAGE.

Robert Edward Turner III, known from childhood by the nickname Ted, was born in Cincinnati, Ohio, on November 19, 1938. His parents were

171

Florence and Ed Turner. When Ted was nine years old, the family moved to the city of Savannah, on the Atlantic Coast of Georgia, where Ed Turner ran a thriving billboard business called Turner Advertising. Ed Turner was an alcoholic who also suffered from mental health problems. He was a harsh and controlling man who dominated his children and his timid wife. But his father's nature only brought out the rebellious spirit in young Ted, who often pulled pranks and did small acts of vandalism that earned him beatings from his father.

As a boy, Turner was small and thin and not well suited for athletics. At the age of eleven, he took up competitive sailing, because the sport rewarded quick wits rather than physical size and strength. Turner competed in sailing races and excelled at the sport. He also did surprisingly well at boxing. He credited his success in this area to his father, who taught him how to take a beating. Turner's rebellious nature eventually convinced his parents to send him away to several military boarding schools, including the Georgia Military Academy in Atlanta and the McCallie School in Chattanooga, Tennessee. Always quick with an argument, Turner won the high school debating championship before graduating from McCallie.

When it came time to enter college, Turner disappointed his father by being rejected by Harvard University. He was forced to settle for his second choice, Brown University in Providence, Rhode Island. During his college years at Brown, Turner continued to earn a reputation as a troublemaker by drinking alcohol and getting into fights. He enjoyed playing the role of a loud, feisty Southern boy among his more serious Northern classmates. He even kept a rifle in his dormitory room, which he occasionally fired out the window. Turner continued his successful debating career in college, becoming vice president of the Brown Debating Union. But he was expelled from Brown in 1959 for sneaking a woman into his dorm room.

Facing loss and taking responsibility

When Turner was twenty years old, his seventeen-year-old sister Mary Jane died. She had been diagnosed with an incurable immune system disease called lupus erythematosus when she was only twelve. Turner had been a devout Christian before witnessing his sister's painful struggle with illness. He had even considered becoming a missionary (someone who spreads the Christian faith among non-Christian people). But after Mary Jane's death, he lost faith in a God who could allow an innocent girl to suffer as his sister had. He remained an atheist (someone who does not believe in God) throughout his life.

In 1960 Turner married Judy Nye, whom he had met through yacht racing. Marriage did not steady his wild nature, however, and he had affairs with other women from the beginning. Turner and Nye had two children, Laura and Teddy, before their divorce in 1963. The following year Turner married Jane Smith, with whom he had three children, Beau, Rhett, and Jennie. Turner remained a difficult husband, however, treating his wife rudely in public and continuing to have affairs with other women. Like his own father, he was distant and frequently harsh with his children.

Turner also went to work in his father's business during this time, and he soon showed a strong talent for sales. In 1962, Ed Turner expanded his billboard advertising company into a number of new cities. Within a short time, however, he became fearful that he could not succeed in the new markets and started selling off some of his acquisitions. Increasingly upset about business pressures and mounting debts, Ed Turner committed suicide on March 5, 1963.

Ted Turner was deeply affected by his father's suicide. The unruly son turned into an aggressive businessman in an attempt to fulfill the expectations of the father he had never been able to please. Turner started by building up the billboard business, selling family property and going into debt to get back into the advertising markets his father had abandoned before his death. Soon Turner Advertising was the largest billboard company in the southeastern United States.

In the late 1960s, Turner began expanding from billboard advertising into other areas of the communications industry. He bought several radio stations in the South, beginning with WAPO Radio in Chattanooga in 1968. Two years later he entered television broadcasting by purchasing a failing UHF station, WJRJ in Atlanta.

Television signals are carried by radio waves, which exist in a range of frequencies called the radio spectrum. The Federal Communications Commission (the U.S. government agency in charge of regulating television) allocated two portions of the radio spectrum for television broadcasting: very-high frequency (VHF) and ultra-high frequency (UHF) channels. Most of the stronger VHF channels were controlled by the powerful national broadcasting networks (ABC, CBS, and NBC). The weaker UHF channels tended to belong to independent commercial stations or nonprofit educational stations. Although Turner's first TV

Time Warner Chairman Gerald Levin

Gerald Levin. AP IMAGES.

From 1992 to 2002, Gerald Levin served as the chairman and chief executive officer (CEO) of Time Warner Inc., one of the largest media and entertainment companies in the world. Over the course of his career, Levin became known as a

bold, strategic leader with a remarkable ability to predict the future direction of business and technology. His ideas contributed to the rapid growth of cable TV services in the 1980s and to the increasing consolidation (the combination of several businesses into one large business) of American media in the 1990s.

Gerald Manuel Levin was born on May 6, 1939, in Philadelphia, Pennsylvania. For much of his youth he planned to become a rabbi (a Jewish religious leader). Levin majored in biblical studies at Haverford College in Pennsylvania, but then he decided against further religious training. Instead, he studied law at the University of Pennsylvania, graduating first in his class in 1963.

Levin started out working as an attorney in a New York City law firm. In 1972 he changed career paths and went to work for Home Box Office (HBO), a regional cable TV service that offered pay-per-view movies and sporting events to viewers on the East Coast. HBO was owned by Time Inc., the publisher of *Time* magazine. Levin started out as the vice president of programming at HBO, and he became president of the company the following year.

station used the inferior UHF portion of the broadcast spectrum, he soon came up with a bold plan to expand the reach of its signal.

Becoming the king of cable

Turner renamed his Atlanta television station WTCG, for Turner Communications Group. He began showing classic TV series, cartoons, old movies, and sporting events to attract viewers, and by 1973 the station was making a profit. Then Turner began thinking about ways that he could broadcast programs to a much larger audience. In 1975, a pay-per-view TV channel called Home Box Office (HBO) started offering its programming to viewers across the United States by bouncing its

In 1975 Levin convinced his bosses at Time to invest $7 million in a plan to distribute HBO's programming nationwide. His plan involved bouncing HBO's signal off a communications satellite orbiting Earth. The signal from the satellite could be received by cable TV systems across the country. Levin's bold idea helped HBO increase its number of customers from 100,000 to 14 million over the next four years. During that time, a number of other cable TV stations began distributing their signals by satellite as well. In this way, Levin's idea contributed to the rapid growth of cable TV in the 1980s.

Levin was named chairman and CEO of HBO in 1976, and three years later he was promoted to vice president of video projects at parent company Time Inc. In 1984 he became the vice president of strategy. In this position, Levin began pushing Time to expand its business beyond magazine publishing and cable TV stations. He wanted the company to enter the movie and music businesses as well.

In 1990, in one of the biggest business deals in U.S. media history, Time Inc. combined its operations with Warner Communications. Levin played an important role in planning and negotiating the merger of the two companies. He supported the deal because it gave Time access to Warner's television, film, and music content. In 1992 he became chairman and CEO of the combined firm, known as Time Warner.

Levin continued expanding Time Warner's communications empire in 1995, when he arranged to purchase Turner Communications. This company, founded by Ted Turner, controlled a number of popular cable TV channels, including TBS and CNN. In 2000 Levin made another huge business deal, this time combining Time Warner with the Internet service provider America Online (AOL). He believed that merging with AOL would give Time Warner access to a valuable new distribution channel for its content: the Internet.

Unfortunately, the AOL deal was widely considered to be a disaster for Time Warner. A few months after it was finalized, investors lost confidence in Internet-related businesses and the price of shares of stock in these companies dropped rapidly. The shares of AOL stock that Time Warner had received in the merger lost half of their value, causing financial trouble for the newly formed AOL Time Warner. Levin came under a great deal of criticism from stockholders, and he stepped down as chairman and CEO in 2002.

signal off communications satellites orbiting Earth. The signal was picked up by cable TV systems and sent through cable lines to their customers. Turner decided to use the same approach.

In 1976, Turner turned his independent station into a national cable TV network. Like HBO had done the year before, Turner arranged to deliver his signal to cable systems across the country via satellite. He changed his call letters to WTBS (for Turner Broadcasting System) and referred to it as a Superstation. He soon convinced national advertisers to place their commercials on his cable network. Within a few years, more than 160 million viewers in over 200 countries were watching Turner's lineup of popular shows from the past.

Turner used the wealth he gained from his broadcast stations to buy the Atlanta Braves professional baseball team and the Atlanta Hawks professional basketball team. He later acquired two Atlanta hockey teams, the Flames and the Thrashers. These purchases turned out to be brilliant business decisions, because they gave Turner the right to broadcast all of the teams' games on WTBS. Of course, the flamboyant Turner also enjoyed the special privileges he gained as a team owner, like playing poker with the players and coaching from the sidelines.

As Turner developed a reputation as an important media person, his private life remained troubled. Considered by many to be ill-mannered and coarse, Turner was known to cheat on his wives, bully his children, and alternately charm and terrorize his business associates. Still a skilled and passionate yachtsman, in 1977 he captained the boat *Courageous* that won the prestigious America's Cup sailboat race. After arriving noticeably drunk to collect the trophy, Turner gained the nickname Captain Outrageous.

Creating CNN

As his business enterprises earned greater profits, Turner became convinced that he had a duty to make the world a better place. He began to envision a television network devoted to presenting news from around the world. He believed that such a global news channel could help people in different nations understand each other better and thus contribute to world peace.

With this ambitious goal in mind, Turner launched an innovative new broadcasting enterprise in 1980. His Cable News Network (CNN) became the first cable television channel to offer news programming twenty-four hours per day. In the beginning, many longtime network news experts ridiculed Turner and his cable news channel. They jokingly dubbed CNN the "Chicken Noodle Network" and complained about the poor quality of its sets and the low pay it offered to reporters. CNN initially struggled to attract viewers, but it gradually began to surprise its critics and live up to its founder's ideals. In 1982 CNN began broadcasting in Asia, and in 1985 it expanded to Europe.

Within a few years of its creation, CNN became famous for its coverage of breaking news events. In 1986, for instance, CNN was the only TV channel to provide live coverage of the launch of the space shuttle *Challenger*. After the first American astronaut walked on the Moon in 1969, the broadcast networks had stopped paying much attention to the U.S. space program. So when *Challenger* exploded 73 seconds after lift-off, killing all seven astronauts on board, CNN achieved a major scoop on the competition. The incident helped make CNN the first choice for many TV viewers when important news broke.

CNN really moved to the front of TV news coverage during the 1991 Persian Gulf War. This conflict began when the Middle Eastern nation of Iraq invaded its smaller neighbor, Kuwait. When Iraqi leader Saddam Hussein (1937–) refused international requests to remove his troops from Kuwait, the United States and a coalition (cooperative group) of other countries sent military forces to the Persian Gulf region. The coalition spent several weeks bombing strategic targets in Iraq, then launched a ground attack that succeeded in forcing the Iraqi troops to leave Kuwait.

On the night the coalition bombing raids began, CNN had three anchors stationed in the Iraqi capital of Baghdad. These men—Peter Arnett (1934–), Bernard Shaw (1940–), and John Holliman (1948–1998)—covered the attacks live from the balcony of their downtown hotel room. Their daring footage attracted 11 million viewers—or about 20 times the normal ratings for CNN. CNN's coverage of the 1991 Persian Gulf War, which was broadcast via satellite, helped the cable network become a prime news source for TV viewers around the world. In fact, news experts started discussing a theory called the CNN effect, in which CNN actually influenced world events by focusing its news cameras on them. Network executives who had laughed at the idea of twenty-four-hour news soon began to develop their own competing cable news channels, such as MSNBC and Fox News.

Rancher and philanthropist

Turner continued expanding his media empire throughout the 1980s. In 1986, following a failed attempt to buy the CBS broadcast network, Turner made a $1.5 billion deal to buy the Metro Goldwyn Mayer (MGM) and United Artists film studios. These purchases gave him access to huge film libraries, which he used to provide programming for his cable TV networks. In 1988 Turner launched a new cable channel called Turner Network Television (TNT), and in 1994 he added Turner Classic Movies (TCM) to showcase the MGM films. Deciding that modern audiences did not like to watch black-and-white movies, he began the process of colorizing (using computerized methods to add color) many of the older films he had bought. Classic film lovers were horrified by the practice, but many viewers enjoyed the colorized films. In 1991,

Ted Turner announces the launch of the cable channel Turner Classic Movies (TCM) in April 1994. © RICK MAIMAN/ CORBIS SYGMA.

Turner bought a library of classic cartoons from the legendary animation studio Hanna Barbera, and the following year he introduced the Cartoon Network in order to present these programs.

During this time, Turner began seeing a mental health professional who diagnosed him with manic-depressive (bipolar) disorder. People who have this condition suffer severe mood swings, with periods of high energy and extreme happiness alternating with periods of deep depression. A doctor prescribed the drug lithium to help Turner control his mood swings. After divorcing his second wife in 1988, Turner married actress Jane Fonda in 1991. During this marriage, Turner became more relaxed and developed closer relationships with his children. He eventually was able to stop taking lithium. Although he and Fonda divorced in 2001, they remained friends afterward.

In 1995, Turner Broadcasting merged with the giant media company Time Warner. While Turner retained some influence over the operation of the business he created, he found it difficult to no longer be the boss. Time Warner's management had little patience with Turner's strict style of leadership or his often embarrassing public displays of temper. When Time Warner merged with the large Internet company America Online (AOL) in 2001, Turner found himself with almost no power. He stepped down from his position as vice chairman of the Time Warner board of directors in 2003, and in 2006 he left the company entirely.

At first Turner was angry about losing control of the company he had built. But he soon turned his attention to other interests. For instance, he became the largest individual landowner in the United States, with more than 200 million acres of land in several western states. Since he was always an avid outdoorsman, Turner's lifelong love of fishing and hunting led him to become an active environmentalist. To help preserve the American bison from extinction, he developed the largest private herd in the world, with more than 40,000 animals. He also started a national chain of restaurants, Ted's Montana Grill, which featured buffalo meat specialties.

Moreover, Turner dedicated his time and money to various charitable causes. He eventually became known as one of the world's leading philanthropists (people who support charities) and publicly challenged other billionaires to follow his example. From 1985 until 1991, Turner operated the Better World Society, which promoted environmental education by making documentary films on subjects such as world hunger and pollution. In 1989 he established the Turner Tomorrow Fellowship Awards to honor writers whose works offered solutions to important world problems. To administer his vast contributions, he created the Turner Foundation in 1990.

In 1997 Turner was honored by the United Nations (UN) for his humanitarian work. That year, in an unprecedented gesture, he donated one billion dollars—a third of his personal fortune—to the UN to help provide food, medicine, and other aid to needy people. In 2000 he contributed $35 million of his own money to help settle a dispute between the UN and the United States.

In Ken Auletta's 2004 biography *Media Man,* Turner summed up his remarkable career in typically folksy fashion. Comparing himself to "a rabbit that's small and fast," he noted that "all my big competitors were like a pack of wolves, and they were all chasing me, but I was fast enough to be out in front of them."

For More Information

BOOKS

Auletta, Ken. *Media Man: Ted Turner's Improbable Empire.* New York: Norton, 2004.

Bibb, Porter. *It Ain't as Easy as It Looks: Ted Turner's Amazing Story.* New York: Crown, 1993.

Goldberg, Robert, and Gerald Jay Goldberg. *Citizen Turner: The Wild Rise of an American Tycoon.* New York: Harcourt Brace, 1995.

Klein, Alec. *Stealing Time: Steve Case, Jerry Levin, and the Collapse of AOL Time Warner.* New York: Simon and Schuster, 2003.

Stark, Steven. *Glued to the Set.* New York: Free Press, 1997.

Williams, Christian. *Lead, Follow, or Get Out of the Way: The Story of Ted Turner.* New York: Times Books, 1981.

PERIODICALS

Auletta, Ken. "The Lost Tycoon." *New Yorker,* April 23, 2001.

Henry, William A. III. "History as It Happens." *Time,* January 6, 1992.

Lewis, Mark. "Levin's Legacy at AOL Time Warner." *Forbes,* May 17, 2002.

Painton, Priscilla. "The Taming of Ted Turner." *Time,* January 6, 1992.

"Ted Turner." *Current Biography,* June 1998.

Waters, Harry F. "Ted Turner Tackles TV News." *Newsweek,* June 16, 1980.

WEB SITES

"CNN." *Bookrags.* http://www.bookrags.com/history/popculture/cnn-bbbb-05/ (accessed on May 24, 2006).

McLeland, Susan. "Ted Turner." *Museum of Broadcast Communications.* http://www.museum.tv/archives/etv/T/htmlT/turnerted/turnerted.htm (accessed on May 24, 2006).

Seel, Peter B. "Gerald Levin." *Museum of Broadcast Communications.* http://www.museum.tv/archives/etv/L/levingerald/levingerald.htm (accessed on June 19, 2006).

"Ted Turner: Young Rebel in Business." *Reference for Business.* http://www.referenceforbusiness.com/businesses/A-F/Turner-Ted.html (accessed on May 24, 2006).

Barbara Walters

BORN: September 25, 1931 • Boston,
Massachusetts

American broadcast journalist, television producer

"Don't complain, don't whine, don't blame anybody. Just
work as hard as you can. I showed that not only can women do what
men can do, but sometimes we do it better, faster, and first."

When respected broadcast journalist Barbara Walters started working in television in the early 1960s, she became one of the first women to break into an industry that had long been considered a boys' club, meaning that it was designed for men only. Over the course of her forty-year career, Walters was the first woman to hold many kinds of jobs. For instance, she served as the first female anchor (the main news presenter) of a major network newscast when she joined the *ABC Evening News* with Harry Reasoner (1923–1991) in 1976.

Walters is probably best known as the host of *The Barbara Walters Specials,* an occasional interview series which has aired on ABC since 1976. During its thirty-year run, Walters has interviewed a wide variety of celebrities and world leaders, including every sitting U.S. president and first lady. Walters has also received seven Emmy Awards and served as a mentor for countless other female reporters, including Connie Chung and Paula Zahn.

Barbara Walters.
AP IMAGES.

181

Becoming a journalist

Barbara Walters was born on September 25, 1931 (some sources say 1929), to Louis Edward Walters and Dena Seletsky Walters. Louis Walters was a Broadway producer who also owned the Latin Quarter, a famous chain of nightclubs. Due to his business interests, the family divided their time between New York and Miami. Her father's job also gave Barbara the opportunity to meet and talk with many celebrities throughout her youth. She has credited this early experience for allowing her to feel at ease in the company of public figures.

Walters attended Miami Beach High School and later received her bachelor's degree in English from Sarah Lawrence College. After she completed college, her family went bankrupt, and her father suffered a heart attack. Walters then took a job as a secretary to help her family. Before long, though, she was able to put her skills as an English major to work by writing for television programs, including *The Dick Van Dyke Show* and *CBS News*. Her success as a writer led to a job as a producer for New York's NBC affiliate station, WNBC-TV.

Although Walters was thrilled to be working in television, she hoped to eventually appear in front of the cameras as a news reporter. She knew that she faced a few obstacles in this field. "I was the kind nobody thought could make it," she admitted. "I had a funny Boston accent. I couldn't pronounce my Rs. I wasn't a beauty."

Reporting in a hostile environment

During the 1950s, Walters was married for a short time to businessman Robert Henry Katz. In 1963, she married her second husband, theater producer Lee Guber, and they adopted a daughter, Jacqueline. Around this time, Walters started working on *Today,* a national morning news and entertainment program that aired on NBC. She started out as a writer for the show and then worked her way up to become a news reporter.

Throughout her early career, however, Walters struggled to prove herself to male co-workers who believed that women were not capable of being good journalists. Because of their sexist attitudes, Walters often could not interview a subject until all of the male reporters had finished asking their questions. She was also discouraged from asking questions about politics or financial issues, which were not considered appropriate for women. It took more than a decade of working behind the scenes on *Today* before she was officially named co-host of the show in 1974.

Despite the challenges Walters faced, she soon became an audience favorite thanks to her regular interview segment on *Today*. Walters interviewed many prominent people, including the families of slain leaders John F. Kennedy (1917–1963) and Martin Luther King Jr. (1929–1968). Walters also became known for doggedly pursuing big news stories. When U.S. president Richard M. Nixon (1913–1994; served 1969–74) traveled to China in 1972, breaking twenty years of political silence between the two countries, Walters was the only woman to cover the story. She returned to China in 1975 to cover a visit by President Gerald R. Ford (1913–2006; served 1974–77). That same year, Walters began to receive recognition for her journalistic excellence. She earned an Emmy Award (an annual honor recognizing excellence in television), Broadcaster of the Year honors from the International Radio and Television Society, and an award from the National Association of Television Programming Executives.

Making a high-profile move to ABC

After fifteen years with the *Today* show, Walters moved to rival network ABC in 1976. She received an annual salary of one million dollars to become the first woman ever to serve as co-anchor of a national evening newscast. Co-anchor Harry Reasoner, however, was not pleased with the idea of sharing his job, particularly with a woman. Walters also came under criticism from viewers and the media. Some people questioned her qualifications or did not like her reporting style, while others disapproved of a woman earning such a lavish salary. Walters pointed out that she actually received $500,000 as the co-anchor of *ABC News* (the same salary as Reasoner) and $500,000 from the network's entertainment division for a series of hour-long, prime-time interview specials.

Walters ignored her critics and continued to prove herself a journalist. In 1977, she conducted the first joint interview with Egyptian president Anwar Sadat (1918–1973) and Israeli prime minister Menachem Begin (1913–1992). At the time, the two Middle Eastern leaders were working on a historic peace treaty between their countries. Despite the seriousness of the proceedings, Walters established a casual, friendly atmosphere in the interview. "Sadat seemed to delight in chiding [teasing] Walters, a trait that served them both well," John Carman wrote in the *San Francisco Chronicle*. "When she tried to pin him down on peace terms during the joint interview, Sadat cut in and playfully remarked, 'You are always like this, Barbara.' Begin roared with laughter."

In 1976 Barbara Walters, pictured with co-anchor Harry Reasoner, become the first woman ever to serve as co-anchor of a national evening newscast. AP IMAGES.

Establishing a reputation as a top interviewer

In 1979, citing low ratings, the network removed Walters from her position as co-anchor of the *ABC Evening News.* Although disappointed, Walters responded by working harder than ever to establish a place for herself in the world of TV news. "I had to work my way back," she told Peter Johnson of *USA Today.* "Don't complain, don't whine, don't blame anybody. Just work as hard as you can. I showed that not only can women do what men can do, but sometimes we do it better, faster, and first."

Shortly after losing her anchor position, Walters became a correspondent for *20/20,* a weekly prime-time news magazine that combined hard-hitting investigative pieces with celebrity interviews and human-interest stories, similar to the different types of articles in a print magazine. In 1984 she became co-anchor of *20/20,* working alongside Hugh Downs (1921–). Twenty years later, the news magazine still used Walters's interviews of public figures as regular features.

Walters's own prime-time interview series, *The Barbara Walters Specials,* first aired in 1976 and continued to receive strong ratings into the 2000s. Her style of personality journalism, which often encourages her subjects to open up and reveal their feelings and beliefs, has long appealed to television audiences. Viewers of the program also appreciate the fact that Walters seems to gain access to every major politician and entertainer of the day. Over its thirty-year history, *The Barbara Walters Specials* has received a number of prominent awards.

Despite the program's popularity, however, it has often served as the target of critics and as the subject of ridicule by comedians. During the 1980s, for instance, comedian Gilda Radner (1946–1989) did a famous impersonation of Walters on the skit-comedy series *Saturday Night Live.* Radner's character, "Baba Wawa," was barely understandable due to a speech impediment and always seemed to find herself much more interesting than her interview subjects. Other people have questioned Walters' integrity as a journalist over the years, claiming that she only asks safe, easy questions.

Regardless of the criticism it has received, Walters's interview program remained highly influential. Walters's intimate talk with actor Christopher Reeve (1952–2004), conducted shortly after the horseback riding accident that left him paralyzed, was watched by twenty-nine million viewers and received a George Foster Peabody Award. Her interview with Monica Lewinsky, the White House intern who had an affair with President Bill Clinton (1946–; served 1993–2001), received the highest ratings of any TV interview in history.

Moving into daytime TV with *The View*

In 1986, Walters married Merv Adelson, the head of Lorimar Television. The marriage ended in divorce six years later. In 1997, Walters created a daytime talk show for ABC called *The View.* Walters selected four women of varying ages, ethnic backgrounds, and beliefs to serve as her co-hosts. "I've always wanted to do a show with women who have very different views," she explained during the series premiere. *The View* provides a casual atmosphere where the hosts and various guests can discuss current events, fashion, and entertainment.

In 2004, Walters retired from her position as co-host of *20/20* to concentrate on other projects. For instance, she created and hosted a 2005 television special called "Heaven. Where is it? How do we get there?" "I've done years and years of specials, but I care more about this one than anything I've ever done," she told Rebecca Phillips of *Beliefnet.* "I think there's a great need and a great soul-searching in this country." Throughout her long career, Walters has faced criticism for her role in shifting the emphasis of TV news away from hard facts and toward entertainment and personality. But her critics cannot dispute the fact that the pioneering female broadcast journalist has attained a position of lasting influence and paved the way for future generations of women to succeed in the field.

For More Information

BOOKS

Gianoulis, Tina. "Barbara Walters." *St. James Encyclopedia of Pop Culture,* Farmington Hills, MI: Gale Group, 2002.

Oppenheimer, Jerry. *Barbara Walters: An Unauthorized Biography.* New York: St. Martin's Press, 1991.

Remstein, Henna, and Martina S. Horner. *Women of Achievement: Barbara Walters.* New York: Chelsea House, 1998.

PERIODICALS

Carman, John. "Walters and Twenty Years of Questions." *San Francisco Chronicle,* May 1, 1996.

Johnson, Peter. "Barbara Walters Looks Back on Her Trailblazing Role." *USA Today,* September 16, 2004.

Lowry, Brian. "A Barbara Walters Special: Heaven. Where Is It? How Do We Get There?" Variety, December 19, 2005.

WEB SITES

"Barbara Walters." *ABC.com.* http://abc.go.com/theview/hosts/walters.html (accessed on May 22, 2006).

"Barbara Walters Leaving 20/20." *CNN.com,* January 26, 2004. http://www.cnn.com/2004/SHOWBIZ/TV/01/26/tv.abc.walters.ap (accessed on May 22, 2006).

McLeland, Susan. "Walters, Barbara." *Museum of Broadcast Communications.* http://www.museum.tv/archives/etv/W/htmlW/waltersbarb/waltersbarb.htm (accessed on May 22, 2006).

Phillips, Rebecca. "Heaven is a Place Where You Are Happy." *Beliefnet.* http://www.beliefnet.com/story/181/story_18118.html (accessed on May 22, 2006).

Senior, Jennifer. "30th Anniversary Issue/Barbara Walters." *NYMAG.com.* http://www.newyorkmetro.com/nymetro/news/people/features/2433/index.html (accessed on May 22, 2006).

Oprah Winfrey

BORN: January 29, 1954 • Kosciusko, Mississippi

American talk show host, television producer

Oprah Winfrey.
© SCOTT MCDERMOTT/
CORBIS.

"I am finally at a point in my life where I'm doing the kind of shows I've always wanted to do, helping people see themselves more clearly and to make choices that lead to more fulfilled lives."

As a successful television talk show host, actress, production company executive, magazine editor, and motivational speaker, Oprah Winfrey is the most powerful woman in the entertainment industry. Since *The Oprah Winfrey Show* made its national TV debut in 1986, the name Oprah has evoked an image of warmth, empathy, frankness, and generosity to millions of viewers in countries around the world. Her high standards of integrity and unique ability to connect with her audience have helped make *The Oprah Winfrey Show* number one in daytime programming for almost twenty years.

But Winfrey is much more than the host of a popular talk show. As the first African American woman to become a billionaire, Winfrey has used her wealth and influence to promote her most cherished values. Through her production company, Harpo Productions, she has created film and television versions of many fictional works by women, especially

187

women of color. While she has sometimes faced criticism for keeping a tight control over her entertainment empire, many people have been charmed by her unaffected manner and inspired by her example.

A lonely childhood

Oprah Gail Winfrey was born on January 29, 1954, in the central Mississippi town of Kosciusko. Her parents, Vernita Lee and Vernon Winfrey, were teenagers whose relationship lasted only long enough to conceive their baby daughter. After giving birth, Vernita Lee moved north to Milwaukee, Wisconsin, to work as a housemaid, leaving Oprah to be raised by her grandmother, Hattie Mae Lee. Vernon Winfrey had been in the army when he met Vernita, and after his discharge he moved to Nashville, Tennessee, and opened a barbershop.

Young Oprah spent her first six years in Mississippi with her grandmother, a strict disciplinarian who taught her to read and told her stories from the Bible. Winfrey loved to read from an early age, and she also enjoyed entertaining friends and family by reciting Bible verses and poems she had memorized.

At the age of six, Winfrey began to divide her time between her mother's home in Milwaukee and her father's home in Nashville. When she was nine, she moved in with her mother full-time. Throughout her childhood, Winfrey was a lonely girl who found comfort and escape in books. Her mother was used to a life of hard work, and she had little patience for her daughter's constant reading and theatrical nature. But a seventh-grade teacher noticed the bright young girl who loved to read and helped Winfrey obtain a scholarship to attend a better school in the suburbs of Milwaukee.

When Winfrey was nine years old, she was raped by a cousin who was babysitting her. This was the first of many painful experiences in her adolescence, which included other incidents of sexual abuse. While barely a teenager, Winfrey became pregnant. At this point, her mother gave up trying to control her behavior and sent her to Nashville to live with her father. Winfrey's baby died in early infancy, and afterward her father and stepmother encouraged her to further her education. While still in high school, she got a job as a reporter on WVOL, a Nashville radio station.

Winfrey earned a scholarship to Tennessee State University, a historically black college in Nashville. She majored in speech, communication, and performing arts. At the age of nineteen, Winfrey got her first television job—as a reporter and news anchor (main presenter) on a local Nashville station, WTVF-TV. In 1976 she moved to Baltimore to take a job as co-anchor of the newscast on WJZ-TV. Her employers found her too emotional to be an effective news anchor, however, and in 1978 they made her the host of *People Are Talking,* a local talk show.

Finding fame as a talk show host

The talk show format provided a perfect way to show off Winfrey's warm, sympathetic personality. She did so well on *People Are Talking* that she attracted the attention of executives at the Chicago television station WLS. In 1984, they hired Winfrey to try to revive a failing local morning talk show called *A.M. Chicago.* The program became an instant success, and within a year it had been renamed *The Oprah Winfrey Show.*

The format of *Oprah* had been pioneered by talk show host Phil Donahue (1935–) in the late 1960s. Before Donahue launched his successful program, talk and variety show hosts had maintained a clear separation between performers and the studio audience. Donahue changed this by strolling through the studio and inviting audience members to ask questions and express opinions. Donahue also tackled more controversial topics than most talk show hosts who had come before him.

Winfrey followed Donahue's lead and addressed some tough topics on *The Oprah Winfrey Show,* but she used a more personal and sympathetic approach. She openly discussed her own personal struggles and hardships, for instance, which helped her form a deeper connection with guests and viewers alike. Her reassuring style also encouraged guests and audience members to share their experiences and feelings.

In 1986, Winfrey expanded the reach of her talk show to a national audience by signing a syndication deal with King World Productions (syndication is an arrangement in which a producer distributes a program independently to TV stations in various markets, instead of selling it to a major broadcast network). Within a year, *The Oprah Winfrey Show* became the most-watched program on daytime television, and it would remain in that position for the next twenty years. In 1987, the program won its first three Emmy Awards (annual honors recognizing excellence in television programming) from the National Academy of Television Arts and Sciences, for Outstanding Talk/Service Program, Outstanding Host, and Outstanding Direction. Winfrey and her show went on to win forty Emmy Awards by 1998.

That year, Winfrey received the Academy's Lifetime Achievement Award and withdrew her name from future award consideration. By the 2000s, her show was watched by nearly fifty million viewers daily, and its success had made her one of the wealthiest and most influential women in the world.

Working to improve the quality of daytime talk

A number of other talk shows tried to copy the successful formula of *The Oprah Winfrey Show* during the 1990s, but no other host was able to duplicate Winfrey's connection with her audience. Then competing shows began trying to use sensational (outrageous or shocking) subject matter to draw viewers away from *Oprah*. Many talk shows set up surprise confrontations between guests in order to create drama and attract viewers. This approach often led to crying, shouting, and fighting between guests.

By the mid-1990s, Winfrey had grown troubled at the outrageous direction some of these talk shows had taken. Not only did some of the shows seem to promote anger and even violence, but she felt that many of the shows presented racial and gender stereotypes (generalized, usually negative views of a group of people). Winfrey was careful to avoid any such tendency in her own show. She not only demanded respectful behavior from her audience and guests, but she made sure her show presented controversial issues in a constructive way. She was particularly determined to counteract racism by presenting the positive aspects of African American culture. "As the years evolved, I grew and wanted to say something with the show," she explained in *Jet*. "Not just be a television announcer or a television performer, but I wanted to say something meaningful to the American public and culture."

One part of Winfrey's plan to ensure that her program had a positive impact on viewers involved sharing her lifelong love of reading with her audience. In 1996, she introduced a new feature called Oprah's Book Club. Each month, she invited viewers to read a book she selected and then tune in to her show for a discussion with the author. Each selection was a book that Winfrey herself had read and enjoyed. Some of the books were written by prominent authors, while others were by practically unknown writers.

Just as Winfrey had hoped, the book club feature had an immediate impact on the American public's reading habits. Oprah's Book Club selections sold hundreds of thousands of copies, giving a boost to authors and publishers, as well as to the pastime of reading. In 2002, Winfrey cut back the Book Club to an occasional feature on her show, but she also introduced Traveling with the Classics, which encouraged viewers to read exceptional novels written in the past. This feature made instant bestsellers of books that modern readers might otherwise not know, such as Leo Tolstoy's 1877 novel *Anna Karenina*.

Founding Harpo Productions

In 1984, as Winfrey's career as a talk-show host was just developing, she also won her first major role as an actress. She appeared in the film version of *The Color Purple*, directed by Steven Spielberg. Based on a 1982 novel by Alice Walker that was one of Winfrey's favorites, the movie tells the story of an African American woman named Celie who overcomes a very difficult childhood in the South during the era of segregation (the forced separation of people by race). Winfrey played the role of Sofia, a tough and fiercely independent black woman who suffers greatly in the white-dominated society in which she lives. Winfrey played the part with intense emotion, and her performance earned Academy Award and Golden Globe Award nominations as Best Supporting Actress. She continued to take on acting roles as her television show developed, earning critical praise for her work in films such as *Native Son* (1986) and television miniseries such as *The Women of Brewster Place* (1989).

In 1986, shortly after her talk show went national, Winfrey founded her own production company to develop theatrical films and television programs. Chicago-based Harpo Productions (the name is "Oprah" spelled backwards) increased Winfrey's power and influence in the entertainment industry. Winfrey not only gained complete creative control over *The Oprah Winfrey Show*, but she also gained the ability to make films based on some of her favorite books. Winfrey bought the movie rights to several acclaimed novels by African American women, including *Beloved* by Toni Morrison (1931–) and *Their Eyes Were Watching God* by Zora Neale Hurston (1891–1960). She appeared as an actress in some of the films she produced.

In 2000, Winfrey entered yet another part of the entertainment industry by introducing a new magazine called *O*. At a time when periodical sales were declining, *O* enjoyed the most successful startup in magazine history and began showing a profit almost immediately. By 2004, the publication had a circulation of over 2.5 million. Winfrey viewed her magazine as a personal growth manual. Like her talk show, it provided

Oprah Winfrey

Oprah Winfrey launched her magazine, O, in 2000. By 2004, the publication had a circulation of over 2.5 million readers. AP IMAGES.

people with constructive ideas about how to increase their health and happiness. Also in 2000, Winfrey joined several other producers in founding Oxygen Media, a new cable television and interactive online network dedicated to providing programming of interest to women.

Many employees of Harpo Productions have found Winfrey to be a demanding boss. Her own energy is seemingly boundless, and she has often required long hours of work from her staff. Although she can be quite open with her audiences, Winfrey is also extremely protective of her privacy, and each of her employees must sign a lifetime confidentiality agreement (a pledge not to reveal any inside information about Winfrey or her business enterprises).

The Angel Network

As Winfrey's wealth increased, so did her commitment to helping various charitable organizations. Winfrey had always donated generously to causes that moved her, but in the late 1990s she began encouraging viewers to join her in helping others. In 1998 she established the Angel Network, a charitable foundation that collected donations and distributed money to people in need around the world. Winfrey herself covered all of the organization's operating expenses, so that 100 percent of viewers' donations could go toward charitable programs. As of 2000, Winfrey's Angel Network had raised over $50 million to help build schools in poor and war-torn areas around the world, buy books and uniforms for students, and support women whose lives have been devastated by war. She has received a number of prestigious awards for her charitable efforts, including the United Nations Global Humanitarian Action Award in 2004 and selection to the National Association for the Advancement of Colored People (NAACP) Hall of Fame in 2005.

A large part of Winfrey's personal appeal on television is based on her upbeat and positive attitude about changing and improving one's life. In 2001 she turned this attitude into another aspect of her business career by launching her "Live Your Best Life" seminars. This series of all-day workshops, during which audiences hear Winfrey speak about her philosophy of personal growth, took her across the United States and around the world. Although tickets cost almost $200 each, the seminars are so popular that tickets usually sell out within a few hours of going on sale.

Despite her various business successes, Winfrey is still best known as the host of *The Oprah Winfrey Show*. Over the course of the program's two decades on television, Winfrey has won over a huge audience of devoted fans by creating a positive, supportive atmosphere for people to discuss personal problems and issues. Winfrey has turned her unique connection with TV audiences into a vast business empire and a billion-dollar fortune. Perhaps her most important contribution to the entertainment industry, however, has been her determination to use her power and influence in a constructive way. "I am finally at a point in my life where I'm doing the kind of shows I've always wanted to do, helping people see themselves more clearly and to make choices that lead to more fulfilled lives," she stated in a press release.

For More Information

BOOKS

Nicholson, Lois P. *Oprah Winfrey.* New York: Chelsea House, 1994.

Westen, Robin. *Oprah Winfrey: "I Don't Believe in Failure."* Berkeley Heights, NJ: Enslow, 2005.

Woods, Geraldine. *The Oprah Winfrey Story: Speaking Her Mind.* Minneapolis: Dillon Press, 1991.

PERIODICALS

Bednarski, P. J. "All About Oprah Inc." *Broadcasting and Cable,* January 24, 2005.

Flamm, Matthew. "The Oprah Factor." *Crain's New York Business,* April 25, 2005.

Harrison, Barbara Grizzuti. "The Importance of Being Oprah." *New York Times Magazine,* June 11, 1989.

Johnson, Marilyn, and Dana Fineman. "Oprah Winfrey: A Life in Books." *Life,* September 1997.

"Oprah Winfrey Reveals the Real Reason Why She Stayed on Television." *Jet,* November 24, 1997.

Rogers, Jackie. "Understanding Oprah." *Redbook,* September 1993.

Sellers, Patricia. "The Business of Being Oprah." *Fortune,* April 1, 2002.

WEB SITES

"About Oprah." *Oprah.com.* http://www.oprah.com/about/press/about_press_bio.jhtml (accessed on May 24, 2006).

Tannen, Deborah. "Oprah Winfrey." *Time.* http://www.time.com/time/time100/artists/profile/winfrey.html (accessed on May 24, 2006).

Timberg, Bernard M. "Talk Shows." *Museum of Broadcast Communications.* http://www.museum.tv/archives/etv/T/htmlT/talkshows/talkshows.htm (accessed on May 25, 2006).

Vladimir Zworykin

BORN: July 30, 1889 • Mourom, Russia
DIED: July 29, 1982 • Princeton, New Jersey

Russian American electrical engineer

"All technology can be used for bad or good. It's up to you how to use it."

Electrical engineer Vladimir Zworykin is one of the most important figures in the creation and development of electronic television technology. During, his twenty-five-year career as the director of television research at the Radio Corporation of America (RCA), he helped make television a reality in the United States.

Growing up in Russia

Vladimir Kosma Zworykin was born on July 30, 1889, in Mourom, Russia. He was the youngest of seven children born to Kosma and Elaine Zworykin. His father was a wealthy merchant who owned a grain business and operated a fleet of steamships on the Oka River. As a boy, Zworykin enjoyed a comfortable life in a huge stone mansion. He spent his spare time horseback riding, playing croquet, attending the opera, and studying art.

Vladimir Zworykin.
© BETTMANN/CORBIS.

Zworykin completed his early education in the local schools in Mourom. He developed a passion for science at an early age, often

195

staying after school to help his teachers in the laboratory. After graduating from high school, he studied physics and electrical engineering at the St. Petersburg Institute of Technology. Zworykin recalled in *Tube: The Invention of Television* that it was an exciting time to study science. "When I was a student, we suddenly underwent a sort of revolution in physics, which produced the new possibility of using technology and science for human welfare," he noted.

In 1910, Zworykin began serving as an assistant to one of his professors, the respected Russian physicist Boris Rosing (1869–1933). At this time, scientists around the world were just beginning to develop systems for transmitting live, moving pictures across a distance. Rosing had become interested in this area of study a few years earlier, and he had made some important discoveries in the new field of television. He encouraged his bright young assistant to help him develop the technology.

Working on early TV systems

Like many other researchers working on the problem in these early years, Rosing's television system used a mechanical transmitter to capture moving images and turn them into electrical signals. Mechanical TV cameras used spinning metal disks with holes in them to continuously measure the amount of light reflected off a moving image. The holes sent electrical signals, which varied in strength depending on the amount of light hitting them, across a wire to a similar device at the other end. The second device reversed the process and turned the electrical signals back into light, creating a crude representation of the moving image at the other end of the wire.

Rosing was one of the first researchers to develop an electronic device (one that had no moving parts and instead worked entirely by using the properties of electricity) called a cathode ray tube to receive television signals and display the images. A cathode is a filament inside a sealed glass tube, sort of like those found in lightbulbs. When the filament is heated, it forms a vacuum, or an empty space that does not contain any matter. A cathode ray is a stream of electrons that pours off the cathode into the vacuum. Rosing and Zworykin used electrical circuits to focus these electrons into a beam and shoot them toward a flat screen at one end of the tube. The inside of the screen was coated in a substance that emitted light, or glowed, when struck by a beam of radiation. They used the mechanical camera and electronic receiver to send a crude television image in 1911.

After graduating from college in 1912, Zworykin chose to continue his education rather than return home to learn the family business. He went to Paris, France, where he spent a year studying X-ray technology under the Nobel Prize-winning physicist Paul Langevin (1872–1946). When World War I (1914–1918) began, Zworykin returned to Russia and was drafted into the army. Thanks to his training in electronics, he became an officer and served as a radio communications expert. Before the war ended, Zworykin married Tatiana Vasilieff, and they eventually had two children.

Moving to the United States

In 1917, Russia experienced a political revolution. Common people rose up to overthrow the government and take away the possessions of the ruling class. Zworykin's family lost their home in Mourom and much of their wealth at this time. Fearing for his safety, Zworykin decided to leave his homeland. He joined an Arctic expedition led by a Russian scientist and traveled from there to England, finally reaching the United States in 1919. When he arrived in the United States, Zworykin had very little money and did not speak English. He initially got a job as an adding machine operator for the Russian Purchasing Commission in New York City, and he studied the English language in his spare time.

In 1920, Zworykin got a job as an electronics researcher with the Westinghouse Electric Corporation in Pittsburgh, Pennsylvania. This position gave him the resources to bring his wife and children to the United States. Over the next several years, the engineer helped developed radio technology and worked on ways to improve the light sensitivity and electrical output of photoelectric cells. Zworykin also worked toward a doctoral degree in electrical engineering at the University of Pittsburgh during this time, receiving his Ph.D. in 1926.

During his years at Westinghouse, Zworykin remained interested in television. In the decade since he had first encountered the technology in Rosing's lab, he had come to the conclusion that mechanical television systems would never be able to scan images fast enough to produce a good picture. In order for television to work well, he decided that both the transmitter and the receiver had to be fully electronic.

Inventing the Iconoscope and Kinescope

Around 1923, Zworykin created an all-electronic television camera tube he called the Iconoscope. The Iconoscope worked by reflecting the light

Vladimir Zworykin

from a moving image onto a special plate. This plate was coated with tiny dots, or pixels, of a chemical that was sensitive to light. When the light swept across the pixels, they would become electrically charged. The charge varied in strength depending on the amount of light that hit each pixel. In this way, Zworykin's Iconoscope television camera converted a visual image into an electrical signal without the need for the spinning wheels used in mechanical television systems.

In 1924—the same year he became a U.S. citizen—Zworykin demonstrated an early version of the Iconoscope for his bosses at Westinghouse. But while the invention broke new ground in television research, it was still far from perfect. The camera produced a small, hazy picture that flickered and then faded out abruptly. As a result, the demonstration failed to impress the decision-makers at Westinghouse. Westinghouse management thought Zworykin should devote his time to what they might see as more useful inventions. Nevertheless, Zworykin continued pursuing his interest in television, even if he had to conduct experiments in the laboratory at night or on weekends.

In 1929, Zworykin invented an improved version of the cathode ray television picture tube he called the Kinescope. He successfully used this device to receive and display the TV signals from his Iconoscope camera. One of the people who heard about Zworykin's television research was **David Sarnoff** (1891–1971; see entry), an ambitious businessman who had recently become the acting president of RCA, the leading producer of radios in the United States. It also held a strong position in radio broadcasting through its ownership of the National Broadcasting Company (NBC). Sarnoff had been interested in television since the earliest mention of the potential new technology. As the head of RCA, he was also concerned that the development of television might cause people to stop buying radios. Once it appeared that TV would become a reality, Sarnoff became determined to make RCA a leader in the television industry as well.

Going to work for RCA

Sarnoff invited Zworykin to RCA headquarters for a meeting. In a famous exchange, Sarnoff asked the engineer what it would take to develop an electronic television system that could be sold to the public. Zworykin estimated that he would need a year and a half and $100,000 to perfect the system. Instead, it ended up taking a decade and costing RCA $50 million before the company introduced television to the public at the 1939 World's Fair.

Since Westinghouse was not supportive of his television research, Zworykin went to work for RCA in 1929. The following year, the U.S. government awarded a patent (a form of legal protection for an invention) to American inventor **Philo T. Farnsworth** (1906–1971; see entry) for an all-electronic television system. A short time later, Sarnoff sent Zworykin to visit Farnsworth's laboratory and check out his inventions. Farnsworth gladly gave the prominent engineer a tour and let Zworykin examine a model of his television camera, called the image dissector.

Following an unsuccessful attempt to buy Farnsworth's invention, Sarnoff decided to challenge Farnsworth's patents in court. RCA filed a lawsuit claiming that Zworykin had invented his electronic television system first. They asked the court to throw out Farnsworth's TV patents and award the rights to the invention to Zworykin instead. The patent battles between Farnsworth and RCA continued throughout the 1930s. After hearing testimony from Farnsworth's high school science teacher, the U.S. Patent Office concluded that Farnsworth had indeed invented electronic television before Zworykin. For the first time in its history, RCA was forced to pay a fee (called a royalty) for the right to use technology created by an independent inventor.

Despite the fact that RCA lost the patent battle to Farnsworth, Zworykin continued making important contributions to the development of television. In the late 1930s, he introduced an improved type of television camera called the Image Orthicon. Since this camera was more sensitive than the Iconoscope, television performers were no longer required to work under extremely bright, hot lights. The Image Orthicon provided the basic technology used in television cameras for the next fifty years.

Using science to help people

Once he had perfected electronic television, Zworykin turned his attention to other problems he felt could be solved with electronic technology. For instance, he directed a team of RCA researchers that created one of the earliest electron microscopes. The first device they built in 1939 was as tall as a house, but within a year they had compressed the technology into a box about six feet tall. The electron microscope applied the principles of television to create a large picture of a tiny object. Instead of using a regular glass lens to magnify small objects, it used a beam of electrons to turn the image into an electrical signal that could be displayed as a picture. The electron microscope revolutionized the fields of molecular and cell biology by allowing scientists to see details twenty to fifty times smaller than was possible using a regular microscope.

During World War II (1939–45) Zworykin served as an advisor to several U.S. government agencies that developed new technology for national defense purposes. In this role, he helped create devices such as the Sniperscope and Snooperscope, which used electronic imaging systems to allow U.S. soldiers to see better in the dark. Zworykin ended up earning over one hundred U.S. patents during his career. Other things he invented include an electric eye for security systems, electronic control systems for weapons and vehicles, an automatic door opener, and a device that helped blind people to read printed words.

After his first marriage ended in divorce, Zworykin married Katherine Polevitsky in 1951. Three years later he retired from active research at RCA, but he remained with the company as a technical consultant. By the time of his retirement, around 30 million television sets in use across the United States included parts that he had helped develop. Zworykin also began pursuing a new area of interest—medical electronics—at Rockefeller University in New Jersey following his retirement from RCA.

Zworykin received a number of prestigious awards over the years for his contributions to television and other important technologies. In 1934, for instance, he received the Morris Liebmann Memorial Prize from the Institute of Radio Engineers. In 1948, the government of France named him a member of its Legion of Honor. In 1952, he won the Edison Medal, the highest honor presented by the American Institute of Electrical Engineers. In 1967, he received National Medal of Science from the National Academy of Sciences, and a decade later he was inducted into the National Inventors Hall of Fame.

Vladimir Zworykin died one day before his ninety-third birthday, on July 29, 1982. He lived long enough to see television expand worldwide and have a major impact on American culture. The great engineer was disappointed in the quality of television programming, however, once describing it as "awful." As he explained in a 1975 interview conducted by the IEEE History Center, "All technology can be used for bad or good. It's up to you how to use it."

For More Information

BOOKS

Abramson, Albert. *Zworykin: Pioneer of Television*. Urbana: University of Illinois Press, 1995.

Fisher, David E., and Marshall J. Fisher. *Tube: The Invention of Television*. Washington, DC: Counterpoint, 2002.

WEB SITES

Benjamin, Louise. "Vladimir Zworykin." *Museum of Broadcast Communications*. http://www.museum.tv/archives/etv/Z/htmlZ/zworykinvla/zworykinvla.htm (accessed on June 5, 2006).

Heyer, Mark, and Al Pinsky. "Vladimir Zworykin Interview," July 4, 1975. *IEEE History Center,* Rutgers University, New Brunswick, New Jersey. http://www.ieee.org/organizations/history_center/oral_histories/transcript/zworykin21.html (accessed on June 5, 2006).

"Vladimir Zworykin" and "Iconoscope Camera Tube." *IEEE Virtual Museum*. http://www.ieee-virtual-museum.org/collection/people.php?taid=&id=1234612&lid=1 (accessed on June 5, 2006).

Where to Learn More

Books

Barnouw, Erik. *Tube of Plenty: The Evolution of American Television.* New York: Oxford University Press, 1975.

Calabro, Marian. *Zap! A Brief History of Television.* New York: Four Winds Press, 1992.

Castleman, Harry, and Walter Podrazik. *Watching TV: Four Decades of American Television.* New York: McGraw-Hill, 1982.

Fisher, David E., and Marshall Jon Fisher. *Tube: The Invention of Television.* Washington, DC: Counterpoint, 1992.

Garner, Joe. *Stay Tuned: Television's Unforgettable Moments.* Kansas City: Andrews McMeel Publishing, 2002.

Gitlin, Todd. *Inside Prime Time.* New York: Pantheon, 1983.

Hilliard, Robert L., and Michael C. Keith. *The Broadcast Century: A Biography of American Broadcasting.* Boston: Focal Press, 1992.

Lichter, S. Robert. *Prime Time: How TV Portrays American Culture.* Washington DC: Regnery Publishers, 1994.

MacDonald, J. Fred. *One Nation under Television: The Rise and Decline of Network TV.* New York: Pantheon, 1990.

McNeil, Alex. *Total Television: The Comprehensive Guide to Programming from 1948 to the Present.* New York: Penguin Books, 1996.

Owen, Rob. *Gen X TV: "The Brady Bunch" to "Melrose Place."* New York: Syracuse University Press, 1997.

Sackett, Susan. *Prime-Time Hits: Television's Most Popular Network Programs, 1950 to the Present.* New York: Billboard Books, 1993.

Schwartz, Evan I. *The Last Lone Inventor: A Tale of Genius, Deceit, and the Birth of Television.* New York: HarperCollins, 2002.

Stark, Steven D. *Glued to the Set: The 60 Television Shows and Events That Made Us Who We Are Today.* New York: The Free Press, 1997.

Stashower, Daniel. *The Boy Genius and the Mogul: The Untold Story of Television.* New York: Broadway Books, 2002.

Web Sites

"Encyclopedia of Television." *Museum of Broadcast Communications.* http://www. museum.tv/archives/etv (accessed on August 9, 2006).

"The FCC History Project," 2003. *Federal Communications Commission.* http://www. fcc.gov/omd/history/tv (accessed on August 9, 2006).

Index

Bold type indicates main entries and their page numbers. Illustrations are marked by (ill.).

A

Aaron Spelling Productions, 159–63
ABC News, 181, 184, 184 (ill.)
ABC's Wide World of Sports, 8–9
Act III, 108
After All (Moore), 121
Ailes, Roger, 1–6, 6 (ill.)
    broadcasting experience of, 2
    childhood and education of, 2
    Fox News Channel development and
      management by, 5–6
    NBC and, 5
    on political bias at Fox News, 5
    political consulting career of, 1–2, 3–4
    television news producing, 4–5
    television producing experience of, 2, 3
    theatrical producing experience of, 3
    on work, 1, 2
Alda, Alan, 76, 76 (ill.), 77
Ali, Muhammad, 13
All in the Family, 101, 105–6, 152
All My Children, 125, 129–30
Allen, Woody, 112
Alterman, Eric, 6
A.M. Chicago, 189
America Online (AOL), 175
American Heritage, 56, 60
American Telephone and Telegraph (AT&T),
    144, 145
America's Intelligence Wire, 54

And the Band Played On (film), 162
Angel Network, 193
Another World, 127
The Apprentice, 37
Arledge, Roone, 7–15, 7 (ill.)
    ABC News leadership and, 11–15
    ABC sports success of, 8–11
    awards won by, 13–14
    childhood of, 7–8
    early television experience of, 8
    education of, 8
    on *Nightline,* 13
    on show business and sports, 7, 8
    television career summarized, 7
Arnaz, Desi, 18–19, 20 (ill.)
Arnaz, Desi, Jr., 22
Arnaz, Lucie, 22
Arnett, Peter, 177
Arthur, Bea, 106
As the World Turns, 126–27
AT&T (American Telephone and Telegraph),
    144, 145
Auletta, Ken, 179

B

Ball, Lucille, 17–23, 17 (ill.), 20 (ill.)
    awards and inspiration of, 22–23
    on being funny, 17
    childhood of, 18
    Desilu Productions and, 21–23

I Love Lucy and, 19–22
on *I Love Lucy* development, 19
on marriage to Desi Arnaz, 19
movie career of, 18–19
radio career of, 19
television career summarized, 17
as television producer, 22
training of, 18
The Barbara Walters Specials, 181, 185, 186–87
Berle, Milton, 25–31, 25 (ill.), 28 (ill.)
awards won by, 30
on failure of television show, 28
on his style of comedy, 25
on his vaudeville years, 26
movie and nightclub work of, 26–27
post-1950s work of, 30
as radio show host, 27
as show business child, 25–26
television career summarized, 25
television show success of, 27
vaudeville background of, 26
BET (Black Entertainment Television), 95–97
BET Holdings, 96–99
BET.com, 97–98
Better World Society, 179
Beverly Hills, 90210, 157, 160–62
The Bill Cosby Show, 51
Black Collegian (magazine), 94, 95, 99–100
Black Enterprise (magazine), 99
Black Entertainment Television (BET), 95–97
Bliss, Edward, Jr., 59
Blue Network, 144
The Boy in the Plastic Bubble, 159
The Brady Bunch, 102, 103
Brill's Content, 5
Brinkley, David, 11, 58
Broadcasting and Cable, 130
Broadway Video, 115
Bunker, Archie, 102, 104
Bunker, Edith, 104
Burnett, Mark, 33–39, 33 (ill.)
on basis of reality show success, 37
books written by, 38
business and military ventures of, 33–34
childhood and young manhood of, 33–34
commercials on reality shows of, 38–39

endurance races and, 34–35
on his work in television, 33
product placement success of, 38–39
reality television invented by, 35–36
on *Survivor,* 35
television career summarized, 33
television production company and
    programs of, 36–38
Business Week, 96

C

Cable News Network (CNN), 171, 176–77
Cable television. *See* Ailes, Roger; Johnson,
    Robert L.; McGrath, Judy; Turner, Ted;
    Winfrey, Oprah
Caesar, Sid, 74–75
Canadian Broadcasting Company (CBC),
    112, 113
Cantor, Muriel G., 159
Carman, John, 183
Carson, Johnny, 113
Cartoon Network, 178
Carugati, Anna, 159, 162
Casting for television roles, 159
Castleman, Harry, 154
Cathode Oscillite Tube television receiver, 65
Cathode ray tube, 196
CBC (Canadian Broadcasting Company),
    112, 113
CBS (Columbia Broadcasting System).
    See Paley, William S.
CBS Evening News, 55
Charlie's Angels, 152, 152 (ill.), 158
Charmed, 163
Cheers, 167
Children's programs. *See* Cooney, Joan Ganz;
    Cosby, Bill
*Classic Sitcoms: A Collection of the Best in Prime-Time
    Comedy* (Waldron), 101, 102, 106
CNBC, 5
CNN (Cable News Network), 171, 176–77
Collins, Scott, 3
The Color Purple (book and movie), 191
Colorization (of movies), 177

Columbia Broadcasting System (CBS).
   See CBS (Columbia Broadcasting System)
Comedy programs. *See* Ball, Lucille; Berle,
   Milton; Cosby, Bill; Gelbart, Larry; Lear,
   Norman; Michaels, Lorne; Moore, Mary Tyler;
   Silverman, Fred
Commercialism, 38–39
Cooney, Joan Ganz, 41–46, 41 (ill.), 45 (ill.)
   awards and achievements of, 44, 45,
      45 (ill.), 46
   childhood and education of, 41–42
   Children's Television Workshop successes of,
      43–46
   documentary production experience of, 43
   research about education and
      television performed by, 43
   social activist motivations of, 41–42
   on television and education, 43
   television career summarized, 41
Corporation for Public Broadcasting (CPB), 94
Cosby, Bill, 47–54, 47 (ill.), 50 (ill.)
   African American family image embodied by,
      52–54
   awards won by, 51, 52
   books written by, 53
   childhood of, 48
   children's television programming and, 51 52
   on common human experience vs. racism,
      47, 49
   education of, 48–49, 52
   as first African American television
      action-adventure star, 50–51, 50 (ill.)
   generosity of, 54
   on negative television stereotypes of African
      Americans, 52–53, 53–54
   stand-up comedy background and
      experience of, 49
   television career summarized, 47
   tragedies endured by, 53
   as trusted product endorser, 51
   values expressed by, 53–54
The Cosby Show, 52–53
Cosell, Howard, 12, 12 (ill.), 13
Crazy Like a Fox (Collins), 3
Cronkite, Walter, 55–62, 55 (ill.), 61 (ill.)
   on American space program, 60

awards won by, 61, 61 (ill.)
   as *CBS Evening News* anchorman, 58–60
   childhood and education of, 56
   on disappointing developments at
      CBS News, 62
   on early days of television news, 55, 58
   early years at CBS television, 57–58
   ethics and values of, 56, 59–61
   image and identity as trusted American,
      55, 58
   journalism experience of, 56–57
   post-anchorman years of, 61–62
   television career summarized, 55
   transition from radio to television of, 136
   wartime reporting of, 57
Culp, Robert, 50, 50 (ill.), 51

D

Daytime dramas. *See* Nixon, Agnes
Desilu Productions, 21–23
Diagnosis Murder, 156
The Dick Van Dyke Show, 120–21, 124
Diller, Phyllis, 112
Donahue, Phil, 189
Donaldson, Sam, 11
Downs, Hugh, 184
Dramatic programs. *See* Silverman, Fred; Spelling,
   Aaron; Tartikoff, Brandon
Dramedy, 77
Dynasty, 157, 160

E

Ebersol, Dick, 114, 168
Eco Challenge, 34–35
The Ed Sullivan Show, 29
Educational programs. *See* Cooney, Joan Ganz;
   Cosby, Bill
Edwards, Douglas, 58
The Electric Company, 45, 51
Electronic Learning, 43
Embassy Communications, 108
ESPN 25 (Hirshberg), 8
Evans, Florida, 106–7

F

Fairness and Accuracy in Reporting (FAIR), 6
Family, 159
Family Ties, 167
Fantasy Island, 158–59
Farnsworth, Kent, 69
Farnsworth, Philo T., 63–71, 63 (ill.), 67 (ill.)
    awards and recognition of work of, 69–70
    childhood and early interest in electronics of,
        63–64
    education of, 64–65
    Farnsworth Radio and television
        corporation years of, 69
    importance to television technology of, 63
    invention of electronic television by, 62, 64–66
    legal battles with RCA (Radio Corporation of
        America), 66, 68, 68–69
    Philco research division work years, 68–69
    research and inventions of later years of, 69–70
    Sarnoff and, 145–46
    Zworykin and, 199–200
Farrell, Mike, 75, 76 (ill.)
Fat Albert and the Cosby Kids, 51–52
Federal Communications Commission (FCC),
    134–35, 148, 173
Feminism, 120, 121–22. *See also* Walters, Barbara
Fernwood 2-Nite, 108
The Fifties (Halberstam), 27
Football, 9–11
Fox News Channel, 5–6, 177
Foxx, Redd, 106
Frawley, William, 20 (ill.), 21
The Fred Silverman Company, 155–56
Fusil, Gerald, 34

G

Game shows. *See* Griffin, Merv
Garner, Joe, 105
Gay and Lesbian Alliance Against Defamation
    (GLAAD), 129–30
GE (General Electric), 144, 145, 149
Gelbart, Larry, 73–79, 73 (ill.)
    awards won by, 75, 77, 78

on British television writing, 75
childhood and education of, 73–74
comedy writing career summarized, 73, 74
on early television writing experience,
    73, 75
early television writing of, 74–75
M*A*S*H writing success for, 75–77,
    76 (ill.)
playwriting experience of, 75
radio comedy writing experiences of, 74
screenplays of, 77–78
General Electric (GE), 144, 145,
    149
Gifford, Frank, 10, 10 (ill.)
Gilligan's Island, 102, 103
GLAAD (Gay and Lesbian Alliance Against
    Defamation), 129–30
Goldberg, Leonard, 158–59
Goldmark Communications, 149
Goldmark, Peter, 134, 148–49
Good Times, 101, 106–7
Griffin, Merv, 81–86, 81 (ill.)
    awards won by, 86
    background and childhood of, 81–82
    business developed outside television
        industry by, 85–86
    early television hosting jobs of, 82
    as game show creator/producer, 84–85,
        85 (ill.)
    on his entrepreneurship, 81, 85
    singing career of, 82
    as talk show host, 83
    television career summarized, 81
Griffith, Andy, 156
Guiding Light, 126, 127

H

Halberstam, David, 27
Hanna Barbera, 178
Happy Days, 153
Harpo Productions, 191–93
Hawn, Goldie, 113
HBO (Home Box Office), 174–75
Hear It Now, 135
Here's Lucy, 22

Hewitt, Don, 87–94, 87 (ill.), 89 (ill.)
awards won by, 92
as broadcast journalism pioneer, 90–92
CBS news documentary direction of, 90
childhood and education of, 87–88
early journalism experiences of, 88
on journalism and confrontation, 87
on political power of television, 89
as presidential debate director, 89, 89 (ill.)
60 Minutes creation by, 90–92
television career summarized, 87
Hill Street Blues, 155, 167
Hirshberg, Charles, 8
Holliman, John, 177
Hollywood Reporter, 37
The Hollywood TV Producer: His Work and His Audience (Cantor), 159
Home Box Office (HBO), 174–75
Hope, Bob, 74
Huntley, Chet, 58

I Love Lucy, 10 (ill.), 20, 23
I Spy, 47, 50–51, 50 (ill.)
Iconoscope, 66, 197–99
Idato, Michael, 162
IEEE History Center, 201
Image Dissector, 66
In the Heat of the Night, 156
Inside Gilligan's Island (Schwartz), 103
Investor's Business Daily, 97

Jackson, Keith, 10
The Jeffersons, 101, 106, 152
Jennings, Peter, 11
Jeopardy (television game show), 84, 85
Jet (magazine), 190
Jiggle TV, 151, 153
Johnson, Peter, 184
Johnson, Robert L., 93–100, 93 (ill.), 98 (ill.)
airline aspirations of, 98–99, 98 (ill.)

Black Entertainment Television (BET) creation and expansion by, 95–97
childhood and early goals of, 94–95
education of, 94
financial power of, 98
on importance of education, 99
on importance of Internet, 97–98
Internet entrepreneurship of, 97–98
magazine and book publishing ventures of, 96–97
on overcoming racism, 93, 99–100
professional sports ownership by, 99
on success, 99
television career summarized, 93

Kinescope, 66, 199
King World Productions, 189
Koppel, Ted, 11, 12–13

L.A. Law, 167, 168 (ill.)
The Last Great Ride (Tartikoff), 169
Late Night with Conan O'Brien, 116
Late Night with David Letterman, 116
Laverne and Shirley, 153
Lear, Norman, 101–9, 101 (ill.), 107 (ill.)
All in the Family and, 104–6
awards won by, 105
black situation comedy development by, 106–7
comedy films of, 104
family background and war experience of, 102–3
influential television programs developed by, 101
1950s comedy writing experience, 103–4
1970 s comedies of, 107–8
as pioneer of socially-conscious television comedy, 105
sitcom (situation comedy) format development and, 105–6
spin-off successes of, 106–7

on television and social issues, 101
  television career summarized, 101
Leonard, Sheldon, 49
Lewin, Gerald, 174
Life magazine, 13–14
Limbaugh, Rush, 5
Littleton, Cynthia, 37
*Live From New York: An Uncensored History
  of "Saturday Night Live"* (Shales, Miller), 111, 112
Live videotaping, 106
"Live Your Best Life" seminars, 193
Looking Ahead: The Papers of David Sarnoff
  (Wiesner), 130
The Love Boat, 157, 159–60
Love, Lucy (Ball), 19
Lowry, Tom, 96
Lucci, Susan, 128 (ill.), 129
The Lucille Ball–Desi Arnaz Show, 22
Lucille Ball Productions, 22
The Lucy Show, 22

M

M*A*S*H, 75–77, 76 (ill.), 152
Marconi, Guglielmo, 142–43
Marconi Wireless Telegraph Company
  of America, 142–43
Mark Burnett Productions (MBP), 36–38
Martin, Dick, 113
Mary Hartman, Mary Hartman, 108
The Mary Tyler Moore Show, 121–23, 122 (ill.), 152
Matlock, 156
Maude, 101, 106, 152
*Maverick Inventor: My Turbulent Years
  at CBS* (Goldmark), 149
McCarthy, Joseph, 136–37
McGrath, Judy, 96–97, 96 (ill.)
McKay, Jim, 9
*Media Man: Ted Turner's Improbable
  Empire* (Auletta), 179
Melrose Place, 157, 161 (ill.), 162
Meredith, Don, 10, 10 (ill.), 13
Merv Griffin Productions, 84–85
The Merv Griffin Show, 82–83
Metro Goldwyn Mayer (MGM) films, 177

Miami Herald, 83
Miami Vice, 167
Michaels, Lorne, 111–17, 111 (ill.)
  awards won by, 117
  Canadian television comedy shows of, 113
  childhood and early influences of, 111–12
  concert and television production
    projects of, 116
  on creating *Saturday Night Live,* 111
  departure from *Saturday Night Live,* 115–16
  early work of, 112–13
  impact of *Saturday Night Live* production on,
    114–15
  movie productions of, 116
  return to *Saturday Night Live,* 116–17
  television career summarized, 111
The Mike Douglas Show, 2
Miller, James Andrew, 111
Miller, Robert G., 94, 99
Milton Berle: An Autobiography (Berle), 26, 30
Milton Berle Show, 30
Miniseries, 153
Mitchell, Pat, 169
The Mod Squad, 158
Monday Night Football, 9–11, 10 (ill.)
Moore, Mary Tyler, 119–24, 119 (ill.), 122 (ill.)
  awards won by, 120, 122, 123
  childhood and family of, 119–20
  on courage and growth, 119
  dance training and experience of, 120
  The Dick Van Dyke Show and, 120–21
  early television work of, 120
  The Mary Tyler Moore Show and, 121–23
  movie and television dramatic roles of, 123, 124
  television career summarized, 119
Morriset, Lloyd, 43
Movie colorization, 177
MSNBC, 5, 177
MTM Enterprises, 119
MTM Productions, 121, 122–23, 167
MTV (Music Television), 96–97
MTV Networks, 96–97
Murdoch, Rupert, 1, 5
Murrow, Edward R., 57, 61, 134–35, 136
Music Television (MTV), 96–97
My Favorite Martian, 102

National Association for the Advancement
of Colored People (NAACP), 162, 193
National Association of Television Programming
Executives (NATPE), 169
National Basketball Association (NBA), 99
National Broadcasting Company (NBC).
See NBC (National Broadcasting Company)
National Cable Television Association (NCTA), 94–95
National Football League (NFL), 9–10
National Urban League, 94
NBA (National Basketball Association), 99
NBC (National Broadcasting Company), 132,
144–45. *See also* Sarnoff, David; Tartikoff,
Brandon
NCTA (National Cable Television Association),
94–95
New York Herald, 142
New York Times, 77
News programs. *See* Arledge, Roone; Cronkite,
Walter; Hewitt, Don; Murrow, Edward R.;
Turner, Ted; Walters, Barbara
Newsweek, 13
NFL (National Football League), 9–10
Nightline, 12–13
Nixon, Agnes, 125–30, 125 (ill.), 128 (ill.)
awards won by, 127, 128–29
childhood and education of, 126
creation and writing of daytime dramas by, 126–29
on drama and storytelling, 125, 130
early television writing experience of, 126
introduction of controversial issues to daytime
drama by, 127–29
television career summarized, 125
on writing soap operas, 130
NOGGIN, 45
Now the News (Bliss), 59

O'Brien, Conan, 116
O'Connor, Carroll, 104, 156
Olympic Games, 9
One Day at a Time, 101, 107–8

One Life to Live, 125, 127, 127–28
The Oprah Winfrey Show, 187, 189–91
Oprah's Book Club, 190
Oxygen Media, 192

Paley, William S., 131–38, 131 (ill.), 137 (ill.)
business talent and decisiveness of, 132
CBS radio network management success of,
132–34
CBS Records and, 135
CBS television beginnings and, 134–36
childhood and education of, 131–32
color television development and, 134–35
diversity of business interest of, 135–36
importance of, 131, 138
McCarthy era and, 136
newscasters and, 133, 136–37
on satisfying the audience, 131
successful transition of CBS from radio to
television led by, 136
television career summarized, 131
television industry leadership of, 137–38
World War II years and, 133
Parsons, Charlie, 35
PBS (Public Broadcasting Service), 43
People (magazine), 101
People Are Talking, 189
Perenchio, Jerry, 108
Person to Person, 135
Petrie, Laura, 120
Philips, Irna, 126
Phyllis, 122
Podrazik, Walter J., 154
Pomerantz, Hart, 112–13
The Potential Uses of Television in Preschool Education
(Cooney), 43
Prime Time Live, 11
Public Broadcasting Service (PBS), 43

R

Radio-Keith-Orpheum (RKO motion picture
company), 144

Raid Gauloises, 34

Rashad, Phylicia, 52

Rather, Dan, 61, 91

RCA (Radio Corporation of America)
    CBS rivalry with, 147–48
    companies founded and later divested by, 144–45
    control of television set market in early years by, 147
    diversity of business of, 148
    founding of, 144
    introduction of television to the world by, 146–47
    Paley and, 147–48
    statistics about, 147
    television technology development and, 145–46, 199–200

The Real World (television program), 97

Reality television shows, 35–39

Reasoner, Harry, 90, 91, 181, 184

Red network, 144

Reiner, Carl, 120

A Reporter's Life (Cronkite), 56, 62

Rhoda, 122

Richards, Mary, 121–22

RKO (Radio-Keith-Orpheum motion picture company), 144

RLJ Development, 99

Rock the Vote campaign, 97

Roots, 153

Rowan and Martin's Laugh-In, 113

Rowan, Dan, 113

S

Safer, Morley, 91

San Francisco Chronicle, 193

Sarnoff, David, 141–50, 141 (ill.), 146 (ill.)
    CBS competition with RCA/NBC and, 147–48
    color television technology race and, 147–48
    communications industry career summarized, 141
    concept of commercial radio and, 143–44
    credit for invention of television and, 69
    family and boyhood of, 141–42

    Farnsworth technology and, 66
    on importance of television, 141, 147
    introduction of television to the public by, 147
    NBC radio network formation and, 144
    RCA leadership of television technology and, 145–47
    RKO motion picture company formation and, 144
    telegraph company experience of, 142–43
    television technology development and, 145–46
    Titanic story and, 143
    World War II and "The General" as title for, 147
    Zworykin and, 199–200

Satellite transmission, 175

Saturday Night Live, 111, 114–15, 114 (ill.), 116, 117

Sawyer, Diane, 11

Schwartz, Evan I., 66

Schwartz, Sherwood, 102–3, 103 (ill.)

Search for Tomorrow, 126, 127

See It Now, 135, 136–37

Sesame Street, 44–45

Seventh Heaven, 163

Shales, Tom, 111, 115

Shaw, Bernard, 177

Shore, Howard, 112

Shuster, Frank, 112

Shuster, Rosie, 112

Silverman, Fred, 151–56, 151 (ill.)
    ABC network programming successes of, 152–54
    background and education of, 152
    CBS programming years of, 152
    children's television programming experience of, 152
    consulting and educational careers of, 156
    independent television productions of, 155–56
    NBC executive experience of, 154–55
    Tartikoff and, 166–67
    television career summarized, 151
    on television programming quality, 151

60 Minutes, 87, 90–92, 138

Smith, Howard K., 136

SNL Studios, 116–17

Soap operas. *See* Nixon, Agnes

Spelling, Aaron, 157–63, 157 (ill.)

    awards won by, 159, 162

    background and childhood of, 158

    on diversity in television programs, 162

    early acting and writing work of, 158

    movie productions of, 160, 162

    on nature of television production work, 159

    production company founding and successes of, 59–160

    teen dramas produced by, 160–62, 161 (ill.)

    television production successes of, 158–59

Spelling Entertainment, 159–63

Sports Illustrated, 14

Sports programs. *See* Arledge, Roone

Stanton, Frank, 133

Stapleton, Jean, 104

Starsky and Hutch, 153, 158

Stay Tuned: Television's Unforgettable Moments (Garner), 105

Straight Forward with Roger Ailes, 5

Sullivan, Ed, 29

Survivor, 35–36, 36 (ill.), 38

Sydney Morning Herald, 160, 162

Syndication, 189

T

Talk shows. *See* Griffin, Merv; Walters, Barbara; Winfrey, Oprah

Tandem Productions, 104

Tartikoff, Brandon, 165–70, 165 (ill.)

    America Online (AOL) venture of, 169

    background and childhood of, 166

    on cancer and his own mortality, 166

    as dramatic development chief of ABC Television, 166–67

    education of, 166

    health challenges of, 166, 169

    legacy of, 169–70

    NBC programming years and, 167–68

    New World Entertainment and, 169

    Paramount Pictures experience of, 169

    Silverman and, 166–67

    television career summarized, 165–66

TAT Communications, 108

TCM (Turner Classic Movies), 177

Television (Winship), 75

Television production, 159. *See also* names of specific television producers

Television technology. *See* Farnsworth, Philo T.; Paley, William; Sarnoff, David; Zworykin, Vladimir

Texaco Star Theater, 25, 27–28, 28 (ill.), 29

Thomas, Danny, 120, 158

Thomas–Spelling Productions, 158

Three's Company, 153

Time (magazine), 65, 69, 147, 154, 174

Time Inc., 174

Time Warner, Inc., 174

Tinker, Grant, 121, 123, 154, 167

Tisch, Lawrence, 138

TNT (Turner Network Television), 177

Toast of the Town, 29

Today, 182–83

Tomlin, Lily, 113

The Tonight Show, 113–14

Travolta, John, 159

Trump, Donald, 37

Turner Classic Movies (TCM), 177

Turner Communications, 175

Turner Foundation, 179

Turner Network Television (TNT), 177

Turner, Ted, 171–80, 171 (ill.), 178 (ill.)

    background and childhood of, 171–72

    billboard advertising company of, 173

    Cable Network News (CNN) success of, 176–77

    cable television career summarized, 171

    cable television impact of, 174–78

    colorization of films and, 177–78

    health challenges of, 178

    as landowner and environmentalist, 179

    movie studio purchases of, 177–78

    as philanthropist, 179

    professional sports teams ownership and, 176

radio broadcasting experience of, 173
Time Warner and, 178–79
UHF television beginnings of, 173–74
United Nations (UN) awards and
donations to, 179
Turner Tomorrow Fellowship Awards, 179
TV History Web site, 147
Twentieth Century, 58
20/20 (television program), 11, 184, 185

U

UHF (ultra-high frequency) television
channels, 173
United Artists films, 177
University of the Air, 135
U.S. News and World Report, 2
USA Today, 184

V

Van Dyke, Dick, 120, 156
Vance, Vivian, 20 (ill.), 21, 22
Variety (newspaper), 169
VHF (very-high frequency) television
stations, 173
Videotaping live, 106
The View, 185
Village Roadshow Pictures, 108
Vincent, E. Duke, 160

W

Waldron, Vince, 101, 102, 106
Walker, Alice, 191
Wallace, Mike, 90, 91
Walters, Barbara, 181–86, 181 (ill.), 184 (ill.)
ABC Television years of, 183–86
awards won by, 181, 183, 185
background of, 182
daytime talk show created by, 185
early television writing and production
experience of, 182

education of, 182
as first woman news co-anchor for *ABC News,*
183, 184 (ill.)
gender discrimination encountered by, 182
as interviewer and news magazine
show co-anchor, 184–85
journalistic excellence of, 183
as mentor, 181
NBC television years of, 182–83
television career summarized, 181
on television specials, 185
on *The View* co-hosts, 185
Today show and, 183
on work ethic and women, 181, 184
Warner Communications, 175
Washington Post, 115
Watching TV: Four Decades of American Television
(Castleman, Podrazik), 154
WCTG (Turner Communications Group cable
television station), 174
Westinghouse, 144, 145
*What Liberal Media? The Truth about Bias
and the Media* (Alterman), 6
Wheel of Fortune (television game show),
84, 85, 85 (ill.)
Wiesner, Jerome B., 150
Winfrey, Oprah, 187–94, 187 (ill.), 192 (ill.)
acting roles of, 191
awards won by, 189–90, 191, 193
background and childhood of, 188
cable television network founded by, 192
charitable contributions of, 193
education of, 188–89
magazine founded by, 191–92
production company founded by, 191
radio experience of, 188
reading and book club feature of, 190–91
as talk show host, 189–91
television career summarized, 187–88
workshops and seminars led by, 193
Winship, Michael, 75
Wired (Schwartz), 66
Worldscreen.com, 159, 162
WTBS (Turner Broadcasting System cable
television station), 175
Wyman, Thomas, 138

Yorkin, Bud, 104, 108
You Are There, 58
Your Show of Shows, 75

Zworykin, Vladimir, 195–201, 195 (ill.), 198 (ill.)
    awards won by, 201
    background and childhood of, 195–96
    early television systems work of, 196

education and training of, 196
electronic television technology career
    summarized, 195
Farnsworth technology and, 66, 199–200
inventions and technologies developed by,
    197–99, 200–201
on physics and electrical engineering, 196
RCA (Radio Corporation of America) years of,
    199–201
Sarnoff and, 145, 199
on uses of technology, 195
Westinghouse years of, 197–99
x-ray technology studies of, 197